Business Threats and Opportunities in the Western Balkans

Business Threats and Opportunities in the Western Balkans

Edited by

Hristina Runcheva Tasev
and Elena Makrevska Disoska

Cambridge Scholars Publishing

Business Threats and Opportunities in the Western Balkans

Edited by Hristina Runcheva Tasev and Elena Makrevska Disoska

This book first published 2021

Cambridge Scholars Publishing

Lady Stephenson Library, Newcastle upon Tyne, NE6 2PA, UK

British Library Cataloguing in Publication Data
A catalogue record for this book is available from the British Library

ISBN (10): 1-5275-7502-0
ISBN (13): 978-1-5275-7502-8

Table of Contents

EDITOR'S NOTE

The current pandemic caused by the COVID-19 virus has affected economies around the globe and highlighted the interdependence of the global risks. For sure it will reshape the world we live in. The risk of a prolonged recession of the global economy will have far-reaching social, environmental, and technological implications. Society is facing public health fears, high unemployment rates, and increased poverty. The pandemic has brought many challenges for governments and the private sector, but it has also created new opportunities and ways to build back better. The organizational aspects of enterprises, changes in consumer behavior, the rise of the informational technologies, and the expansion of the digital market can create economic growth based on lower carbon consumption and sustainable growth based on green and clean solutions. The length and depth of the current economic crisis will depend on a combination of effective policies, incentives, and management systems that can balance the protection of public health and economic well-being.

This book offers readers a comprehensive outlook on the expected long-term changes, inspiration for decision-makers, and ways to leverage the opportunities of this pandemic, even though the articles were written before the beginning of the pandemic. The articles present issues related to entrepreneurship, digitalization, labour market incentives, non-standardized financial metrics for measuring business performance, techniques to improve customer satisfaction, digitalization and machine-learning algorithms, employee satisfaction, and energy consumption. In general, all the issues address the challenge of increasing the competitiveness of European companies and therefore the competitiveness of countries. The book presents economic problems and their possible solutions from the standpoints of researchers in Europe. In particular, I would like to point out the following questions:

1. *How can new opportunities rise for businesses in times of turbulence and consumer behavior changes?*

- The emergence of new business models will encourage new ways of extracting and sharing value from information. Such an ongoing business and economic context will clearly favor countries and organizations that have the capacity to mobilize relevant entrepreneurial talents.

- Use new techniques, such as data extraction techniques, that support the extraction of different representations of knowledge from such large databases, such as machine-learning algorithms.
- Abolishing administrative procedures, reducing corporate levies, and creating an atmosphere of legal certainty can improve the business and investment climate while fostering scientific and entrepreneurial cooperation can simultaneously strengthen the technological readiness of the economy to apply new knowledge to the creation of innovative products and services, all of which will foster and contribute to innovation and competitiveness performance.
- Improve the measurement of business performance by using new financial metrics; for example, non-standardized financial metrics in the analysis of cost and management of the companies.
- Customer satisfaction plays a crucial role in sustaining and increasing the market share of companies and expanding the customer base.
- In order to choose a quality strategy, it is necessary to consider the situation on the European market. Countries that are not members of the EU can attract European tourists by developing so-called medical and dental tourism, with combination of the spa tourism due to the high costs of medical treatment in these countries.

2. How can businesses best use human capital potential?

- Firms should try to implement more innovative recruitment methods and channels to increase their applicant pool and improve their organizational image on the labor market. A proactive and targeted approach to training and extensive training is also a way to create a competitive base of cutting-edge multidisciplinary skills within firms.
- Entrepreneurial talent should be seen as a state of mind that can be developed, enhanced, and nurtured with a mix of policies, incentives, and management approaches that need to be tailored to the specific context of individual countries.
- The better the assessment of the employees' motivation, career development, training, and internal communication ability, the more they were satisfied with their work, earnings, and the possibility of career advancement.

3. How to achieve sustainability growth with low-carbon emissions?

- A direct connection between the degree of digitization, efficiency, and financial parameters in product development can be established. A high degree of digitalization results in cost savings and shorter project lead times.
- European countries are diverging in primary energy consumption per capita and need to pursue policies to make their primary energy supply more stable.

It is certain that new business and employment opportunities are being created in sectors such as telecommunications, informational technologies, and digital market, but a greater dependence on technology has also increased cyber security risks. Numerous academic studies and indications from practice have pointed to the need to find ways to detect fraud early to prevent the negative effects that may arise for decision-makers.

These are some of the perceived problems and proposed solutions from the standpoint of the European researchers. I believe that this book will be an inspiration and open new perspectives for the policy makers, business community, and academics since the current crisis emphasizes the urgent need for effective actions.

Finally, I would like to thank all of those engaged in the process of research, selection, and publishing of this book for their effort and devotion.

Prof. Hristina Runcheva Tasev
Prof. Milena Apostolovska-Stepanoska
Prof. Snezana Knezevic

Elena Makrevska Disoska, Ph.D.

CHAPTER ONE

DETERMINANTS OF EMPLOYEE SKILLS' LEVEL AND UTILIZATION IN SMES IN THE REPUBLIC OF NORTH MACEDONIA

IRENA PIPERKOVA MAJOVSKI[1]
ALEKSANDRA LOZANOSKA[2]
ELENA DAVITKOVSKA[3]

Abstract

Recent research shows that continuous skill upgrading is paramount to achieving competitiveness and sustainability for individuals in the labour market and firms. Due to the dynamic business changes, firms expect higher levels of creativity, innovation, and initiative from their employees, hence ensure that they possess cutting-edge knowledge, skills, and abilities. Nevertheless, firms cannot capitalize solely on employees' skills i.e., the full utilization of employees' skills is necessary to achieve competitiveness. Thus, the determinants that influence the level and utilization of employee skills are crucial for firms as well. In this paper, the recruitment process and training are recognized as factors that affect skill level whereas the methods of motivation determine skill utilization.

The results of the empirical analysis on a sample of SMEs in the Republic of North Macedonia indicate that the challenges firms face during the process of recruitment pertain to the lack of applicants' skills and the small number of applicants. Also, almost 60% of the firms either announce only primary vacancy requirements or, although thoroughly

[1] Institute of Economics-Skopje, Ss. Cyril and Methodius University
[2] Institute of Economics-Skopje, Ss. Cyril and Methodius University
[3] Institute of Economics-Skopje, Ss. Cyril and Methodius University

defined, do not include the requirements in the vacancy announcement. As for the upgrading of skills, about 50% of the firms had organized one to three training sessions in the last three years, mainly pertaining to the improvement of job-specific skills of primary employees. Almost one-fifth of firms had not organized any training.

The motivation methods are highly important not only to boost employees' willingness to upgrade their skills but also to fully utilize them in their working activities. The findings indicate that more than half of the firms motivate their employees by providing bonuses and rewards, and by taking employees' opinion into account. An additional motivating factor refers to employee participation; in particular, including employees in the process of new product/service development.

Keywords: *employee skills level, skills utilization, skill determinants, recruitment, training, motivation*

1. Introduction

Human capital is a focal point in today's economy. Human resources can contribute to a firm's competitive advantage only if they possess high levels of knowledge and skills, have sufficient motivation, and the means to participate in achieving organizational goals. In this regard, firms should create an overall management philosophy, specifically covering human resource policies and practices, to support the use and development of employees' skills in order to maximize the benefits of their human capital.

The global trends that have emerged in the last decades, such as mass digitalization and a wider use of technology, tight competition as a result of globalization and deregulation, more sophisticated customer demands, and the growth of the service sector, have imposed dramatic changes on business processes and working methods. Hence, firms have upgraded their business processes, changed their organizational structure to achieve higher flexibility, and redesigned many jobs within their organizations. Subsequently, this has imposed new skill requirements for employees and to meet them, employees should possess a complementary set of cognitive and non-cognitive skills and be able to deal with non-routine activities in unpredictable situations.[4] At the same time, they should be able to comprehend new ideas and concepts and adjust quickly to changes.

[4] OECD, *Skills for Jobs*, 2018,

Global market changes, as well as the changes in the way business operations are conducted, have put knowledge and skills at the centre of corporate policies and increased the importance of employees' skills level and utilization. This has imposed a need for firms to redesign their human resource strategy and shift their focus to creating high skill levels among employees through the recruitment and selection process and intensive training and on identifying ways to utilize these skills more effectively. This paper discusses the determinants of employee skill levels and utilization and analyses these determinants in SMEs in the Republic of North Macedonia.

2. Determinants of skills level and utilization

Research has confirmed the importance of human capital for the performance of firms in terms of higher productivity, higher innovation, more profit, and better overall results as well as increased market competitiveness. Nevertheless, human resources can contribute to achieving organizational goals and increasing the market competitiveness of firms only if certain preconditions are met. First, employees should possess adequate skills levels. Second, they should be highly motivated to use their discretionary efforts or give their best, and third, they should have the means or opportunity to use their skills.[5] The mass digitalization, continuous technology improvements, redesigned business processes, growing competition, and customer orientation of firms have imposed new requirements for employees' skills. To meet these requirements, employees should possess a complementary set of job-specific, soft, digital, and entrepreneurial skills. Firm-level needs for specific employee skills depend on several factors such as the industry, long-term and short-term organizational goals, business strategy, the firm's technology development, competition, and so on. With the rising importance of human capital, building a sufficient pool of advanced skills has become one of the priorities of firms today. Thus, firms continuously strive to sophisticate their recruitment process and use cutting-edge selection methods while focusing their human resource strategy on upgrading their skills bases through systematic employee training programs.

[https://www.oecdskillsforjobsdatabase.org/methodology.php]

[5] Appelbaum, Eileen, Thomas Bailey, Peter Berg, Arne L. Kalleberg, and Thomas Andrew Bailey. *Manufacturing Advantage: Why High-Performance Work Systems Pay Off.* Cornell University Press, 2000.

Creating a firm's skills base alone does not add value to the firm. To maximize the potential value of a competitive skills base, employees should use these skills for organizational goals. In this regard, employee knowledge, skills, and abilities (or the human capital) should be "effectively used to achieve a competitive advantage."[6] Also, this transformation from human to intellectual capital is mainly dependent on the context in that companies should create a supportive environment that will enable the upgrading, utilization, and exchange of knowledge.[7] Therefore, creating appropriate conditions for skill utilization is as important as building those skills. Firms should create an environment, i.e., develop methods and mechanisms, that will encourage and enable employees to apply their knowledge and skills. Hence, developed motivational methods and employee participation mechanisms are essential elements in creating an organizational environment that supports skill utilization.

2.1. Determinants of skills level

Recruitment and training are considered to be the main determinants of the skill levels of employees in a firm as they directly affect the firm's skills base. In the human resource management literature, there is still debate on whether creating a firm's skills base should be through external recruitment or intensive employee training. However, these are not mutually exclusive. In reality, these determinants co-exist to build the necessary pool of knowledge and skills. On one hand, a successful recruitment process enables firms to select the candidate who possesses the required set of skills, and on the other hand, proactive employee training enables firms to meet their current and future skill requirements.

The recruitment process is especially important for jobs that require highly specialized skills as well as in the sectors that are technologically advanced and in firms that have innovative processes. As the complexity of the workplace increases, so does the difference in employee performance, which is closely related to the individual's ability, skills, knowledge, and experience. It is for these reasons that companies strive to

---

6 Youndt, Mark A., Mohan Subramaniam, and Scott A. Snell. "Intellectual capital profiles: An examination of investments and returns." *Journal of Management Studies* 41, no. 2 (2004): 335–361.

7 Swart, Juani. "HRM and knowledge workers." In *The Oxford Handbook of Human Resource Management,* edited by Boxall, Peter F., John Purcell, and Patrick M. Oxford: Oxford University Press, 2007.

attract and retain employees who have the competencies required to increase the firm's performance and achieve a competitive advantage.

The recruitment process is mainly dependent on, but also directly affects, the quantity and quality of applicants, and thus the potential human capital of the firm. The success of the recruitment process depends on several factors, including the ability of the firm to determine the required employee profile and identify different methods and channels for attracting applicants as well as the firm's organizational image and its labour market power. Probably the most important organizational aspects that directly affect the success of the recruitment process, and especially the quantity and quality of applicants, refer to determining the appropriate candidate for the job, identifying crucial requirements in the vacancy advertisement, and identifying recruitment channels to attract applicants. A detailed job and needs analysis is the first step in profiling a suitable candidate. By determining the requirements in this way, the required skills and the desired behavior of the potential employee are accurately identified. Therefore, job analysis and needs assessment are inevitable aspects in determining the required profile as well as the cognitive and non-cognitive skills that applicants should possess. In addition, this process enables the firm to adequately identify the vital requirements in the vacancy advertisement and determine the appropriate recruitment channels.

The appropriate definition of job criteria in advertisements is especially important for the successful attraction of candidates who have the necessary skills and abilities and also possess the identified individual characteristics. According to Breaugh and Starke,[8] vacancy advertisements with specific information that emphasizes the attractiveness of the vacancy have a positive effect on the number of applicants in the recruitment process. In this context, the vacancy advertisement should highlight the most important requirements for the position as well as present the advantages offered by the firm. The former should improve the organizational image of the firm in the labour market, which is as important as the financial power of the firm to offer competitive salaries—aspects considered crucial for the firm's capacity to attract a large applicant pool.

[8] Breaugh, James A., and Mary Starke. "Research on employee recruitment: So many studies, so many remaining questions." *Journal of Management* 26, no. 3 (2000): 405–434.

The ability of a company to improve its organizational image affects both the quantity and quality of applicants in the recruitment process. Harrell-Cook and Ferris[9] indicate that firms that do not have a good reputation in the labour market face more difficulties in attracting highly skilled staff, which directly affects the competitive advantage of the firm in the long run. Small and medium-sized enterprises should build their recruitment strategies based on their strengths and use a variety of recruitment channels to attract applicants with different profiles, especially in terms of age, experience, and personal characteristics. In this regard, SMEs should attract skilled applicants by emphasizing the aspects that are specific for this type of firm—the opportunity for dynamic and diverse work, greater employee involvement in the firm's processes, flexible working hours, etc.

The recruitment process is a vital phase in creating a firm's human capital; that is, the knowledge, skills, and abilities of a firm. Supported by continuous employee training, it would enable a firm to build and develop a competitive skills base, which is considered to be one of the prerequisites for sustainability in 21st-century business.

A strategic approach to employee training and development enables a firm to up-skill its workforce. This is especially important for skills that are not easily available in the labour market and yet are essential for firm's competitiveness. These investments, in terms of type and intensity of training, depend on factors such as the firm's goals and strategy, its specifics, the industry, and the organizational culture. A proactive approach to continuous training, however, enables a firm to anticipate future needs and build the necessary skill levels of its workforce.

New ways of doing business require not only extensive training in job-specific skills but also skills that would enable employees to change their traditional approach to work, become more flexible, and adapt easily to change. In this context, training improves employees' skills and abilities and directly affects their performance. Research has confirmed the positive impact of formal training on productivity, profitability, product quality, market share, and sales.[10] Nevertheless, human resource literature implies

---

[9] Harrell-Cook, G. and G. R. Ferris. "Competing pressures for human resource investment." In *Strategic Human Resource Management,* edited by R. S. Schuler and S.E. Jackson. Blackwell Publishers Ltd, 1999.

[10] Bartel, Ann P. "Productivity gains from the implementation of employee training programs." *National Bureau of Economics Research Series*. Working paper no. 3893, 1991. https://www.nber.org/papers/w3893; Hansson, Bo. "Company-based determinants of training and the impact of training on company

that employee training should not be comprehended as a series of interventions. In today's business context, employee training and development cover a wider concept since the requirements for employee skills change at a fast pace, imposing the need for their continuous development. A proactive approach to upgrading employees' skills will reduce the mismatch between the existing and required skills in firms in the long run. Those firms that implement employee training only to meet their short-term needs are more likely to face a skill gap that could hinder their very existence.

Eurostat's research[11] shows that 72.6% of firms in the EU conduct some type of training for their employees, which is a significant increase compared to 59.7% in 2005. Considerable differences are identified among firms based on their size; that is, small firms lag behind large firms in terms of conducted training. This is mainly due to the specifics of small firms such as the lack of human resource plan and budgets, lack of adequate training needs assessment, etc. In addition, small firms face more obstacles in implementing employee training as a result of limited financial power, higher training costs, and lack of information on training opportunities among others. Taking these obstacles into consideration, small and medium firms that cannot implement a continuous investment in employee training should seek alternative methods that will enable them to upgrade their employees' skills and maintain a competitive skills base.

2.2. Determinants of skills utilization

The intensive utilization of employee skills directly affects the potential benefits that firms can derive from their human capital. Firms can achieve this only through an adequate organizational environment that will support and encourage the efficient use of employees' knowledge and skills. Employee performance levels and, subsequently, their contribution to organizational goals are a result of a complex system that includes different levels of employee motivation, i.e., their willingness to contribute to a firm's goals, as well as differences in the context in which they work, i.e., the ability of the firm to develop appropriate mechanisms for greater

---

performance." *Personnel Review*, 2007; Kalleberg, Arne L., and James W. Moody. "Human resource management and organizational performance." *American Behavioral Scientist* 37, no. 7 (1994): 948–962.

[11] Eurostat. Accessed March 15, 2020. https://ec.europa.eu/eurostat/statistics-explained/index.php?title=Vocational_education_and_training_statistics&oldid=464069

employee involvement. Thus, the conditions that firms develop to support skills utilization also determine the effects of the same. The motivation of employees to apply their knowledge and skills and the opportunity provided by firms to use these skills are considered to be the main determinants in the process of creating an organizational environment for skill utilization.

The motivational methods developed by firms determine the level of discretionary effort employees put into utilizing their knowledge and skills for the achievement of organizational goals. Therefore, it is paramount that firms offer various motivational methods that include both internal and external rewards. Aligning organizational goals with the individual interests and aspirations of the employees is essential for the success of these motivational methods. Compensation and rewards systems (for example, pay for performance, bonuses, profit/gain sharing), teamwork, employee participation, two-way communication and information, career development, job design (such as job rotation, job enrichment), job security, job autonomy, and self-management (through self-managed teams) are some of the most widely used methods for employee motivation. Indeed, research has shown, especially in the last two decades, that there is a close connection between these methods and organizational performance. In fact, companies that show high organizational and market performance have incorporated these methods into their human resource management strategy.

The complexity of the motivation process is reflected in the necessity to create a developed system of different methods that positively affects employee levels of motivation. This is primarily due to the fact that employees expect both external and internal rewards that are consistent with the perception of individual contribution and performance. Individuals are motivated by financial rewards, additional benefits, status, job security, job satisfaction, the opportunity for career development, job decision-making autonomy, recognition, acknowledged contribution to the overall organizational goals, and so on. These aspects have different impacts on the overall employee motivation.

In addition, employee participation is central to skills utilization and, along with motivational methods, provides the required organizational context for the intensive utilization and free flow of knowledge and skills. In fact, employee involvement mechanisms are also some form of motivational methods, i.e., they are closely related to them. Employees will not be motivated to apply their skills when performing an activity or overcoming a problem if they are not "heard" by the management. So, employee participation is a crucial element in the equation of skills utilization.

Depending on the national, industrial, and organizational context, firms develop different methods for employee participation, ranging from informal mechanisms to systematically developed systems where employees participate equally in the decision-making process, thus providing incentives for the full utilization of their knowledge, skills, and abilities. Employee participation includes a variety of methods, such as a vertical communication system, where ‘bottom-up’ communication is as important as ‘top-down’ communication, self-managed teams, quality control cycles, etc. These methods and techniques are particularly important for firms that operate in dynamic, fast-growing industries and those that implement an innovation strategy. In fact, the possibility for greater employee involvement is much higher in small and medium enterprises, due to loosely defined roles and job descriptions and a flatter hierarchy, as opposed to large firms. In fact, SMEs should use this advantage to develop an efficient employee involvement system. Adequately implemented employee participation systems will provide these firms with multiple benefits, including greater skills utilization, an organizational culture based on cooperation, learning and advancement, and a better organizational image that could strengthen their labour market position and subsequently increase their ability to attract applicants with the right skills.

Developed motivational methods and employee participation mechanisms, as determinants of skills utilization, provide twofold benefits for firms. First, firms will have positive effects from their investments in their human capital (those made by the recruitment process and the employee training), and second, these mechanisms will enable employees to utilize their knowledge and skills and achieve organizational goals.

3. Methodology

The objective of this paper is to assess the methods and mechanisms most frequently used by small and medium enterprises in the Republic of North Macedonia that determine and increase employee skill levels and utilization. A survey questionnaire was distributed to business owners or senior managers of private firms in different sectors in North Macedonia. The questionnaire included aspects pertaining to different factors that determine the level and use of employee skills in a firm. Hence, aspects of the recruitment process, employee training, and motivational factors, including employee participation, were part of the questionnaire.

Lack of skills can often be the result of inappropriate recruitment practices in terms of hiring inappropriate applicants for certain jobs, low labour market power, or the inability to identify and attract the appropriate candidate. In addition, employee training, if not implemented continuously or in line with a firm's present and, even more importantly, future needs, will not generate the anticipated results. Also, a variety of developed motivational techniques is a main prerequisite to achieve the full utilization of employees' skills. Therefore, the questionnaire covered different aspects of the recruitment process, employee training, and motivational techniques implemented in firms. Such an analysis will produce in-depth knowledge of the methods and mechanisms used by SMEs in North Macedonia and highlight the biggest impediments to the process of creating a skills base and developing an organizational context that would maximize skill utilization.

4. Results

A sample of 133 SMEs was included in the analysis, out of which 37% were micro, 43% small, and 20% medium enterprises. Most of these firms (78.2%) operate in the domestic market and have been active in the market for more than 5 years. In fact, 40% of the firms have existed for between five and ten years, and 49% for more than ten years. A total of 51% of the survey sample are firms that offer services, while 26% are in production, and 23% in trade.

The results of the empirical research show that one of the greatest challenges for firms in the recruitment process is the number of applicants for a job vacancy. About 35% of the firms have an average number of applicants for a vacancy, while almost 19% attract an insufficient number of applicants during the recruitment process (Figure 1-1). There are several reasons for the dearth of potential applicants for a vacancy: for example, a lack of interest in a specific position, industry, or firm, then the firm's weak labour market power, and so on.

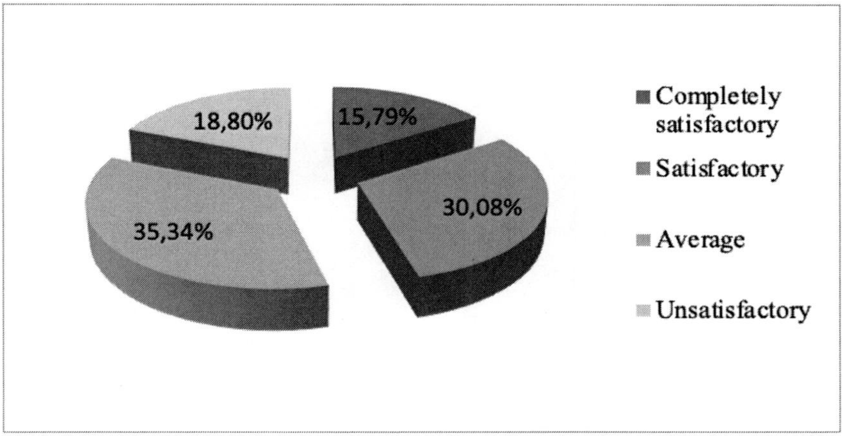

Figure 1-1. Number of applicants for vacancy, % of firms

Few applicants for a job can also be the result of inappropriately specified requirements. Namely, the quantity and quality of applicants for a vacancy are often related to the job requirements specified in the advertisement. A lack of information or ill-defined requirements in the advertisement can result in lack of applicants for the vacancy; it can also produce a reverse effect such as a huge number of applicants whose knowledge and skills do not correspond to those needed for the job. This will not only impede the recruitment process but also result in time-consuming, costly, and often unsuccessful recruitment. Therefore, companies should clearly and thoroughly define the required skills for the specific position and publish them transparently.

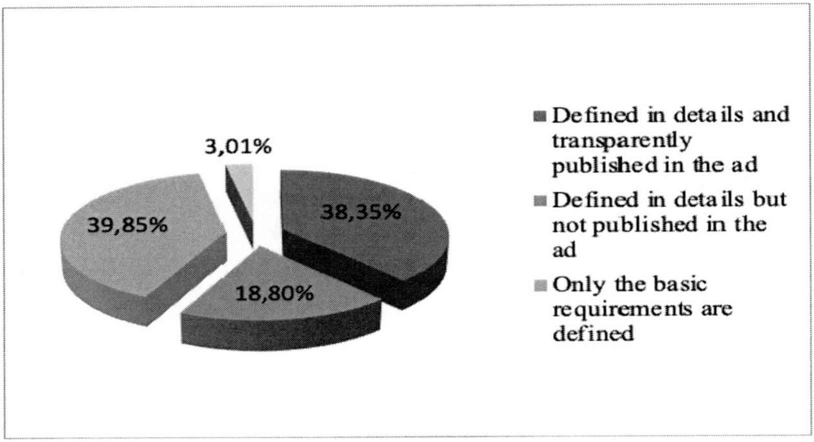

Figure 1-2. Skills requirements in job advertisements

However, only about 38% of the firms define skills requirements in detail and publish them transparently. A significant share of almost 40% of analysed firms define only the basic requirements for the vacancy (Figure 1-2).

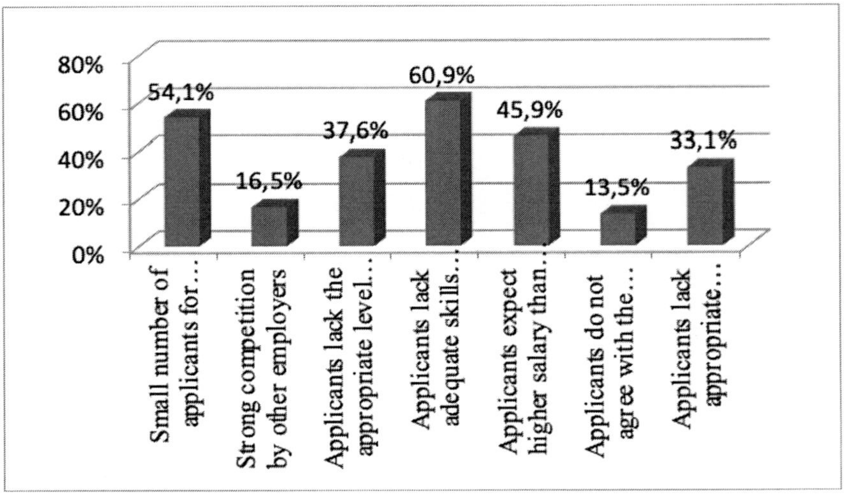

Figure 1-3. Main recruitment barriers, % of firms

Taking into consideration the above, it comes as no surprise that one of the biggest challenges faced by firms is the lack of adequate skills for a specific vacancy among the applicants. In fact, more than half of the analysed firms indicate few applicants (54.1%) and lack of skills (60.9%) as major obstacles in the recruitment process (Figure 1-3). Some of the reasons for these recruitment impediments are labour market skill mismatch as well as the firm's inability to appeal to adequate applicants. Also, for about 46% of the firms, their lack of financial power, reflected in non-competitive salaries, also imposes difficulties and undermines their labour market power, hampering their appeal to adequate applicants. Firms should, therefore, offer alternative methods and techniques to attract skilled applicants such as more employee involvement in decision making, career development opportunities, professional growth, flexible working time, etc.

Recruitment barriers considerably undermine the process of building adequate skill pools in firms and directly affect firms' human capital and their subsequent performance. This highlights even more the importance of continuous employee training in firms. A systematic and proactive approach to employee training would compensate for the drawbacks derived from the recruitment process, strengthening firms' skills pools.

Employee training is another determinant of the level of employees' skills. In this context, the frequency of employee training offered by firms is very important for up-skilling and acquiring skills that are aligned with firms' present and future needs. The results show that about 50% of firms conducted one to three training courses in the last three years, while one-fifth of the firms did not offer any training to their employees (Figure 1-4).

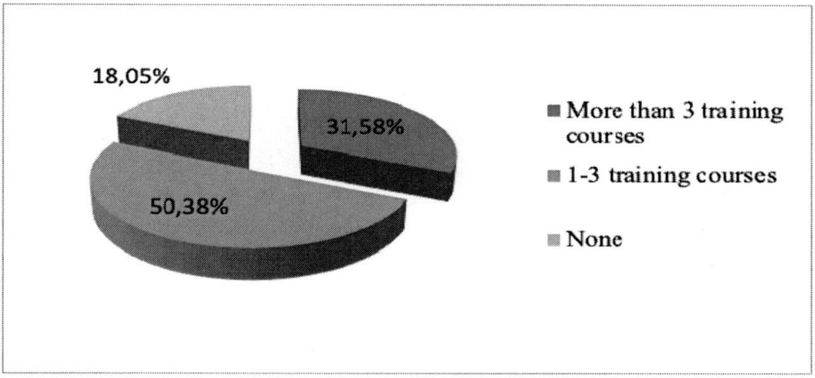

Figure 1-4. Frequency of conducted training, % of firms

Additionally, the majority of the firms organized training for their core employees (those who perform activities closely related to the core business) whereas less than half organized training to supporting employees (those who perform supporting activities to the core business) and managers (Figure 1-5).

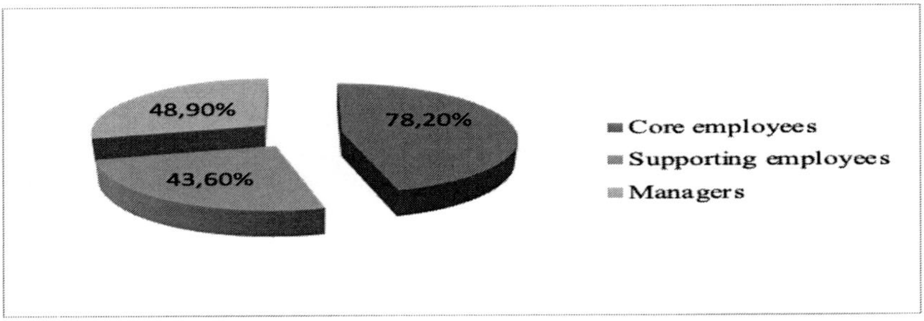

Figure 1-5. Employees for which training was conducted, % of firms

Training courses were mainly conducted to upgrade job-specific skills (36% of the firms conducted such training). Some of the firms organized training on digital and entrepreneurial skills, and an insignificant percentage of firms organized training on soft skills as well (Figure 1-6). These findings are consistent with other studies in this area, which conclude that small and medium enterprises do not invest much in employee training as opposed to large firms. This could be for several reasons, some of which are due to the specifics of such firms. Nevertheless, investment in human capital is a primary prerequisite for competitiveness today, and with the rapid changes in the markets and the way business is conducted, continuous training provides firms with the necessary skills to meet current and future targets and goals.

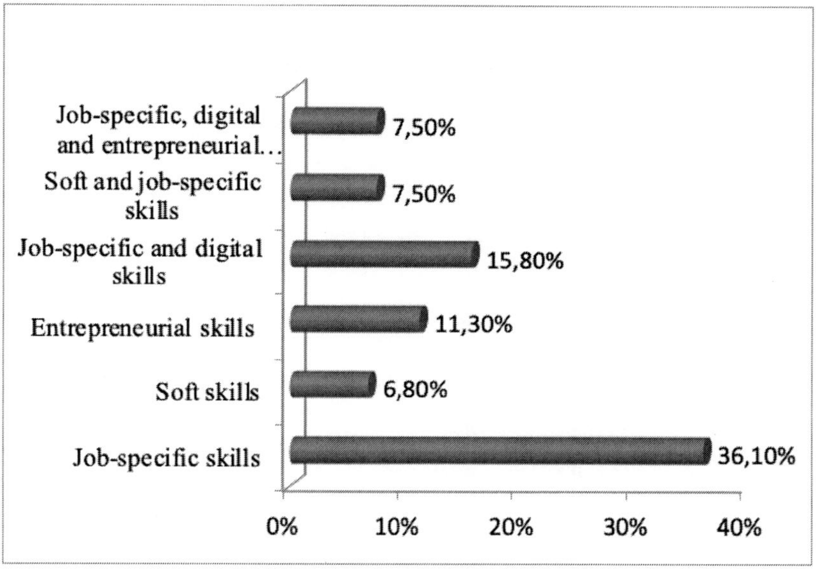

Figure 1-6. Type of training provided, % of firms

However, firms can only benefit from their human capital through an intensive utilization of their knowledge, skills, and abilities so it is crucial that they create appropriate conditions. Employees should be motivated enough to apply their knowledge and firms should ensure they have the opportunity to use it for the benefit of the firm. So, the main determinants of employee skill utilization are, in fact, the motivational methods and employee involvement mechanisms developed by firms.

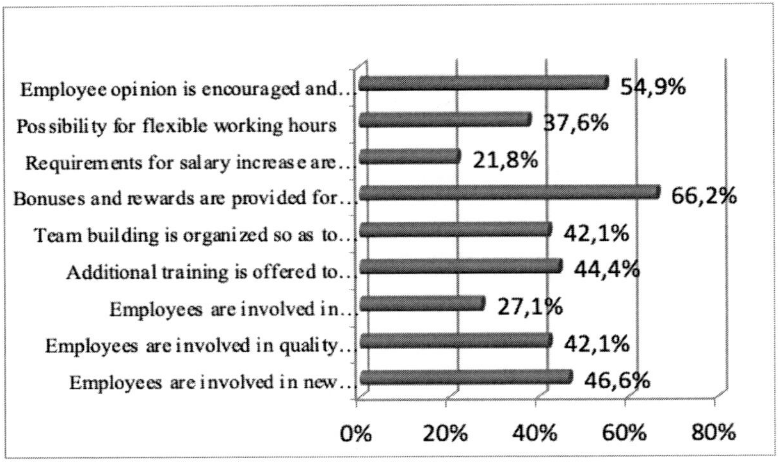

Figure 1-7. Motivational methods implemented by firms

Small and medium enterprises in the Republic of North Macedonia primarily motivate their employees through bonuses and rewards (about 66% of firms) and additional training (almost 45% of the firms). Firms do not believe that they can motivate their employees through transparent and clear rules and requirements for increased salaries. In fact, this is the least-used motivational technique used by firms (Figure 1-7).

Employee participation is not only a considerable motivational factor but also enables skill utilization. As such, this represents a major determinant of skill use in a firm. About 55% of firms indicate that they respect their employees' opinion yet less than 47% include their employees in new product or service development, and only 27% of firms include them in establishing working procedures. Such results clearly point to the need to introduce a larger variety of both motivational methods and wider employee participation in the decision-making process.

Conclusion

The success of the recruitment process, i.e., the quantity and quality of applicants, as well as employee training investments determine the level of skills in a firm. Firms should improve their recruitment process and training investments so they can build a skills base that is aligned with their current and future needs and turn their human capital into a competitive advantage. In this regard, firms should try to implement more innovative recruitment methods and channels to increase their applicant pool and improve their organizational image on the labour market. A proactive and targeted approach to training and extensive training is also required as a way to create a competitive base of cutting-edge multidisciplinary skills within firms.

Firms can, however, capitalize on their employees' skills only if they create an environment that supports the full utilization of these skills. Motivational methods and employee participation are some of the most serious impediments to SMEs fully utilizing their workforce skills. The lack of mechanisms that would enable the full utilization of employee skills, such as insufficient or inadequate motivational methods or low levels of employee participation, can generate several negative implications. Not only do they demean the effects of the recruitment and training process but also undermine the firm's growth and impede its market competitiveness. Therefore, small and medium enterprises in North Macedonia should create an organizational context that would improve both motivational levels of their employees and employee participation in the decision-making process of their firms more vigorously. Firms should set different organizational mechanisms (such as job enrichment, team working, ad hoc groups, etc.) to increase employee autonomy in performing job-related activities and increase employee participation in business processes, product or service development, quality improvement, and alike.

References

Appelbaum, Eileen, Thomas Bailey, Peter Berg, Arne L. Kalleberg, and Thomas Andrew Bailey. *Manufacturing Advantage: Why High-Performance Work Systems Pay Off.* Cornell University Press, 2000.

Bartel, Ann P. "Productivity gains from the implementation of employee training programs." *National Bureau of Economics Research Series.* Working paper no. 3893, 1991. https://www.nber.org/papers/w3893.

Breaugh, James A., and Mary Starke. "Research on employee recruitment: So many studies, so many remaining questions." *Journal of Management* 26, no. 3 (2000): 405–434.

Eurostat. Accessed March 15, 2020. https://ec.europa.eu/eurostat/statistics-explained/index.php?title=Vocational_education_and_training_statistics&oldid=464069

Hansson, Bo. "Company-based determinants of training and the impact of training on company performance." *Personnel Review*, 2007.

Harrell-Cook, G. and G. R. Ferris. "Competing pressures for human resource investment." In *Strategic Human Resource Management,* edited by R. S. Schuler and S. E. Jackson. Blackwell Publishers Ltd, 1999.

Kalleberg, Arne L., and James W. Moody. "Human resource management and organizational performance." *American Behavioral Scientist* 37, no. 7 (1994): 948–962.

OECD, *Skills for Jobs*, 2018 [https://www.oecdskillsforjobsdatabase.org/methodology.php]

Swart, Juani. "HRM and knowledge workers." In *The Oxford Handbook of Human Resource Management,* edited by Boxall, Peter F., John Purcell, and Patrick M. Oxford: Oxford University Press, 2007.

Youndt, Mark A., Mohan Subramaniam, and Scott A. Snell. "Intellectual capital profiles: An examination of investments and returns." Journal of Management Studies 41, no. 2 (2004): 335–361.

CHAPTER TWO

KEY NON-STANDARDIZED FINANCIAL METRICS BASED ON THE INCOME STATEMENT FOR MEASURING HOTEL PERFORMANCE AND THE POSSIBILITY OF FRAUD

ALEKSANDAR GRGUR[1]
STEFAN MILOJEVIĆ[2]

Abstract

Non-standardized metrics are one of the key metrics that can have a big impact on the operations of hotel companies. In today's environment, it is necessary to identify the parameters to properly determine the direction of movement of hotel companies, given that their performance depends on the success of their business. The information contained in financial statements is of great importance to decision makers and enables them to create direction for the company's future operation. Standardized metrics do not have the flexibility required by today's environment and cannot be properly subject to business policy changes so non-standardized metrics are created that serve managers as a tool when measuring a company's financial performance. For a company to survive in today's market, it must adapt to changes and manage costs in an adequate way. The aim of this paper is to identify key non-standardized financial metrics that can serve hotel companies in measuring their business performances. The subject of the paper is the financial reports of hotel companies that operate in the Serbian market and are listed on the Belgrade Stock

---

[1] MSc, Financial Analyst, NCKE, Belgrade, Serbia
[2] MSc, PhD student, Belgrade, Serbia

Exchange. The research is based on the application of the case study method and the content analysis method.

Keywords: *non-standardized financial measures, hotel companies, financial reports, fraud*

1. Introduction

The goal of financial reporting is to provide useful information to business decision makers, and such information is a central part of market information.[3] Relevant financial information is information that distinguishes between the decisions of the users of financial statements. If it was not available, users would probably make other decisions.[4] The information must have a confirmatory or predictive value in order to be able to influence the decisions of the financial statement users. One can speak about the confirmatory value of information if it indicates the correctness of previous assessments in the sense of confirming or denying them. The predictive value of information exists if it can be used to predict the future. An important aspect of relevance, which is specific to each entity, is significance (materiality), which depends on the nature or size of the item in the context of the entity's financial statements. Information is considered significant if its omission or misrepresentation could affect economic decisions. The data from the financial statements do not allow companies to measure their performance in relation to the market; therefore, market parameters must be included in order to determine the complete position of the company.

In this regard, the financial statements provide an insight into the operations to various stakeholders. Among the most important group of stakeholders, in addition to customers, suppliers, and regulatory bodies, are shareholders.[5] The company's shareholders are most interested in the predictive values of the information in the financial statements and seek to use that information to increase the value of the company as a whole. The managers of the companies have an opposite orientation because they are

---

[3] Knežević, Snežana. *Finansijsko izveštavanje.* Beograd: Samostalno izdanje autora. 2019.

[4] Škarić-Jovanović, Kata and Dejan Spasić. *Specijalni bilansi.* Beograd: Centar za izdavačku delatnost, Ekonomski fakultet u Beogradu. 2014.

[5] Altman, Edward I. "Financial ratios, discriminant analysis and the prediction of corporate bankruptcy." *The Journal of Finance* 23, no. 4 (1968): 589–609.

most interested in the company's liquidity and solvency.[6] Liquidity and solvency ratios are generally opposite in relation to the company's profitability, and therefore shareholders are not very interested in them. Profitability indicators such as earnings before interest, taxes, depreciation, and amortization – EBITDA, earnings before interest and taxes – EBIT, earnings before taxes – EBT, and, finally, net profit, are the most important to shareholders and so they strive to maximize these metrics.

In this regard, companies that do not achieve a high performance based on these parameters are often the subject of shareholder research and all previously made decisions are examined at the general meeting. When you look at hospitality companies, which are characterized by a high amount of capital expenditures (Eng. CAPEX), the goal of the company is to make the highest possible net profit in order to return the invested funds to its operation.[7] However, it would be necessary to gain insight into all those non-standardized financial metrics that are not characteristic of day-to-day reporting to find the shortcomings of financial performance management in hotel companies.

Although some standard financial ratios show the degree of profitability of the company, such as profit margin, business margin, ROA, and ROE, they cannot properly provide insight into the cost structure that burdens the operation the most.[8] It is measures such as EBITDA, EBIT, and EBT that provide, through a vertical analysis of the income statement and its positions, insight into the profits of the company that best reflects its operation.[9] These types of measures are intended to control the functions in companies and so, in addition to standard reporting, it should be possible to present non-standardized financial metrics. Further, as Knežević et al.[10] point out, if we keep in mind that distortive accounting and the financial effects on company earnings are not taken as factors in EBITDA, then it is a good way to compare company performance not only within business activities but also outside them. However, one should also keep in mind

---

[6] Knežević, Snežana. *Finansijsko izveštavanje.* Beograd: Samostalno izdanje autora. 2019.

[7] Melville, Alan. *International Financial Reporting: A Practical Guide*. Pearson Education, 2008.

[8] Horrigan, J. (1968). "A short history of financial ratio analysis." *The Accounting Review*, pp. 284–294.

[9] Knežević, Snežana. *Finansijsko izveštavanje.* Beograd: Samostalno izdanje autora. 2019.

[10] Knežević, Snežana, Aleksandra Mitrović, Milan Vujić and Aleksandar Grgur, A. *Analiza finansijskih izveštaja.* Beograd: Samostalno izdanje autora. 2019.

the possibility of fraudulent actions when it comes to the financial metrics of the company. The scientific and practical discipline of forensic accounting is a growing segment of accounting practice. In today's environment, which is characterized by an increase in the number of frauds, the demand for forensic accountants is high both in litigation and in expertise.

2. EBITDA measure

EBITDA is a commonly used by financial analysts and represents earnings less interest, tax income, and depreciation. Therefore, costs that do not cause cash outflows, such as depreciation, are excluded from this value. In hotel companies, this indicator is significant because it shows the profit reduced by the amount of depreciation, which represents a high cost in hotel companies. EBITDA is calculated as follows:

$$\text{EBITDA} = \text{Operating income} + \text{Depreciation}$$

Another important standardized financial metric is the EBITDA margin, which is calculated as a percentage of EBITDA relative to revenue. It allows comparing the real performance of the company relative to others in the industry.

$$\text{EBITDA margin} = \frac{\text{EBITDA}}{\text{Revenue}}\, x$$

According to our calculations, the Park Hotel in Novi Sad has the highest amount of EBITDA. However, it is necessary to consider the data in previous years, i.e., whether the amount of EBITDA increased or decreased over time. We have the answer to that question in the following figure.

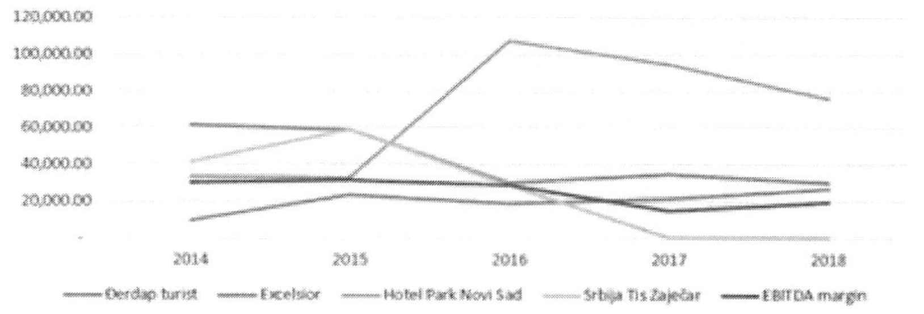

Figure 2-1 EBITDA over time

Based on figure 2-1, we can conclude that all companies, over a period of five years, have a lower EBITDA except for the Park Hotel in Novi Sad. This hotel alone has performed better in the last year compared to other companies. What is characteristic for all hotel companies is the low EBITDA margin in relation to operating incomes. As hotel companies are burdened with high capital expenditures, a satisfactory EBITDA margin could only be found by applying the benchmarking technique, which means that hotel companies compare themselves with each other and draw a conclusion based on which companies have the highest EBITDA margin. In our case, this means that the Park Hotel in Novi Sad in relation to other companies has the highest EBITDA margins, with the Excelsior Hotel coming second. Compared to these two hotels, other hotels have more accessible EBITDA metrics, in both percentages and cash.

2.1. EBITDA/EBIT indicator

EBITDA/EBIT is a non-standardized financial metric that provides insight into earnings before interest, taxes, depreciation, and amortization as well as earnings before interest and taxes.[11] This financial metric best shows what amount of depreciation improves the EBITDA image, and looks at the real picture of a company's profits when all operating costs are deducted from the revenue. Operating costs can put a lot of strain on a company, but it would be necessary to consider other non-standardized

[11] Iotti, Mattia, and Giuseppe Bonazzi. "EBITDA/EBIT and cash flow based ICRs: A comparative approach in the agro-food system in Italy." *Financial Assets and Investing* 3, no. 2 (2012): 19–31.

financial metrics in order to get a complete picture of overall financial performance. The table below provides an overview of the EBIT measure and EBITDA/EBIT ratio of five hotel companies in Serbia, observed for a five-year period. This ratio is also applied by rating agencies and banks to assess the creditworthiness of companies. Banks specifically use this ratio to determine the ability to pay debts (they also use the interest coverage ratio as well as cash flow measures), profitability (return on equity (ROE) and return on assets (ROA)), and the leverage ratio (debt-to-asset ratio, as well as the debt and equity ratio).[12]

Table 2-1. EBIT and EBITDA/EBIT of hotel companies for a five-year period

EBIT	Hotel companies over a five year period				
	2014	2015	2016	2017	2018
Đerdap turist	- RSD	15,058.00 RSD	10,251.00 RSD	12,783.00 RSD	17,063.00 RSD
EBITDA/EBIT	0%	64%	54%	59%	63%
Excelsior	37,194.00 RSD	34,062.00 RSD	5,475.00 RSD	9,727.00 RSD	4,348.00 RSD
EBITDA/EBIT	61%	58%	18%	28%	14%
Hotel Park Novi Sad	- RSD	6,862.00 RSD	82,429.00 RSD	70,627.00 RSD	52,223.00 RSD
EBITDA/EBIT	0%	21%	77%	74%	68%
Rimex	2,067.00 RSD	1,938.00 RSD	5,797.00 RSD	1,280.00 RSD	4,266.00 RSD
EBITDA/EBIT	29%	28%	55%	13%	37%
Srbija Tis Zaječar	17,502.00 RSD	19,276.00 RSD	16,180.00 RSD	- RSD	- RSD
EBITDA/EBIT	58%	60%	56%	0%	0%

Source: Author`s calculations

Based on the presented results, we can conclude that the EBITDA/EBIT ratio affected the hotel companies Excelsior, Rimex, and Srbija-Tis Zaječar

[12] Dothan, Michael. "Costs of financial distress and interest coverage ratios." *Journal of Financial Research* 29, no. 2 (2006): 147–162.

the most. The EBITDA in table 2-1 shows that the companies' financial performance is at a satisfactory level overall. However, it can be seen that depreciation greatly affects the amount of total profit. This is a cost that does not represent an outflow of money, and for that reason it is necessary to pay attention to hotels that have high depreciation costs because these costs allow the EBITDA to be manipulated. As in the first case, Hotel Park Novi Sad has the highest EBITDA/EBIT ratio and thus has the best ratio of operating income and operating expenses.

3. EBT/EBIT indicator

Another indicator of great importance in determining the overall financial performance is the EBIT & EBT ratio. EBT represents earnings before taxes, and EBIT earnings before interest and taxes. With this indicator, one can get an insight into the company's financial expenses as it shows the ratio of profit before tax and profit before tax and interest. It shows what percentage of EBIT remains after the payment of interest expenses and other financial expenses. In order to increase the return on equity, the company must reduce interest costs, as in the case when the EBT/EBIT ratio is at a high level.[13] The name of this ratio indicates that we are looking for the impact of interest costs on return on equity. As can be seen in the formula, we can find how much taxable profit remains after interest costs are deducted from the operating profit.

$$\frac{Taxable\ profit}{Operating\ profit}$$

In this regard, companies strive to keep their interest costs low. This means that companies will use low amounts of debt or will pay low interest rates on the money they borrow.[14] Companies that are largely financed by debt have a big problem with this ratio. The financial leverage factor can also help in determining this ratio, but the ratio provides insight into interest expense only, not negative exchange rate differences or other financial expenses. The EBT/EBIT indicator has a wide range of insights into financial expenditure management. The main goal of this indicator is

---

[13] Soliman, Mark T. "The use of DuPont analysis by market participants." *The Accounting Review* 83, no. 3 (2008): 823–853.
[14] Taparia, Jay. *Understanding Financial Statements: A Journalist's Guide*. Marion Street Press, Inc., 2004.

the percentage of EBT that remains after the payment of interest on the debt of this company. Attached is table 2-2, which shows EBT and EBT/EBIT for the five-year period.

Table 2-2. EBT and EBT/EBIT of hotel companies over five years

EBT	2014	2015	2016	2017	2018
Đerdap turist	- RSD	10,691.00 RSD	65,590.00 RSD	12,679.00 RSD	14,803.00 RSD
EBT/EBIT	0%	71%	640%	99%	87%
Excelsior	15,107.00 RSD	24,663.00 RSD	0.00 RSD	6,960.00 RSD	0.00 RSD
EBT/EBIT	41%	72%	0%	72%	0%
Hotel Park Novi Sad	0.00 RSD	0.00 RSD	59,664.00 RSD	116,013.00 RSD	46,402.00 RSD
EBT/EBIT	0%	0%	72%	164%	89%
Rimex	16,867.00 RSD	16,679.00 RSD	17,135.00 RSD	0.00 RSD	0.00 RSD
EBT/EBIT	96%	87%	106%	0%	0%
Srbija Tis Zaječar	0.00 RSD	0.00 RSD	1,331.00 RSD	1,491.00 RSD	684.00 RSD
EBT/EBIT	0%	0%	23%	116%	16%

Source: Author`s calculations

Table 2-2 shows us the financial performance of the hotels, which is most reflected in financial income and expenditures. It is acceptable for this ratio to be above 0%; however, it is also necessary to strive for financial revenues to be higher than expenditures. In this case, the best EBT/EBIT ratio is in the Park Hotel in Novi Sad. Based on the table, we conclude that there are hotels that have a percentage higher than 100%. This means that the company has more income than expenses, which indicates that it will have a higher profit before tax due to financial income compared to profit before interest and taxes. This ratio is one of the most important ratios for determining the return on shareholders' capital. According to the DuPont analysis, the extended version of the return on shareholders' capital was obtained as follows:

Return on equity =

$$\frac{\text{Net profit}}{\text{EBT}} \times \frac{\text{EBT}}{\text{EBIT}} \times \frac{\text{EBIT}}{\text{Sales Revenues}} \times \frac{\text{Sales Revenues}}{\text{Total assets}} \times \frac{\text{Total assets}}{\text{Equity}}$$

The EBT/EBIT ratio is one of the main indicators of the size of return on equity.[15] This indicator can be an excellent driver in reducing the financial expenses of companies and enabling the obtaining of borrowed funds from financial institutions at lower interest rates.

In the end, shareholders are most interested in the net profit because the level of dividend they will receive at the end of the business year depends on it. Net profit, on the other hand, is the main driver of the company's development and thus represents the amount that the company can dispose of for future investments. The accumulated net profit is transferred to the capital for the next year and thus increases, reducing the cost of equity, which allows for a potentially higher return in the future for the company. Figure 2-2 shows the net profit for five hotel companies on the Serbian market.

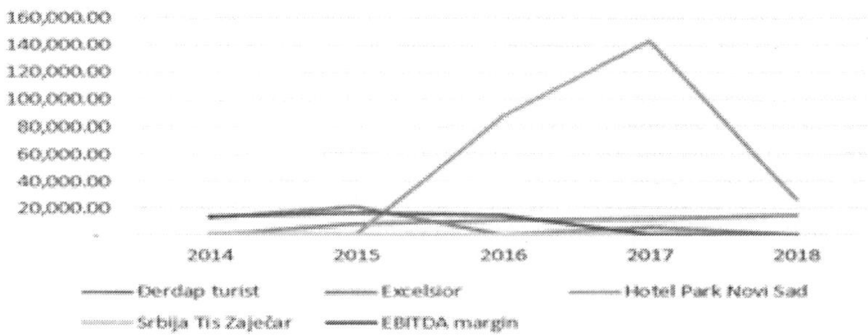

Figure 2-2. Net profit of the hotel companies over time

In figure 2-2 we see that the net profit of all companies is declining, while at the Park Hotel we can see many oscillations. The net profit for Djerdap Turist is at the input level, which means that the company manages its costs and makes an increasing net profit over time. The companies that have a downward net profit trajectory must find a way to improve the periodic result and achieve sustainable profits, primarily through the reduction primarily of operating costs and then financial expenses wherever possible. The best way to change these trends is to reduce costs and reorient the hotel business market through knowing the company's opportunities and strengths and making the most of them.

---

15 Jin Kim, Dong. "A comparative study of financial ratios between hotels and restaurants." *International Journal of Tourism Sciences* 6, no. 1 (2006): 95–106.

Conclusion

Through this comparative analysis of all non-standardized types of ratios, it is concluded that they must be a mandatory part of the analysis of financial statements because they provide insight into the types of costs that are not visible by applying standardized analysis. Data related to EBITDA, EBIT, EBT, and i earnings often make it possible to identify the main points of restraint for companies. Metrics that use comparative types of costs and orient business towards market share can also be of great importance in the process of financial analysis. An indicator such as EVA (economic value added) and a concept such as MEVA (market value added) allow the proper assessment of a company's position in the market, and thus how efficiently and effectively the company is managed. In this context, it is pointed out that non-standardized financial metrics have the highest degree of significance in the analysis of costs and their management not only in hotel companies but also beyond. Most studies define earnings management as a way to influence a company's revenue. [16] The research that has dealt with this issue, as a brief review of the literature on earnings management, show that earnings management is affected by the amount of cash flows from operating activities that lead to false financial reporting.

Bibliography

1. Altman, Edward I. "Financial ratios, discriminant analysis and the prediction of corporate bankruptcy." *The Journal of Finance* 23, no. 4 (1968): 589–609.
2. Copeland, Tom, Time Koller, and Jack Murrin. *Valuation: Measuring and Managing the Value of Companies*. New York, John Wiley& Sons. (2000).
3. Dothan, Michael. "Costs of financial distress and interest coverage ratios." *Journal of Financial Research* 29, no. 2 (2006): 147–162.
4. Horrigan, J. (1968). "A short history of financial ratio analysis." *The Accounting Review*, pp. 284–294.

[16] Safta, Ioana Lavinia, and Monica Violeta Achim. "Quality score on earnings management: Case study on the Romanian companies." In *RSEP CONFERENCES*, p. 230, 2020.

5. Iotti, Mattia, and Giuseppe Bonazzi. "EBITDA/EBIT and cash flow based ICRs: A comparative approach in the agro-food system in Italy." *Financial Assets and Investing* 3, no. 2 (2012): 19–31.
6. Jin Kim, Dong. "A comparative study of financial ratios between hotels and restaurants." *International Journal of Tourism Sciences* 6, no. 1 (2006): 95–106.
7. Knežević, Snežana. *Finansijsko izveštavanje.* Beograd: Samostalno izdanje autora, 2019.
8. Knežević, Snežana, Aleksandra Mitrović, Milan Vujić and Aleksandar Grgur, A. *Analiza finansijskih izveštaja.* Beograd: Samostalno izdanje autora, 2019.
9. Melville, Alan. *International Financial Reporting: A Practical Guide.* Pearson Education, 2008.
10. Škarić-Jovanović, Kata and Dejan Spasić. *Specijalni bilansi. Beograd:* Beograd: Centar za izdavačku delatnost, Ekonomski fakultet u Beogradu, 2014.
11. Safta, Ioana Lavinia, and Monica Violeta Achim. "Quality score on earnings management: Case study on the Romanian companies." In RSEP conferences, p. 230, 2020.
12. Soliman, Mark T. "The use of DuPont analysis by market participants." *The Accounting Review* 83, no. 3 (2008): 823–853.
13. Taparia, Jay. *Understanding Financial Statements: A Journalist's Guide*. Marion Street Press, Inc., 2004.

CHAPTER THREE

CUSTOMER EXPERIENCE IN THE TELECOMMUNICATIONS INDUSTRY: ASSUMPTIONS AND PERSPECTIVES

BIANKA CHORVATOVA[1]
ANDREJ MIKLOSIK[2]

Abstract

Companies looking at growing and increasing their market share rely on the loyalty of their existing customers and the expansion of the customer base. In both cases, customer satisfaction plays a crucial role in sustaining and improving their market position. In the telecommunications industry, mobile operators compete on the B2C and B2B markets, operating a variety of customer touch points. The objective of this paper is to provide insights into the specifics and situation in the Slovak telecommunications market and its development. On top of describing the current situation, it focuses on determining the trends affecting customer experience. Its results will assist in further research aiming at identifying the strengths and weaknesses of customer experience management by selected telecommunications operators and designing a methodological handbook that will enable mobile operators to systematically enhance their customer experience.

Keywords: *Customer experience, telecommunications industry, mobile network operator (MNO), mobile virtual network operator (MVNO), Slovakia*

---

[1] Faculty of Management, Comenius University in Bratislava, Slovakia
[2] Faculty of Management, Comenius University in Bratislava, Slovakia

1. Introduction

In most cases, start-ups lack capital and are in a vulnerable competitive position. Companies that are already established on the market want to grow and increase their market share, gain and build loyal customers, and invest profits in their own development. Thus, companies get to a state where they look into portfolio expansion or consider growth strategies such as licenses or strategic alliances. One such strategy is franchising, which has become established in the telecommunications industry and has created many specifics in the area of customer experience management.

The research presented in this paper forms part of a bigger project aimed at identifying the strengths and weaknesses in managing customer experience by selected telecommunications operators to design a methodological handbook that will identify factors affecting the customer experience. The objective of this paper is to share partial results, assisting the researchers to achieve the aim of the project. Specifically, it provides insights into the unique specifics and situation in the Slovak telecommunications market, its development, and an overview of actively operating mobile network operators and mobile virtual network operators along with their market position.

2. Background Current situation and directions in the telecommunications sector

Telecommunications refers to the exchange of information by electronic and electrical means at a certain (mostly considerable) distance. It is a universal term used for a wide range of information transmission technologies such as mobile phones, landlines, VoIP, and broadcast networks. In telecommunications, data is transmitted in the form of electrical signals known as carrier waves, which are modulated into analogue or digital signals for the transmission of information. Telecommunications and broadcasting are managed worldwide by the International Telecommunication Union (ITU). Most countries have their own telecommunications enforcement and compliance agencies. In Slovakia, for example, it is the Telecommunications Office of the Slovak Republic (Office for the Regulation of Electronic Communications and Postal Services).

In recent years, there has been a steady increase and change in the requirements of the communications industry. To be successful in this area, companies must also focus on new trends and markets such as IoT.

Many companies doing business in the field of IoT are starting to deal with their IT infrastructure. For example, by providing a cloud service, companies can effectively deploy and expand their business models while significantly reducing the total cost of owning physical assets such as servers and the like. Two of the most common means of communication are mobile phones/-smartphones and Wi-Fi, which is why companies tend to reach for innovations in the field to expand their portfolio of customers and the products they provide.

The characteristics of the telecommunications industry in the market fall within the definition of an oligopoly. This type of market does not compete at the European level but in each country separately, where the composition of the market is dominated by a small group of companies to ensure a quality distribution of services on the market. The oligopoly corresponds to the market structure of imperfect competition, is characterized by the fact that the market is dominated by a small number of companies, and that one company has the power to influence the price. In an oligopoly, products and services may be homogeneous or show some differences as competition is generally at the highest level of factors such as quality, customer service, or loyalty, but not the price level. An important feature of an oligopoly is that oligopolies are located in sectors with significant barriers – high input costs, a very high-quality minimum, strong economic experience, and legal restrictions among others. Oligopolies are common on the market; in the communications sector, we can find them precisely because of significant barriers to entry into the telecommunications market. The development trends of oligopolies concern secret agreements (or cartels) in which oligopolists organize and jointly decide on supply and prices. This type of practice is usually illegal under antitrust law due to its adverse effects on the economy and the harm it causes consumers.

3. Selected aspects of customer experience management

Companies are aware of the growing importance of providing customer experience. Thanks to this experience, they differentiate themselves from their competitors. However, not all companies realized this in time – United Airlines experienced a brand crisis during which it lost $1.4 billion overnight when customers shared their unpleasant experiences with the company on social media.[3] Whether it's customer service, product quality,

[3] Hyken, Shep. "Customer experience is the new brand." 2018b.

or just what customers think of the companies they do business with, customer experience is rising in the ranking of variables that determine which brand the customer chooses. Nowadays, 89% of companies compete mainly on the basis of customer experience; in 2010 it was only 36%[4]; 80% of companies believe that they provide a great customer experience but only 8% of customers agree.[5] This ultimately means that there is a huge opportunity for competitors to gain another company's customer base.

Everything the brand does (marketing, research, advertising, etc.) plays a role in shaping the customer experience. Focusing on customer experience management (further as "CXM") may be one of the most important investments a brand can make in today's competitive business environment. For example, Sprinklr has created a CXM platform that allows all the channels through which the company communicates with the customer to be combined into one.[6] The company's solutions enable customer support centres to unify 25 different communication channels, such as Twitter, Facebook, and Instagram. All interactions and data should be in one place – whether the customer wants to communicate by phone, receive advice via chat, or communicate via social networks. Customers don't care which department they talk to when they need help; they just want answers to their questions and to solve their problems. A company may have different teams that help customers with different issues, but this is not the customer's concern. When all interactions are transferred to one place, teams can also work together more effectively.[7]

At present, consumers use an average of almost six contact points, with 50% regularly using more than four, creating the need for a customer service strategy.[8] According to LivePerson, 82% of customers say that solving their problem quickly is a number one factor for a great

---

https://www.forbes.com/sites/shephyken/2018/07/15/customer-experience-is-the-new-brand/#773df31b7f52

[4] Sorofman, Jake. 2014. "Gartner surveys confirm customer experience is the new battlefield." 2014. https://blogs.gartner.com/jake-sorofman/gartner-surveys-confirm-customer-experience-new-battlefield/

[5] Hyken, Shep. "Customer experience is the new brand." 2018b. https://www.forbes.com/sites/shephyken/2018/07/15/customer-experience-is-the-new-brand/#773df31b7f52

[6] Ibid

[7] Ibid

[8] Gautam, N. 2017. "List of innovative customer service ideas to create happier customers." 2017. https://www.ameyo.com/blog/innovative-customer-service-ideas.

experience; Nielsen-McKinsey claims that only 33% of consumers would recommend a brand that provides a quick but ineffective response and 75% of online customers expect help within five minutes.[9] Most customers nowadays expect "more" from companies.[10]

Processes are key to transforming the customer experience as the lack of consistent and interconnected processes (e.g., back office and front office) leads not only to customer frustration but also to the demotivation of front-line employees who are in direct contact with customers. If a company wants to build sustainable differentiation, it is necessary to create a customer-focused organization. Among the skills related to customer experience, purposeful leadership, convincing brand values, employee involvement, and connection with the customer should be included.[11]

The benefits of managing customer experience include strengthening brand preferences, reducing the number of new customers (the cost of a new customer is higher than retaining an existing customer), increased revenue, channel flexibility, customer route maps, omnichannel marketing, faster adaptation, and faster customer identification.[12]

Companies are losing more than $75 billion yearly due to poor customer service.[13] Some innovative ideas for improving customer service include:

- Chatbots – according to Juniper Research, chatbots will save companies $8 billion a year by 2022, and 40% of customers don't care if they are answered by a chatbot or a person.[14]
- Self-service – 45% of companies offering self-service web or mobile services reported an increase in site traffic and a reduction in telephone enquiries.[15]

---

[9] Ibid

[10] Ibid

[11] I-Scoop. 2014. "Customer experience (CX): The guide to customer success." 2014. https://www.i-scoop.eu/customer-experience.

[12] Ameyo. 2018. "What is customer experience? Guide to customer experience management." 2018.
https://www.ameyo.com/customer-engagement/what-is-customer-experience.

[13] Hyken, Shep. "Businesses lose $75 billion due to poor customer service." 2018a. https://www.forbes.com/sites/shephyken/2018/05/17/businesses-lose-75-billion-due-to-poor-customer-service/#21b66a4416f9.

[14] Trips, Reddy. 2017. "Chatbots for customer service will help businesses save $8 billion per year." 2017. https://www.ibm.com/blogs/watson/2017/05/chatbots-customer-service-will-help-businesses-save-8-billion-per-year/.

- Creation of a "hall of fame" based on customer feedback.
- Customer engagement – a survey by Rosetta Consulting found that engaged customers are five times more likely to buy from the same brand in the future.[16]
- Simplification of switching channels for customers during the provision of services – fifteen years ago, the average consumer usually used two contact points when buying goods, and only 7% of consumers regularly used more than four.[17]

4. Methodology

This paper used secondary research to identify and process sources relevant to the examined topic. There is a lot of already published secondary data available that can assist in achieving the objective of this research. In particular, data extraction, synthesis, and comparison were used to aggregate data about the situation in the telecommunications industry in Slovakia and Europe. This has assisted the researchers to identify the current situation in the industry along with relevant trends that can significantly affect perceived customer experience. Resources were identified, examined, and processed between October 2019 and April 2020, with the results summarized in May 2020.

5. Findings

Slovak telecommunications sector in the European context

In Slovakia, telecommunications belong to the NACE division's 61 code (J Information and communication, 61 Telecommunications, 61.1 Wired telecommunications activities, 61.2 Wireless telecommunications

---

[15] Jones, Colleen. "5 customer experience statistics that will change your content focus." 2019. https://review.content-science.com/5-customer-experience-statistics-that-will-change-your-content-focus/.

[16] Bansal, Chetna. 2015. "Why engaged customers are your best customers: Facts & figures on the value of engagement." 2015.
https://www.linkedin.com/pulse/why-engaged-customers-your-best-facts-figures-value-chetna-bansal/

[17] V12. 2020. "25 amazing omnichannel statistics every marketer should know." 2020.
https://v12data.com/blog/25-amazing-omnichannel-statistics-every-marketer-should-know/.

activities, 61.3 Satellite telecommunications activities, 61.9 Other telecommunications activities). This division includes providing telecommunications and related services, which are the transmission of voice, data, text, sound, and images. Transmission equipment that performs these activities may be based on a single technology or a combination of these technologies. The common ground of the activities classified in this section is the transfer of content without being involved in its creation; the breakdown depends on the type of infrastructure performing the activities. In the case of transmission of television signals, a package of complete program channels (created in division 60) in program packages intended for distribution may also be included here.

In figures 3-1 to 3-4, an overview of the Slovak and European telecommunications industry is provided. Figure 3-1 illustrates the development of the industry's annual turnover over the past years, which has been quite steady and above €2 billion.

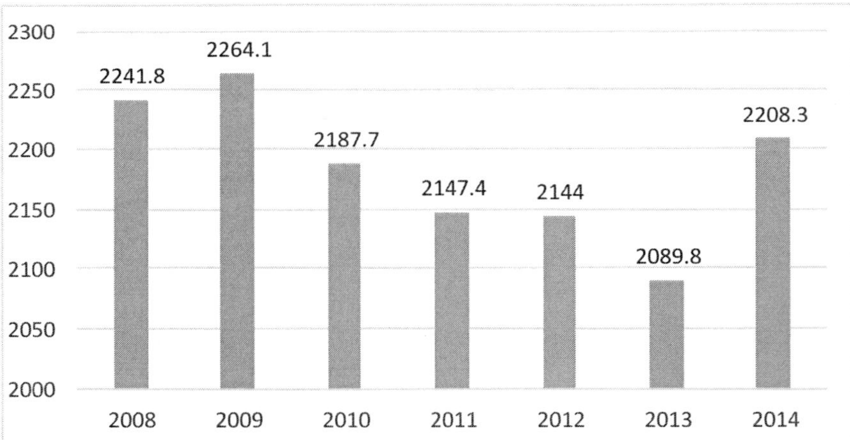

Figure 3-1. Annual turnover of the telecommunications sector in Slovakia in millions of EUR

Source: Processed by the authors, based on data by Statista, "Global no.1 Business Data Platform." 2020. https://www.statista.com/

In figure 3-2, the operating income of Slovak companies in the telecommunications industry is put into perspective with personnel costs.

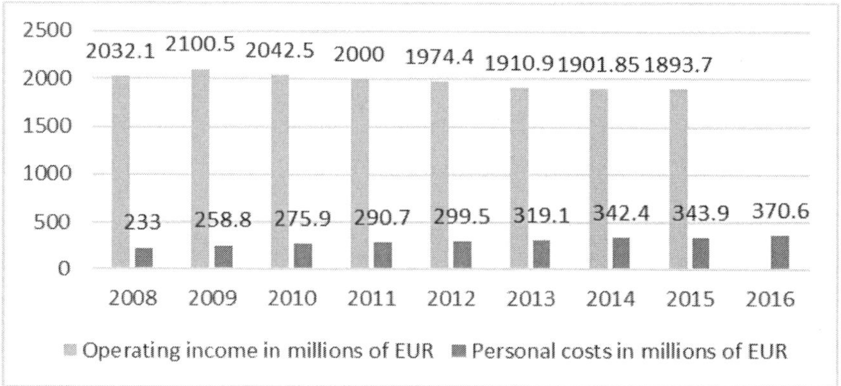

Figure 3-2. Operating income and personnel costs in the telecommunications sector in Slovakia
Source: Processed by the authors, based on data by Statista, "Global no.1 Business Data Platform." 2020. https://www.statista.com/

The situation in the European telecommunications market is illustrated in figure 3-3, which displays the aggregated annual revenues of companies in the telecommunications sector in billions of euros. By 2015, revenues were declining, which could be caused by investments in a new and higher quality network, more comprehensive coverage, or a change in the portfolio of large telecommunications companies.

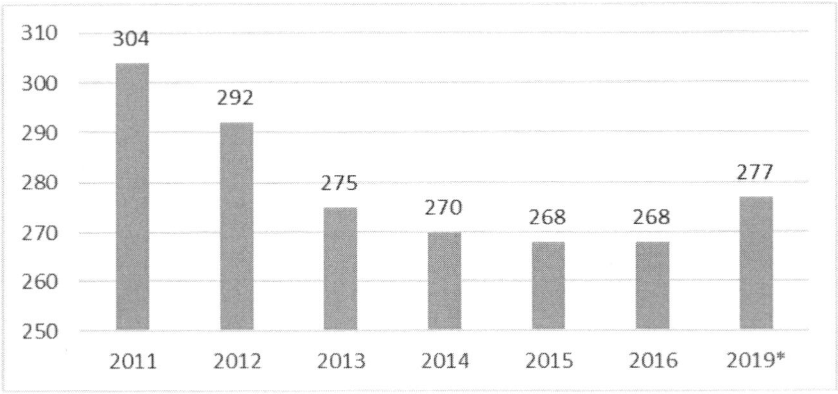

Figure 3-3. Revenue from telecommunications services in Europe in billions of EUR
Source: Processed by the authors, based on data by Statista, "Global no.1 Business Data Platform." 2020. https://www.statista.com/

A similar tendency in the development of operating revenue can be seen when looking at the individual data of selected operators. For example, Telefonica, the second-largest telecommunications operator in Europe, had the lowest revenues in 2015 but has since bounced back (figure 3-4).

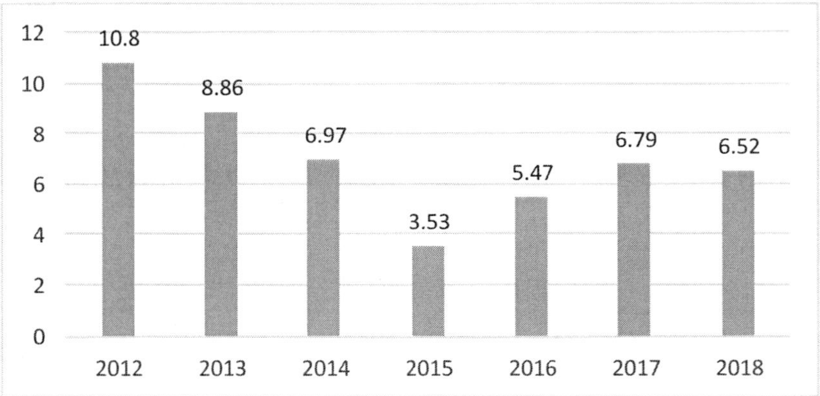

Figure 3-4. Operating income of Telefonica worldwide in billions of EUR
Source: Processed by the authors, based on data by Statista, "Global no.1 Business Data Platform." 2020. https://www.statista.com/

The telecommunications industry is changing quickly in short time intervals. This is because it is based on technological progress, which is one of the fastest-growing phenomena today. Therefore, it is important to find answers to emerging questions such as the determinants of revenue growth, including customer satisfaction, and turn them into knowledge applicable by telecommunications companies.

6. Analysis of mobile network operators in Slovakia

A telecommunications company is a company that operates Internet, data, and voice services in a selected area. This includes companies that provide audiotext and SMS services, sell mobile phones, accessories, and software for mobile phones, telephone exchanges, telecommunications technology, and mobile network operators (further as "MNOs"). MNOs are telecommunications operators with a mobile operator's license. There are other companies offering mobile telecommunications services which do not own mobile networks but are in direct contact with customers, referred to as mobile virtual network operators (further as "MVNOs").

There are four MNOs in the Slovak market – Slovak Telekom, Orange, O2 Slovakia, and 4ka and three MVNOs – Tesco Mobile (O2), FunFon (Orange), and Juro (Slovak Telekom). Table 3-1 gives an overview of the Slovak mobile telecommunications market.

Table 3-1. MNOs and MVNOs in the Slovak market

Mobile network operators (MNOs)	Mobile virtual network operators (MVNOs)
Slovak Telekom	Tesco Mobile (O2)
Orange	FunFon (Orange)
O2 Slovakia	Juro (Slovak Telekom)
4ka	

Slovak Telekom is the oldest MNO in the Slovak market. The operator offers fixed and mobile network products and services as well as voice services. Slovak Telekom started in the Slovak market as the operator EuroTel Bratislava, a.s. on November 16, 1990. It was the leader in 4G network coverage for many years, but in September 2017, O2 became the market leader in 4G network coverage.

Orange Slovakia has been operating in the market since 27 March 2002 (before as Globtel a.s. since 15 January 1997). The France Telecom Group owns 100% of Orange Slovakia shares through Atlas Services

Belgium. Orange was the first MNO to offer a mobile phone for one Slovak crown (an equivalent of 3.3 Euro cents). They introduced tariffication based on seconds, rather than minutes, so that customers could talk to each other cheaper. They were the first to introduce a 24-hour customer line. They brought to the market the opportunity for people to call each other for free. They automatically made the 4G network available to their customers free of charge.[18] .[19] In 2019, Orange replaced the 2G, 3G, and 4G networks by using Nokia technology taken from Alcatel technology, which resulted in an expansion of LTE network coverage. The operator's plan is to increase 4G LTE coverage to 99.8% of the population within two years. The transmitters of this operator are connected to optical cables, and thus the connectivity will be provided by microwave links – the 4G speed when the network is busy can be significantly lower.[20]

O2 Slovakia (hereinafter referred to as O2) entered the Slovak market as the third operator in February 2007. Since the beginning of its operation, this company has presented itself with open communication and fairness to customers – related to the launch of O2 Fair, which changed the rules of mobile communication in Slovakia. It was the first product of MNOs without commitment, extra charges, and non-transparent contract sections. This MNO was also the first to bring to the market the opportunity to buy a phone without a contract, the opportunity for customers to call nationally and internationally for the same price (before cancelling roaming in the EU) and contributed to the availability of automatic number portability between operators. It was also the first Slovak MNO to launch a pilot operation of a 4G LTE network in 2012. Values that characterize O2 are fairness, simplicity, and transparency. This MNO adheres to the motto "fans, fair, fun" and, in addition to social commitments, annually supports social responsibility projects through the O2 Fair Foundation.[21] In 2019, O2 stated that at the end of March, 96.4% of the population had been covered by the 4G network and 99.5% by the 2G network. Building a network is one of the operator's priorities as the

---

[18] Orange Slovakia. 2020. "About us." 2020. https://www.orange.sk/orange-slovensko/kto-sme/

[19] Orange Slovakia. 2020. "About us." 2020. https://www.orange.sk/orange-slovensko/kto-sme/

[20] Maxa, F. "Orange's ambitious plan: 4G wants 2G wherever it is. We know the timing." 2019b. https://zive.aktuality.sk/clanok/140095/ambiciozny-plan-orangeu-4g-chce-vsade-kde-ma-2g-vieme-termin/

[21] O2 Slovakia. 2020. "O2 Slovakia." 2020. https://spolocnost.o2.sk/

quality of the network is one of the most common demands of this operator's customers.

4ka was originally a Slovak mobile operator but is now a trademark under which mobile communication services are provided by SWAN Mobile, which belongs to the portfolio of the Slovak telecommunications holding DanubiaTel. 4ka is the fourth mobile operator in Slovakia and provides large volumes of data at affordable flat rates without obligation. 4ka has the largest network of shops in Slovakia. 4ka entered the Slovak telecommunications market on October 4, 2015. Unlike virtual operators, 4ka has its own nationwide infrastructure, usually of a newer generation.[22] So far, this MNO has relied heavily on national roaming from Orange.[23] In 2018, 4ka declared that it had 600,000 customers.[24] The operator plans to improve coverage in locations where it already has its network by building approximately 50 new BTS stations, the construction of which has so far cost 80 million euros. They wanted to increase customer satisfaction after conducting a representative survey[25] in which O2 did best in terms of customer experience.

The first virtual operators launched their services in Slovakia more than ten years ago. In 2009, O2 provided the network to the operators Tesco Mobile and Naymobile; in 2010 Orange introduced FunFon. In the same year, MVNO Mphone, created by the company Metro Cash and Carry (Slovak Telekom), was launched, and in 2016, Slovak Telekom launched the operator Juro. Today, three virtual operators operate in Slovakia – Tesco Mobile, FunFon, and Juro.[26] GMS-Railways represents a

---

[22] 4ka. "4ka has revealed plans, declares 600,000 clients." 2019. https://zive.aktuality.sk/clanok/135217/4ka-prezradila-plany-deklaruje-600-tisic-klientov

[23] Maxa, F. "4ka will again offer unlimited data. With a condition." 2019a. https://zive.aktuality.sk/clanok/140772/4ka-bude-opat-ponukat-neobmedzene-data-s-podmienkou/

[24] 4ka. "4ka has revealed plans, declares 600,000 clients." 2019. https://zive.aktuality.sk/clanok/135217/4ka-prezradila-plany-deklaruje-600-tisic-klientov

[25] Maxa, F. "4ka will again offer unlimited data. With a condition." 2019a. https://zive.aktuality.sk/clanok/140772/4ka-bude-opat-ponukat-neobmedzene-data-s-podmienkou/

[26] Mitro, Matus. "Virtual operators in Slovakia: The two largest players have a stable customer portfolio and news is coming continuously." 2019. https://fontech.startitup.sk/virtualni-operatori-na-slovensku-dvaja-najvacsi-hraci-maju-stabilne-portfolio-zakaznikov-a-novinky-prichadzaju-priebezne

special type of mobile operator; it is Slovak Railways' network to manage railway traffic or make emergency stops.[27]

Brand store belongs directly to the ownership of the operator, either MNO or MVNO. Its employees are (or through a third party) employees of the operator and the same services are offered in each branded store. The range of products can vary as it depends on the needs of customers in a given area but on the website of the mobile operator it is possible to find all the products provided by the operator.

Some of the stores are operated using the franchising license. A partner or franchising store is a store owned by a third party that manages its own recruitment. It offers the same products and services as the franchisor; it also uses the same marketing and visuals. In real life, however, there may be a slight change compared to the products and services in the brand store.

Analysing the customer touch points and their contribution to customer satisfaction represents the next phase of the research and as such is out of scope of this paper. It will be based on the results presented in the previous two chapters, along with other relevant findings.

Discussion and Conclusion

The results of the research revealed the situation in the Slovak telecommunications market in the context of the European market and its development. Slovakian MNOs and MVNOs are working on expanding their services and coverage in their attempts to sustain or improve their market positions.

Each of the seven companies on the market operates a network of customer touch points, enabling them to offer their services to prospective and existing customers. These touch points can be run by the operator or by franchisees. The form of their operation influences how customer relationships are managed and how customer satisfaction can be measured and influenced.

The results of this research contribute to the body of knowledge in the telecommunications industry by providing unique insights into the situation and trends on the market, systemizing the fragmented secondary

---

[27] SITA. 2008. "The railways are testing their own GSM network. GSM definitions of GSM Abbreviation 1 Global System (or Standard) for Mobile, a Standardized International System for Digital Mobile Telecommunication." 2008. https://tech.sme.sk/c/3747679/zeleznice-testuju-vlastnu-gsm-siet.html.

data available in different resources. The findings create a basis for the next part of the research project aiming at identifying and managing the determinants of customer satisfaction in the telecommunications industry.

Acknowledgement: This paper originated as the result of working on the grant scheme KEGA 016EU-4/2019: The innovative learning texts from marketing for secondary schools.

References

4ka. "4ka has revealed plans, declares 600,000 clients." 2019. https://zive.aktuality.sk/clanok/135217/4ka-prezradila-plany-deklaruje-600-tisic-klientov

Ameyo. 2018. "What is customer experience? Guide to customer experience management." 2018. https://www.ameyo.com/customer-engagement/what-is-customer-experience

Bansal, Chetna. 2015. "Why engaged customers are your best customers: Facts & figures on the value of engagement." 2015. https://www.linkedin.com/pulse/why-engaged-customers-your-best-facts-figures-value-chetna-bansal/

Gautam, N. 2017. "List of innovative customer service ideas to create happier customers." 2017. https://www.ameyo.com/blog/innovative-customer-service-ideas

Hyken, Shep. "Businesses lose $75 billion due to poor customer service." 2018a. https://www.forbes.com/sites/shephyken/2018/05/17/businesses-lose-75-billion-due-to-poor-customer-service/#21b66a4416f9

Hyken, Shep. "Customer experience is the new brand." 2018b. https://www.forbes.com/sites/shephyken/2018/07/15/customer-experience-is-the-new-brand/#773df31b7f52

I-Scoop. 2014. "Customer experience (CX): The guide to customer success." 2014. https://www.i-scoop.eu/customer-experience

Jones, Colleen. "5 customer experience statistics that will change your content focus." 2019. https://review.content-science.com/5-customer-experience-statistics-that-will-change-your-content-focus/

Maxa, F. "4ka will again offer unlimited data. With a condition." 2019a. https://zive.aktuality.sk/clanok/140772/4ka-bude-opat-ponukat-neobmedzene-data-s-podmienkou/

Maxa, F. "Orange's ambitious plan: 4g wants 2g wherever it is. We know the timing." 2019b.

https://zive.aktuality.sk/clanok/140095/ambiciozny-plan-orangeu-4g-chce-vsade-kde-ma-2g-vieme-termin/

Mitro, Matus. “Virtual operators in Slovakia: The two largest players have a stable customer portfolio and news is coming continuously.” 2019. https://fontech.startitup.sk/virtualni-operatori-na-slovensku-dvaja-najvacsi-hraci-maju-stabilne-portfolio-zakaznikov-a-novinky-prichadzaju-priebezne

O2 Slovakia. 2020. “O2 Slovakia.” 2020. https://spolocnost.o2.sk/

Orange Slovakia. 2020. “About us.” 2020 https://www.orange.sk/orange-slovensko/kto-sme/

SITA. 2008. “The railways are testing their own GSM network. GSM definitions of GSM abbreviation 1 global system (or standard) for mobile, a standardized international system for digital mobile telecommunication.” 2008. https://tech.sme.sk/c/3747679/zeleznice-testuju-vlastnu-gsm-siet.html

Sorofman, Jake. 2014. “Gartner surveys confirm customer experience is the new battlefield.” 2014. https://blogs.gartner.com/jake-sorofman/gartner-surveys-confirm-customer-experience-new-battlefield/

Statista. 2020. “Global no.1 business data platform.” 2020. https://www.statista.com/

Trips, Reddy. 2017. “Chatbots for customer service will help businesses save $8 billion per year.” 2017. https://www.ibm.com/blogs/watson/2017/05/chatbots-customer-service-will-help-businesses-save-8-billion-per-year/

V12. 2020. “25 amazing Omnichannel statistics every marketer should know.” 2020. https://v12data.com/blog/25-amazing-omnichannel-statistics-every-marketer-should-know/

CHAPTER FOUR

EVALUATION OF THE FINANCIAL PERFORMANCE OF A COMPANY: CASE STUDY

MARIJA MILOJIČIĆ[1]

Abstract

The aim of this study is to evaluate the key financial performances of a domestic company in the field of tourism. Ratio analysis was applied as a frequently used technique of financial analysis. Four years are covered by the analyzed period, and financial reports of the observed tourism company (balance sheet and income statement) were used as empirical data. Performance measurement is of special significance for the performance assessment, and identification of achievements in relation to the planned measures. The analysis identified trends that are relevant for identifying opportunities and threats in company performance management.

Keywords: *tourism company, evaluation, ratio analysis, financial reports*

1. Introduction

During financial reports analysis, it is necessary to know well the conditions in which companies from certain areas operate.[2] Also, the

---

[1] *PhD student Faculty of Organizational Sciences, University of Belgrade, Republic of Serbia*

[2] Brown, Andrijana, Marko Milasinovic, Aleksandra Mitrovic, and Snezana Knezevic. "Are audit opinions related to bankruptcy forecasting of companies listed on the sector a-agriculture, forestry and fisheries?" *Fresenius Environmental Bulletin* 29, no. 11 (2020): 9899–905.

quality of financial statements is of special importance for high-quality business decision making. The auditing profession guarantees the reliability of financial reports whereby auditors should apply in their work some of the existing models for predicting company bankruptcy, and in case of signs of financial trouble inform users through the audit report.[3]

The analysis was conducted by applying ratio indicators to financial items incorporated in balance sheet and income statement. The financial analysis using four groups of ratio numbers provided insight into the liquidity, solvency, profitability, and efficiency of a tourism company operating in Serbia. The company was founded in 1991 and performs travel agency business – tourist guiding, i.e., initial tourism. To a lesser extent, it is also engaged in receptive tourism. In its area, the company belongs to micro-enterprises in all the observed years.

2. Material and methods

The research conducted in this paper refers to a case study of the selected company for the period 2016–2019. Empirical data are available on the website of the Business Registers Agency.[4]

For the purposes of this research, an analysis of liquidity, activity, solvency, profitability, and efficiency was applied, and the selected financial ratios for the application of the case study method are given in the following table.

---

[3] Milašinović, Marko and Mitrović, Aleksandra (2020). Internal determinants of agricultural profitability. *Agroeconomics*, 49(88), 1–9, Available at: https://agroekonomika.rs/images/Brojevi/ae88/Agroekonomika_88.pdf

[4] Knežević, Snezana, Aleksandra Mitrović, Marko Vujić, and Aleksandar Grgur. *Analiza finansijskih izveštaja*, Valjevo: Valjevoprint, 2019.

Table 4-1. Application of financial ratios in the evaluation of company performance

Liquidity Ratios	Solvency Ratios	Profitability Ratios	Efficiency Ratios
Current ratio	Interest coverage ratio	Gross profit margin	Average time of collection of trade receivables in days
Quick ratio	Debt ratio	Profit margin	Average trade payables time in days
Cash ratio	Debt-to-equity ratio	Return on assets	Turnover ratio of total assets
Net working capital		Return on equity	

Source: Summarized by the authors

3. Results and discussion

Liquidity ratios (short-term solvency ratios) focus on the company's ability to pay its short-term liabilities (debts). This group of ratios is calculated solely on the basis of balance sheet data known as the liquidity ratio. Those who grant corporate loans deal specifically with the company's liquidity. It is not uncommon for a company to show a profit in its income statement even though it does not have enough money to pay off creditors, i.e., the company has unhealthy liquidity ratios. The following liquidity indicators indicate this type of problem:

Table 4-2. Analysis of the enterprise's liquidity (2016–2019)

Indicators	2016	2017	2018	2019
Current Ratio	1.1443	2.1615	2.4778	9.4372
Quick Ratio	0.5627	0.6895	2.4321	9.3449
Cash Ratio	0.1102	0.2497	0.4694	4.9818

Source: Authors' research based on financial statements 2016–2019

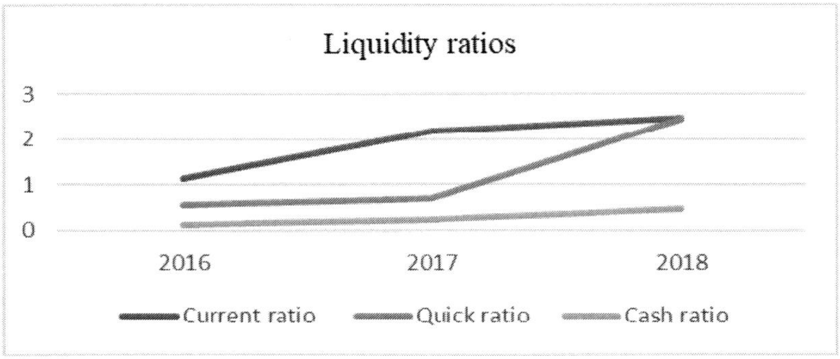

Figure 4-1. Dynamics of liquidity indicators (2016–2019)

According to the data presented in table 4-1 and figure 4-1, extreme values can be observed in the movement of current ratios in 2019, which was almost nine times higher in 2016. The trend is almost identical when looking at the quick ratio. In 2016, the current ratio was below the desired value (2:1). The quick ratio is below normal value (1:1) in 2016 and 2017. The current ratio is within the desired normal value while in 2018 and 2019, the situation worsened because the ratios are lower than 1. Accelerated liquidity ratios are below the desired value, and all are lower than 1 in all observed years (2016–2019). The cash ratio shows growth by each year, which is a favourable trend.

Table 4-3. Net working capital (2016–2019) (in 000 dinars)

Indicators	2016	2017	2018	2019
Net working capital	754	3.344	3.167	5.577

Source: Authors' research based on financial statements (2016–2019); www.apr.gov.rs

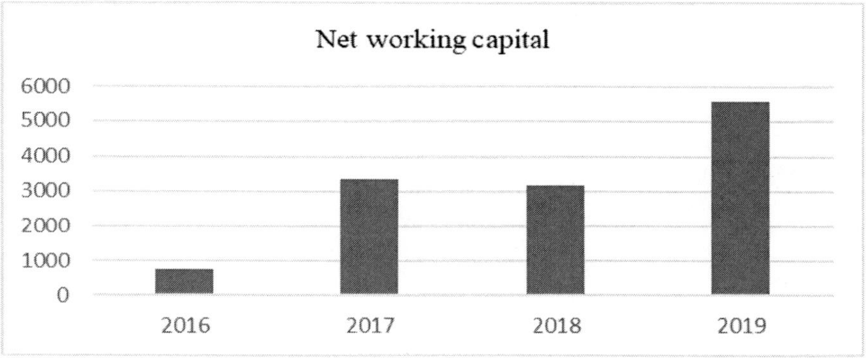

Figure 4-2. Dynamics of net working capital (2016–2019)

Table 4-3 and figure 4-2 present that the net working capital in all observed years was positive, considering that the maximum value was in 2019 and the minimum in 2016.

Table 4-4. Solvency ratios

Indicators	2016	2017	2018	2019
Interest coverage ratio (in number of times)	22.3793	2.0287	2.454	2.6343
Debt ratio (in number of times)	0.8871	0.712	0.6427	0.6659
Debt-to-equity ratio (%)	786.0403	247.1996	179.9011	199.3162

Source: Authors' research based on financial statements (2016–2019); www.apr.gov.rs

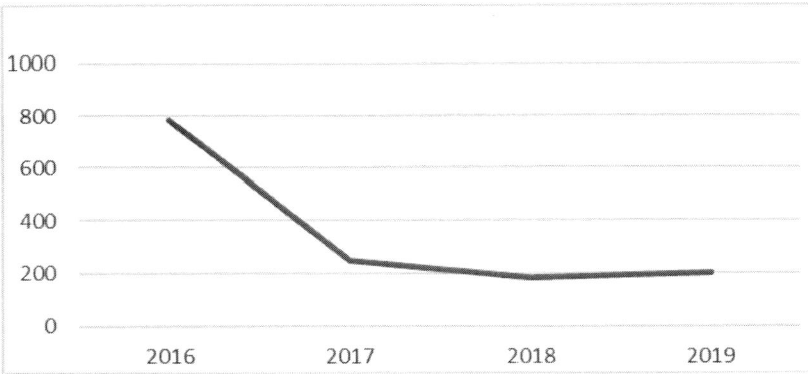

Figure 4-3. Debt-to-equity ratio
Source: Authors' research based on annual report – financial statements (2016–2019); www.apr.gov.rs

Observing the obtained values of solvency ratios, it can be noticed that the interest coverage ratio was the highest in 2016 – 22.38, and the lowest in 2017 (2.02). This indicator shows how easily the company can pay all its interest-related obligations. The debt ratio on average shows a declining trend, with the exception of the last year where there was an increase. The orientation value of this ratio is 1, and the values of this ratio throughout the observed years are below the normal value, which indicates a low level of indebtedness. The debt-to-euity ratio shows the highest value in 2016, followed by a decline in the next two years and an increase in 2019. This ratio showed a steep decline in 2017.

According to Milašinović and Mitrović,[5] one of the tasks of a company's management is to identify which factors affect the level of profitability of the company they manage. This is also the final test of the business efficiency of the analyzed company. Profitability ratios are used to test the success of companies in generating profits. The profitability ratios gross and net profit margin, return on assets, and return on equity are shown.

[5] Milašinović, Marko and Mitrović, Aleksandra (2020). Internal determinants of agricultural profitability. *Agroeconomics*, 49(88), 1–9, Available at: https://agroekonomika.rs/images/Brojevi/ae88/Agroekonomika_88.pdf

Table 4-5. Profitability testing

Indicators	2016	2017	2018	2019
Gross profit margin (%)	66.4714	-1.1625	38.0946	56.9959
Return on sales (ROS) (%)	2.0305	2.2702	1.7789	1.4918
Return on assets (ROA) (%)	2.2039	2.9883	2.0033	1.7537
Return on equity (ROE) (%)	23.4059	14.6083	6.2601	5.0833

Source: Authors' research based on annual report – financial statements (2016–2019)

According to the data presented in table 4-5, it can be concluded that gross profit margin steeply declined in 2017 but returned in the next year to 57% of the 2016 value. The net profit margin shows value oscillations during the observed time period (2016–2019).

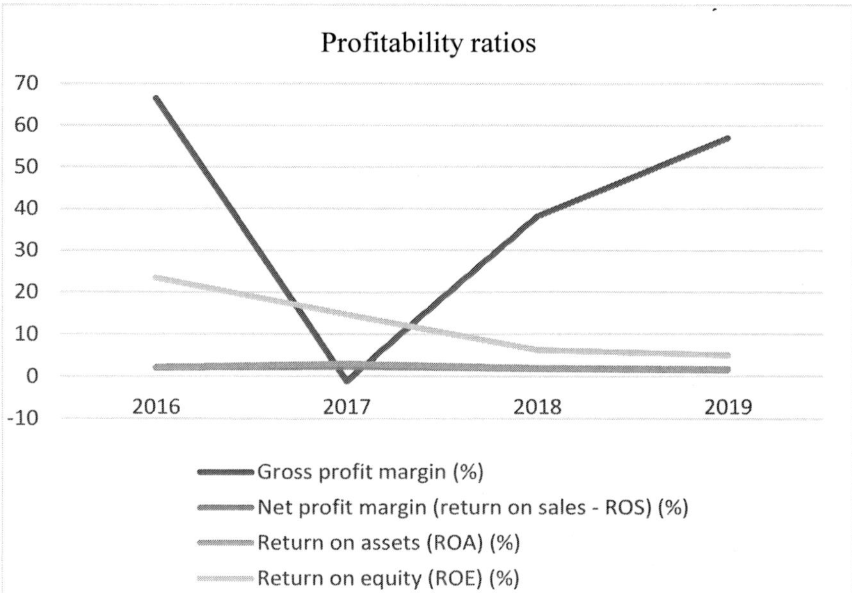

Figure 4-4. Profitability analysis

Return on assets was highest in 2017 – 2.99%, and lowest in 2019 – 1.75%. Return on equity showed a negative tendency since it declined over the observed years.

The movement of revenues from the services sale, based on the internal accounting data, is shown in the following table.

Table 4-6. Revenues by month in 2019. and 2020.

Month	2019	2020	Revenue increase/decrease
January	429,000	389,000	decrease
February	410,000	301,000	decrease
March	447,000	88,000	decrease
April	590,000	0	decrease
May	510,000	0	decrease
June	671,000	493,445	decrease
July	1,144,521	345,000	decrease
August	1,300,627	516,667	decrease
September	1,382,954	258,298	decrease
October	300,127	113,272	decrease
November	287,707	127,541	decrease
December	310,001	0	decrease

Source: Internal data of the company

Based on the given data, an extremely negative tendency can be noticed because the decline is the same phenomenon in all observed months for 2019 and 2020. In three observed months, there was no revenue at all (April, May, and December 2020). This means it was difficult for the company to cover its operating costs in the observed months. The seasonal character of the revenue from the services sale is specific for tourism activities.

"Financial efficiency ratios, i.e. activity ratios are measures of company's ability to convert its assets from balance sheet to cash or sales revenue. By analyzing activity ratios, it is possible to determine how efficiently and well the company is managed".[6] Table 4-6 and figure 4-5 present the results related to the efficiency analysis.

[6] Financial reports, www.apr.gov.rs, Accessed on 12.2.2021.

Table 4-7. Efficiency analysis

Indicator	2016	2017	2018	2019
Average time of collection of trade receivables (in days)	143.6626	45.875	87.5825	123.1214
Average trade payables time (in days)	86.2908	37.5345	34.637	36.698
Total assets turnover ratio	1.0854	1.3163	1.1261	1.1756

Source: Authors' research based on financial reports (2016–2019); www.apr.gov.rs

The turnover ratio of total assets was highest in the last observed year (2019) and lowest in 2016. The higher the turnover ratio of total assets, the better and more efficiently a company uses its asset base to generate sales. The average collection time of trade receivables, as well as trade payables, fluctuates by year.

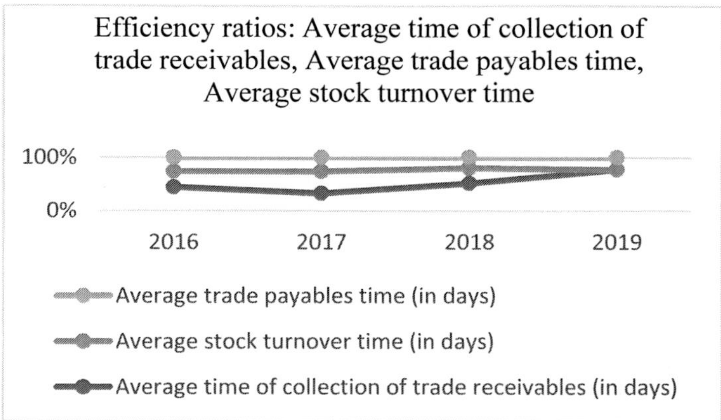

Figure 4-5. Dynamics of ratios: Average time of collection of trade receivables, average trade payables time, average stock turnover time

An efficient way of using the measurement of the duration of collection of trade receivables is to monitor the trend line throughout the months, and if it is a seasonal business, there is a possibility of a comparison of measures on the same basis for the same month in the previous year, which provides the basis for comparison. A negative tendency has been identified, showing that on average the observed company in all the years observed collects its trade receivables from customers more slowly than it pays its trade payables. In some cases, the calculated average time period in which uncollected balances on the company's accounts are stated in receivables can provide a lot of information regarding the nature of the company's cash flow.

Conclusion

Based on the application of this case study of a tourism company's financial data, trends were observed that served as a basis for drawing appropriate conclusions regarding the financial performance of the company. In other words, an assessment of the financial health of the observed company was formed.

The dynamics of liquidity indicators indicate that in 2019, liquidity was extremely high in terms of both current ratios and quick ratios. Profitability analysis showed that the gross profit margin was negative in 2016, and that return on equity declined over the observed years, which is a bad sign for investors. The company is not over-indebted and has a high level of interest coverage by its earnings. Special attention should be paid to the policy of collection of trade receivables so the company does not have a lack of funds to cover short-term liabilities, which would have further negative implications for the financing of operating activities.

The limitations of this analysis are reflected in the fact that no comparison was made to related economic entities (from the so-called peer group) and a bankruptcy test. Future research should focus on the inclusion of non-financial measures in the analysis of financial performance, and comparison with key competitors and leaders in the industry in which the observed company operates. Future research could focus on examining whether the profitability of this and competing companies from a related group is influenced by firm size, liquidity, indebtedness, and sales growth.

References

Brown, Andrijana, Marko Milasinovic, Aleksandra Mitrovic, and Snezana Knezevic. "Are audit opinions related to bankruptcy forecasting of companies listed on the sector a-agriculture, forestry and fisheries?" *Fresenius Environmental Bulletin* 29, no. 11 (2020): 9899–905.

Milašinović, Marko and Mitrović, Aleksandra (2020). Internal determinants of agricultural profitability. *Agroeconomics*, 49(88), 1–9. Available at: https://agroekonomika.rs/images/Brojevi/ae88/Agroekonomika_88.pdf

Knežević, Snezana, Aleksandra Mitrović, Marko Vujić, and Aleksandar Grgur. *Analiza finansijskih izveštaja*, Valjevo: Valjevoprint, 2019.

Financial reports, www.apr.gov.rs, Accessed on 12.2.2021.

PROFESSIONAL PAPER

CHAPTER FIVE

INNOVATION AND COMPETITIVENESS DYNAMICS OF EUROPEAN UNION MEMBER STATES

VLATKA BILAS[1]
LANA TRIFUNIĆ[2]
MARIO KOVAČIĆ[3]

Abstract

The purpose of this paper is to qualitatively and quantitatively compare and describe the innovation and competitiveness performance of European Union member states. A comparative analysis of statistical data and five different methodologies was: Global Innovation Index; Bloomberg Innovation Index; European Innovation Scoreboard; Global Competitiveness Index 4.0; and Global Talent Competitiveness Index. The research shows that Sweden has been categorized as an innovation leader by the European Innovation Scoreboard and why it has achieved the best results according to all five methodologies of research. Finland, Denmark, and the Netherlands are also among the top five EU countries according to all methodologies, while Romania, Malta, Cyprus, and Croatia record the poorest results among the EU countries. There is a record of very uneven

[1] Department of International Economics, Faculty of Economics & Business, University of Zagreb, Croatia
[2] Notitia d.o.o., Zagreb, Croatia
[3] Notitia d.o.o., Zagreb, Croatia

economic performance and a heterogeneous level of competitiveness among EU member states, which is why the new cohesion policy and its accompanying financial perspective for the period 2021–2027 is expected to facilitate a more convergent and homogeneous development of EU countries.

Keywords: *innovation, competitiveness, economic development, economic growth, EU*

1. Introduction

The key to progress and ultimately competitiveness is the continuous implementation of strategic activities to improve all aspects of the economy. For this purpose, it is necessary to regularly monitor, evaluate, and analyse national progress and compare it with the performance of benchmark countries in order to identify areas for improvement. The aim of this paper is to qualitatively and quantitatively compare and describe the state and progress of European Union member states in the field of research, development, and innovation and competitiveness through statistical data and five different methodologies: (1) The Global Innovation Index; (2) The Bloomberg Innovation Index; (3) The European Innovation Scoreboard; (4) The Global Competitiveness Index 4.0; (5) The Global Talent Competitiveness Index.

The paper consists of four sections. After the introduction, the second section describes the meaning and importance of innovation and competitiveness and how they are intertwined. The third section provides an overview of the innovation and competitiveness performance of European Union member states, with deeper insights into methodologies for assessing innovation and competitiveness as well as human resources and investments in research and development. The fourth and final section is the conclusion.

2. Innovation and competitiveness – chains interlinked

In order to be competitive, countries must create factors and develop policies that will create the conditions for a better position in the global market. The factors and policies that affect competitiveness are the business environment, economic and technological infrastructure, education, entrepreneurship, creativity, and innovation.[4] Innovation in the broadest sense implies the creation of new knowledge and new technologies as well as the acquisition of knowledge and technologies that have been developed elsewhere.[5] It is precisely the creation and adoption of new knowledge and new technologies that represent an effective solution for market survival, successful competition, and gaining greater market shares. Therefore, innovation is important for survival on the market and improving competitiveness, which is why more and more companies are turning to innovation to create competitive advantages and added value and to improve their economic performance and competitiveness.

Innovation is a concept that is much wider than is popularly believed and does not belong exclusively to the business sector. More specifically, innovation is present in all ranges of society, from the business sector, public sector, and non-profit organizations to households.[6] The concept of innovation is multidimensional so it does not merely represent the final product, service, process, business model, or business organization as innovation. Innovation involves both process segments and certain activities that ultimately lead to innovation as their ultimate outcome. In short, innovation is considered to be something new and significantly different from previous products and processes. Therefore, innovation activities are activities that include all development, financial, and commercial activities undertaken with the aim of creating innovation.[7]

Innovation is the key to achieving sustainable development, which also makes innovation the key to the competitiveness of the European Union.[8] In a time of major demographic changes and increased competition on a global level, Europe's competitiveness depends on the ability to develop

---

[4] Duspara, Lena, Knežević, Sanja and Mladen Turuk. "Competitiveness and innovation challenge in Croatia", *Poslovna izvrsnost Zagreb*, XI no. 2 (2017): 41–58. https://hrcak.srce.hr/file/284317

[5] Bilas, Vlatka and Sanja Franc. *Innovation and Development*. Zagreb: Notitia d.o.o. 2018.

[6] OECD/Eurostat. *Oslo Manual 2018: Guidelines for`Collecting, Reporting and Using Data on Innovation, 4th Edition, The Measurement of Scientific, Technological and Innovation Activities*. Luxembourg: OECD Publishing, Paris/Eurostat. 2018.

[7] Ibid.

[8] European Commission. "Eco-innovation: The key to Europe's future competitiveness". 2012. Brussels: European Commission. Accessed April 15, 2020. http://ec.europa.eu/environment/pubs/pdf/factsheets/eco_innovation.pdf.

innovation,[9] which is why innovation has been the centre of the Europe 2020 strategy for the smart, sustainable, and inclusive growth of a competitive economy.[10] In all countries, especially in developing countries, innovation is considered to be a starting point for addressing social problems such as environmental pollution, health, poverty, and unemployment, which is why innovation and competitiveness are intertwined. The competitiveness of countries and companies depends on the orientation towards technology and information and the ability to develop innovation[11] so there has been increasing interest in how companies innovate and therefore contribute to international competitiveness.[12] Competitiveness cannot be observed as merely an attribute of a specific country; it is rather a cumulative quality since it reflects the state of its companies.[13] With proper understanding and use, innovation can help achieve a more homogeneous level of competitiveness among the European Union member states.[14]

---

[9] Ibid.

[10] European Commission. "Communication from the Commission: Europe 2020. A strategy for smart, sustainable, and inclusive growth", 2010. Brussels: European Commission. Accessed April 22, 2020.
http://ec.europa.eu/eu2020/pdf/COMPLET%20EN%20BARROSO%20%20%20007%20-%20Europe%202020%20-%20EN%20version.pdf

[11] Dogan, Ebru. "The effect of innovation on competitiveness", *Istanbul University, Faculty of Economics, Department of Business Administration, Istanbul, Ekonometri ve İstatistik Sayı*, 24 (2016): 60–81.
http://static.dergipark.org.tr/article-download/e228/6dfc/9d38/587d11a314943.pdf?

[12] Ferreira, Joao J., Fernandes, Christina I., and Vanessa Ratten. "Entrepreneurship, innovation and competitiveness: What is the connection?", *International Journal of Business and Globalisation*, 1, no. 18 (2017): 73–95.
https://www.researchgate.net/publication/312117305_Entrepreneurship_innovation_and_competitiveness_What_is_the_connection

[13] Camison, Cesar. "Competitiveness and sustainability in tourist firms and destinations", *Competitiveness, Sustainability and Tourism*, 6, no. 12 (2020): 1–6.
file:///C:/Users/Vlatka/Downloads/sustainability-12-02388.pdf

[14] Farinha, Luis, Ferreira, Joao J. M., and Sara Nunes. "Linking innovation and entrepreneurship to economic growth". *Competitiveness Review*, 4, no. 28 (2018): 451–475.
https://www.researchgate.net/publication/325578655_Linking_innovation_and_entrepreneurship_to_economic_growth

3. Overview of the innovation and competitiveness performance of European Union member states

3.1 Innovation performance of European Union member states

The innovation dynamics of European Union member states can be observed through various methodologies that are different yet equally insightful. For example, the Global Innovation Index 2019 (GII 2019)[15] provides insights into the multidimensional aspects of innovation-based growth. Through the presentation of 80 detailed metrics for 129 economies in 2019, GII is one of the leading references for measuring innovation performance in the economy. GII is a benchmarking tool that can facilitate public-private dialogue and where policy makers, business leaders, and other stakeholders can evaluate progress in innovation annually. Each year, the GII analyses a thematic component that tracks global innovation. Through three indices (the overall GII, Innovation Input Sub-Index, and Innovation Output Sub-Index), the 2019 edition analyses the landscape of medical innovation for the coming decade, observing how technological and non-technological medical innovation will transform healthcare delivery across the globe. The overall GII score is the average of the Input and Output Sub-Index scores. The Innovation Input Sub-Index is comprised of five pillars that capture elements of the national economy that enable innovative activities: (1) Institutions, (2) Human capital and research, (3) Infrastructure, (4) Market sophistication, and (5) Business sophistication. The Innovation Output Sub-Index provides information about outputs that are the result of innovative activities within economies: (6) Knowledge and technology outputs, and (7) Creative outputs.

According to the overall GII for 2019,[16] Sweden holds the first position among EU countries (while ranked 2nd overall) as well as in the Innovation Input and Innovation Output Sub-Index. In overall GII, Sweden is immediately followed by Netherlands, United Kingdom, Finland, and Denmark. Croatia ranks 44th in the world, one of the EU countries with the lowest results, after which comes only Romania (50th). In the Innovation Input Sub-Index, Sweden is followed by Denmark, United

---

[15] Cornell University, INSEAD, and WIPO. "The Global Innovation Index 2019: Creating healthy lives – The future of medical innovation, Ithaca, Fontainebleau, and Geneva". 2019. Accessed April 30, 2020, https://www.wipo.int/publications/en/details.jsp?id=4434.

[16] Ibid.

Kingdom, Finland, and the Netherlands, and in the Innovation Output Sub-Index by the United Kingdom, Finland, Germany, and Ireland.

Furthermore, the Bloomberg Innovation Index (BII 2020)[17] measures the intensity of research and development (R&D) investment, which is defined as R&D expenditure as a percentage of GDP; the added value of production; productivity defined as GDP per employee over 15 years of age; high technology (comprising the share of domestic high-tech public companies such as airlines and renewable energy companies); tertiary education; the concentration of researchers or the percentage of the population involved in R&D; and the number of patents per capita. According to the BII,[18] in 2020 Germany came 1st with a score of 88.21, while Sweden, Finland, Denmark, and France were among the top ten EU countries. Croatia is ranked one place higher (43rd) compared to the year before and is among the three EU countries with a low score of 55.00, which is still a slight improvement from the previous year (54.98), while only Malta and Cyprus are behind Croatia. The EU leader in R&D intensity was Sweden, Ireland was the leader in productivity, France in high-tech density, and Denmark in researcher concentration.

The European Innovation Scoreboard (EIS 2019)[19] provides a comparative assessment of the research and innovation results of EU member states and selected third countries and the relative strengths and weaknesses of their research and innovation systems. With its methodology, it assists countries in assessing areas where they need to concentrate their efforts to increase innovation. The EIS measurement framework distinguishes four main types of indicators and 10 innovation dimensions, with 27 different indicators. The *Framework condition* covers the main external drivers of innovation performance and encompasses three dimensions of innovation: (1) Human resources, (2) Attractive research systems, and (3) Innovation-friendly environment. *Investments* cover both public and

---

[17] Bloomberg. 2020. "Bloomberg Innovation Index 2020". Accessed April 16, 2020. https://www.bloomberg.com/news/articles/2020-01-18/germany-breaks-korea-s-six-year-streak-as-most-innovative-nation

[18] Bloomberg. 2020. "Bloomberg Innovation Index 2020". Accessed April 16, 2020. https://www.bloomberg.com/news/articles/2020-01-18/germany-breaks-korea-s-six-year-streak-as-most-innovative-nation

[19] Maastricht Economic and Social Research Institute on Innovation and Technology (MERIT). 2020. "European Innovation Scoreboard 2019". Accessed April 18, 2020.
https://ec.europa.eu/docsroom/documents/38781/attachments/1/translations/en/renditions/native

private investment in research and innovation and include two dimensions: (1) Finance and support, and (2) Firm investment. *Innovation activities* include enterprise-level innovation divided into the following three dimensions of innovation: (1) Innovators, (2) Linkages, and (3) Intellectual assets. *Impacts* capture the effects of enterprise innovation activities in two dimensions of innovation: (1) Employment impacts, and (2) Sales impact.

Member states are classified into four groups based on average results. Denmark, Finland, the Netherlands, and Sweden are innovation leaders with results well above the EU average. Austria, Belgium, Estonia, France, Germany, Ireland, Luxembourg, and the United Kingdom are strong innovators with an effect above or near the EU average. Results from Croatia, Cyprus, Czech Republic, Greece, Hungary, Italy, Latvia, Lithuania, Malta, Poland, Portugal, Slovakia, Slovenia, and Spain are below the EU average and these countries are therefore moderate innovators. Bulgaria and Romania are modest innovators with a performance well below the EU average. In this year's edition, Estonia (formerly a moderate innovator) joins the group of strong innovators. Luxembourg and the United Kingdom (both countries were previously innovation leaders) are now among the strong innovators this year, and Slovenia (formerly a strong innovator) is one of the moderate innovators. Performance differences between individual innovation leaders and strong innovators are relatively small.

According to EIS 2019[20], EU leading countries in innovation are, respectively, Sweden, Finland, Denmark, the Netherlands, and Luxembourg. Romania holds the lowest overall position among EU countries. On the other hand, Croatia holds the last and lowest position of the 28 EU countries in the sales effects segment but is ranked best in the corporate investment dimension (11th). However, the EIS index has been growing steadily since 2014, and for the first time Croatia has moved closer to the average of 60%, bringing it closer to Poland with a higher position.

[20] Maastricht Economic and Social Research Institute on Innovation and Technology (MERIT). 2020. "European Innovation Scoreboard 2019". Accessed April 18, 2020.
https://ec.europa.eu/docsroom/documents/38781/attachments/1/translations/en/renditions/native.

Table 5-1. Rankings and results of Global Innovation Index (2019), Bloomberg Innovation Index (2020), and European Innovation Scoreboard (2019)

Global Innovation Index 2019			Bloomberg Innovation Index 2020			European Innovation Scoreboard 2019		
R	**Country**	**Score**	**R**	**Country**	**Score**	**R**	**Country**	**Score**
2	Sweden	63,65	**1**	Germany	88,21	**1**	Sweden	147,74
4	Netherlands	61,44	**5**	Sweden	85,50	**2**	Finland	145,87
5	United Kingdom	61,30	**7**	Finland	84,00	**3**	Denmark	140,94
6	Finland	59,83	**8**	Denmark	83,22	**4**	Netherlands	134,99
7	Denmark	58,44	**10**	France	82,75	**5**	Luxembourg	129,20
9	Germany	58,19	**11**	Austria	82,40	**6**	Belgium	128,06
12	Ireland	56,10	**13**	Netherlands	81,28	**7**	United Kingdom	127,82
16	France	54,25	**14**	Belgium	79,93	**8**	Germany	126,88
18	Luxembourg	53,47	**16**	Ireland	78,65	**9**	Austria	124,82
21	Austria	50,94	**18**	United Kingdom	76,03	**10**	Ireland	117,63
23	Belgium	50,18	**19**	Italy	75,76	**11**	France	111,01
24	Estonia	49,97	**21**	Slovenia	73,93	**12**	Estonia	103,75
26	Czech Republic	49,43	**24**	Czech Republic	70,00	**13**	Portugal	97,63
27	Malta	49,01	**25**	Poland	69,98	**14**	Czech Republic	89,40
28	Cyprus	48,34	**28**	Hungary	68,24	**15**	Slovenia	87,61
29	Spain	47,85	**30**	Greece	66,30	**16**	Cyprus	86,78
30	Italy	46,30	**31**	Luxembourg	65,41	**17**	Malta	85,69
31	Slovenia	45,25	**32**	Romania	65,25	**18**	Italy	84,94
32	Portugal	44,65	**33**	Spain	65,11	**19**	Spain	84,77
33	Hungary	44,51	**34**	Portugal	65,08	**20**	Greece	81,62
34	Latvia	43,23	**36**	Estonia	62,79	**21**	Lithuania	81,08
37	Slovakia	42,05	**37**	Latvia	62,03	**22**	Slovakia	69,10
38	Lithuania	41,46	**38**	Lithuania	61,97	**23**	Hungary	69,03
39	Poland	41,31	**41**	Slovakia	59,36	**24**	Latvia	65,66
40	Bulgaria	40,35	**42**	Bulgaria	56,59	**25**	Poland	61,10
41	Greece	38,90	**43**	Croatia	55,00	**26**	Croatia	59,58
44	Croatia	37,82	**47**	Malta	53,48	**27**	Bulgaria	48,72
50	Romania	36,76	**48**	Cyprus	51,56	**28**	Romania	34,13

Source: According to GII (Cornell University, INSEAD, World Intellectual Property Organization 2019), EIS (Maastricht Economic and Social Research Institute on Innovation and Technology – MERIT 2019), and BII (Bloomberg 2020).

A very important factor in innovation performance is the human resources in R&D, which represent a basis for knowledge and innovation-based economy. In order to define and differentiate the human resources that implement and participate in R&D activities, according to the Frascati Manual[21] the following R&D staff activities can be used: (1) performing scientific and technical work in R&D projects; (2) planning and managing R&D projects; (3) preparing interim and final reports for R&D projects; (4) providing internal services for R&D projects; and (5) supporting the management of financial and personnel aspects of R&D projects.

Observing from the human resources aspect, in 2017 Germany had the largest number of R&D employees, with almost one million employees in this segment, followed by the other two largest EU economies – the United Kingdom and France.[22] Furthermore, EU countries with the fewest R&D employees in 2017 were, respectively, Croatia, Latvia, Estonia, Luxembourg, Cyprus, and Malta.[23]

In order to make it easier to compare data with respect to different sizes of countries and population, it is necessary to observe the statistical size of human resources in science and technology (HRST) as the share of active population in the 25–64 age group. Data showing an active population in the 25–64 age group classified as HRST (or as having successfully completed tertiary education or employed in science and technology) demonstrate the continuous growth in all EU countries over the years, which indicates the growing perception of R&D significance. In 2016 and 2019, Luxembourg was the EU country with the largest number of HRST while Romania recorded the least, which indicates a steady trend and still a rather heterogeneous growth[24] (Figure 5-1).

[21] OECD/Eurostat. *Oslo Manual 2018: Guidelines for Collecting, Reporting and Using Data on Innovation, 4th Edition, The Measurement of Scientific, Technological and Innovation Activities*. Luxembourg: OECD Publishing, Paris/Eurostat. 2018.

[22] Eurostat. "Business expenditure on R&D (BERD) by NACE Rev. activity". 2020. Accessed April 22, 2020.
http://appsso.eurostat.ec.europa.eu/nui/show.do?dataset=rd_e_berdindr2&lang=en

[23] Ibid.

[24] Eurostat. "HRST by category, sex and age". Accessed April 23, 2020, https://ec.europa.eu/eurostat/web/products-datasets/product?code=hrst_st_ncat

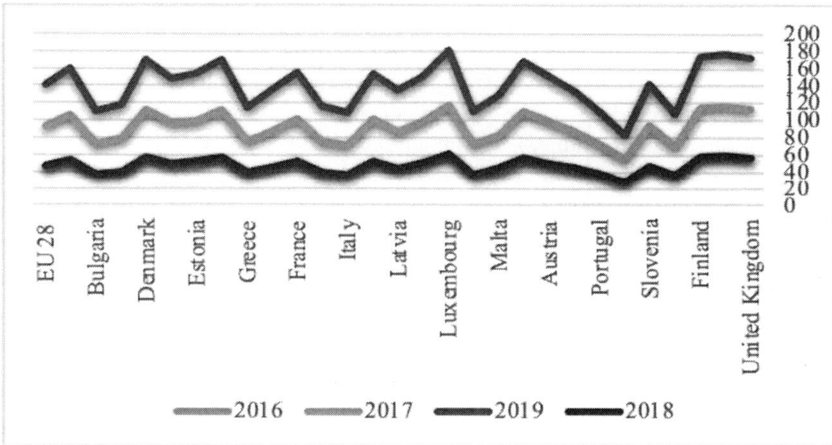

Figure 5-1. Number of R&D employees in the period 2012–2018 as share of active population aged 25–64, EU28
Source: Eurostat (2020)

Furthermore, another useful indicator of the potential of human resources is the research conducted by the Organization for Economic Co-operation and Development[25] as part of the Program for International Student Assessment (PISA). It is a three-year international survey that aims to evaluate education systems around the world by testing the skills and knowledge of 15-year-old students nearing the end of compulsory education. PISA assesses how well students can apply what they learn in schools to real-life situations. To date, more than 90 countries have participated in the evaluation that began in 2000. Every three years, students are tested in key skills and areas: reading literacy, math, and science. In addition to the three core subjects, students are tested in an innovative area such as collaborative problem solving, which was the case in 2015, or, for example, global competency skills, implemented in 2018, as well as in aspects that provide insight into how students' backgrounds and school environment can influence their performance. According to this

[25] OECD. "PISA 2018 Results COMBINED EXECUTIVE SUMMARIES VOLUME I, II & III". 2019. Accessed April 27, 2020. https://www.oecd.org/pisa/Combined_Executive_Summaries_PISA_2018.pdf

study, the average value for OECD member countries is 487 in the field of reading literacy and 489 in mathematics and science.[26]

Estonia, Finland, and Ireland were the highest-performing OECD countries in reading while the Netherlands, Estonia, and Poland in mathematics, and Estonia, Finland, and Poland in science.[27]

Furthermore, investment in R&D is not only crucial for fostering innovation and strengthening competitiveness but also a precondition. Without investment in all aspects of R&D, there is no prospect for economic development. Fortunately, recent data shows that this has been recognized by both companies and governments, which, over time, have been focusing their efforts into facilitating R&D.

One of the main indicators of R&D investments, gross domestic expenditure on R&D (GERD), includes expenditure on research and the development of business enterprises and institutions of higher education as well as government and private non-profit organizations. R&D expenditure is believed to be linked to the country's future ability to innovate and generate economic growth, especially when investments are made by enterprises. According to the Frascati Manual,[28] R&D includes creative work carried out on a systematic basis to maximize the stock of knowledge, including knowledge about people, culture, and society, and the use of that knowledge to develop new applications. GERD covers all R&D expenditures made in the territory of the country in a given year. It therefore includes "domestic" R&D funded abroad but excludes R&D funds paid abroad, especially to international agencies.

The level of R&D investment relative to GDP is the highest in Sweden and stood at 3.32% in 2018. The Europe 2020 Strategy sets a target of increasing EU R&D investment to 3% by 2020.[29] The EU recorded a long-term stagnation in gross domestic expenditure on R&D in 2002–2007. By 2009, at the beginning of the economic crisis, R&D intensity had increased to

---

[26] OECD. "PISA 2018 Results COMBINED EXECUTIVE SUMMARIES VOLUME I, II & III". 2019. Accessed April 27, 2020.
https://www.oecd.org/pisa/Combined_Executive_Summaries_PISA_2018.pdf

[27] Ibid.

[28] OECD. "Frascati Manual 2015 - Guidelines for Collecting and Reporting Data on Research and Experimental Development". 2015. Accessed April 26, 2020, https://www.oecd.org/sti/frascati-manual-2015-9789264239012-en.htm

[29] Eurostat. "Gross domestic expenditure on R&D (GERD)". Accessed April 18, 2020.
https://ec.europa.eu/eurostat/tgm/table.do?tab=table&init=1&plugin=1&language=en&pcode=t2020_20

1.93%.[30] It has continued to grow slightly since 2011, stabilizing at 2.02% in 2014. Despite an increase in public and private R&D expenditure from 2007 to 2014, the EU is not well on track to reach its 3% of GDP target for R&D investment. Globally, the EU is still lagging behind other players, such as the United States, Japan and South Korea, in terms of R&D expenditure.[31] According to the latest data, only Sweden, Austria, Germany, and Denmark have reached this target in the EU, with Austria and Denmark exceeding it already in 2014 and 2015, respectively.[32]

The historical overview of GERD shows that in 2013, the highest GERD was recorded in Denmark (2.97%) and the lowest in Romania (0.39%) (Eurostat 2020) (Figure 5-2). However, in 2018, Sweden recorded the highest GERD (3.32%) while Romania was still recording the poorest results (0.5%) (Eurostat 2020). Croatia has modest results, and R&D investment is expressed as a percentage of GDP from 2015 to 2017 at about the same level of 0.84% – 0.86% (Eurostat 2020). However, significant growth was recorded in 2018 (0.97%). The target in Croatia is lower (1.40%); however, according to the trends shown, it will not be reached by 2020.

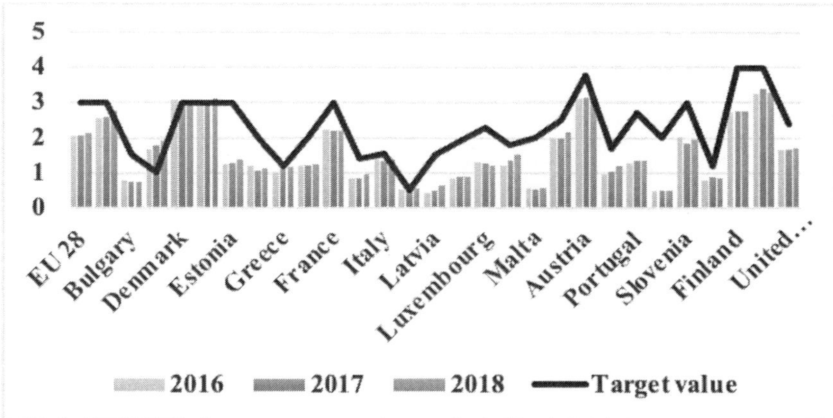

Figure 5-2. Share of R&D expenditure in GDP in % (GERD), 2016 – 2018.
Source: Eurostat (2020)

[30] Eurostat. "Total R&D personnel by sectors of performance, occupation and sex". Accessed April 19, 2020.
http://appsso.eurostat.ec.europa.eu/nui/show.do?wai=true&dataset=rd_p_persocc
[31] Ibid.
[32] Ibid.

According to the GERD indicator expressed in EUR per capita, Sweden has been in the EU's top spot regularly since 2011, and in 2018 Denmark took this position with an average amount of EUR 1,581.[33] Sweden is almost at the same level and invests an average of EUR 1,545 per capita. Bulgaria and Romania are at the forefront, spending EUR 60 per capita and EUR 52, respectively, on R&D in 2018.[34] Only Latvia, with an average of EUR 96, invests less than Croatia. At EUR 122, Croatia is ranked 25th in the EU and would have to invest almost four times as much in R&D to reach, for example, Slovenia.[35]

The main indicator used to describe R&D results within the business sector is business enterprise expenditure on R&D (BERD) expenditures. BERD represents a component of gross domestic expenditure on research and development (GERD) incurred in units belonging to the business sector. It is a measure of internal R&D expenditure over a given reference period. When collecting and reporting on the source of funds for BERD, five main sources are considered, according to the sector from which the resources originate: the business sector (which includes internal and external funds received from other companies), state and local government and self-government, higher education, private non-profit organizations, and abroad.

In 2018, GERD and BERD showed similar results in the means of highest and lowest-achieving EU countries. The highest BERD *per capita* in 2018 was again recorded in Sweden (EUR 1,096), Denmark (EUR 1,016), and Austria (EUR 970), while the lowest BERD *per capita* was achieved in Bulgaria (EUR 43,2), Romania (EUR 31,1) and Latvia (EUR 23,9) (Eurostat, 2020). According to the share in GDP, BERD for 2018 was the highest in Sweden (2.35%), Austria (2.22%) and Germany (2.16%), while Romania (0.3%), Cyprus (0.2%), and Latvia (0.16%) recorded the lowest BERD[36] (Figure 5-3).

[33] Eurostat. "Intramural R&D expenditure (GERD) by sectors of performance". Accessed April 16, 2020.
http://appsso.eurostat.ec.europa.eu/nui/show.do?dataset=rd_e_gerdtot&lang=en

[34] Ibid.

[35] Ibid.

[36] Eurostat. "Research and development expenditure, by sectors of performance". Accessed April 18, 2020. https://ec.europa.eu/eurostat/web/science-technology-innovation/data/main-tables

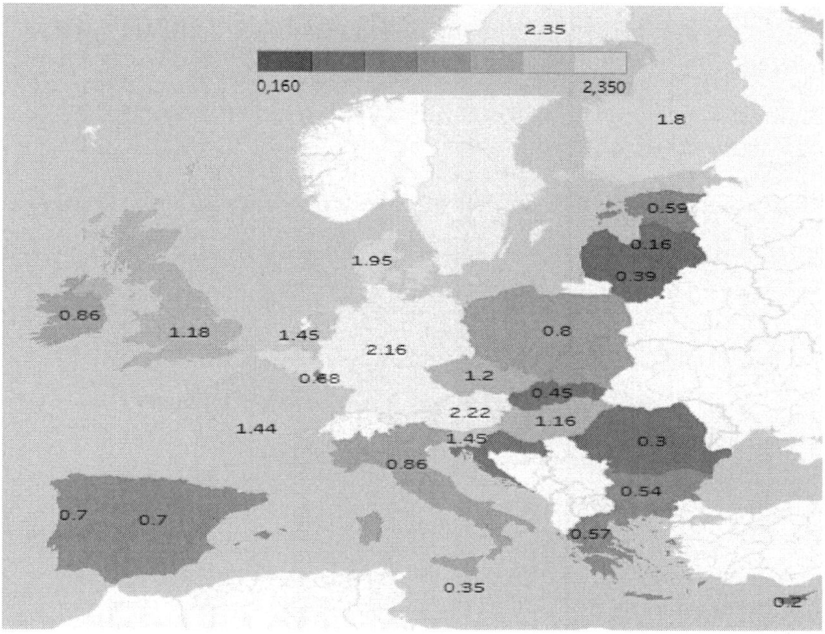

Figure 5-3. Business enterprise R&D expenditure (BERD) share as a percentage of GDP, 2018.
Source: European Commission, Joint Research Centre – Research and Innovation Observatory (2020)

3.2 Competitiveness performance of European Union Member States

Moreover, countries and policy makers also need to think beyond the short-term as well as beyond only responsive measures, and instead evaluate their progress against a range of factors and productivity determinants. The Global Competitiveness Index 4.0 (GCI 4.0)[37] provides a framework for evaluation and a long-term vision through an annual benchmark of key factors and productivity determinants on a global level. These factors are divided into four groups with 12 pillars: (I) Enabling

[37] World Economic Forum. "The Global Competitiveness Report 2019". 2019. Accessed April 16, 2020.
http://www3.weforum.org/docs/WEF_TheGlobalCompetitivenessReport2019.pdf

environment (Pillars: (1) institutions; (2) infrastructure; (3) ICT adoption; (4) macroeconomic stability); (II) Human capital (Pillars: (5) health; (6) skills); (III) Markets (Pillars: (7) product market; (8) labour market; (9) financial system; (10) market size); (IV) Innovation ecosystem (Pillars: (11) Business dynamism; (12) Innovation capability).

Table 5-2. The Global Competitiveness Index 4.0 rankings and results, EU28, 2019

Rank	Country	Score	Difference compared to 2018		
			Rank	Score	Difference
4.	Netherlands	82,4	+2	-	↑
7.	Germany	81,8	-4	-1,0	↓
8.	Sweden	81,2	+1	-0,4	↑
9.	United Kingdom	81,2	-1	-0,8	↓
10.	Denmark	81,2	-	+0,6	—
11.	Finland	80,2	-	-	—
15.	France	78,8	+2	+0,8	↑
18.	Luxembourg	77,0	+1	+0,4	↑
21.	Austria	76,6	+1	+0,3	↑
22.	Belgium	76,4	-1	-0,2	↓
23.	Spain	75,3	+3	+1,1	↑
24.	Ireland	75,1	-1	-0,6	↓
30.	Italy	71,5	+1	+0,8	↑
31.	Estonia	70,9	+1	+0,2	↑
32.	Czech Republic	70,9	-3	-0,3	↓
34.	Portugal	70,4	-	+0,2	—
35.	Slovenia	70,2	-	+0,6	—
37.	Poland	68,9	-	+0,7	—
38.	Malta	68,5	-2	-0,2	↓
39.	Lithuania	68,4	+1	+1,2	↑
41.	Latvia	67,0	+1	+0,7	↑
42.	Slovakia	66,8	-1	-0,1	↓
44.	Cyprus	66,4	-	+0,8	—
47.	Hungary	65,1	+1	+0,8	↑
49.	Bulgaria	64,9	+2	+1,3	↑
51.	Romania	64,4	+1	+0,9	↑
59.	Greece	62,6	-2	+0,5	↓
63.	Croatia	61,9	+5	+1,8	↑

Source: World Economic Forum (2019)

According to the 2019 GCI 4.0 (WEF 2019), Singapore is ranked number one in the world with an average score of 84.8, while the EU's best-ranked country is the Netherlands, in 4th place. Germany, Sweden, and Denmark are also in the top ten EU countries (Table 5-2). Furthermore, Croatia ranks 63rd in the world with an average score of 61.9 and is last among EU countries. In front of Croatia are Bulgaria (49th),

Romania (51st) and Greece (59th).[38] However, Croatia has improved its placement by five places compared to the previous issue of the GCI, which represents the biggest improvement among EU countries. Ultimately, the results of GCI 4.0[39] show that abolishing administrative procedures, reducing corporate levies, and creating an atmosphere of legal certainty can improve the business and investment climate while fostering scientific and entrepreneurial cooperation can simultaneously strengthen the technological readiness of the economy to apply new knowledge to the creation of innovative products and services.

Talent is also a decisive factor in the global competitiveness struggle. As the world of work changes rapidly, it is imperative to have information about the talent available to see where we stand in relation to competition and understand the trends that affect talent flows and competitiveness of talent in order to improve performance. The findings of the Global Talent Competitiveness Index 2020 report (GTCI 2020)[40] shows that talent inequality has only grown over the years. Looking at the results of the first six years and comparing the available data over time, it is evident that the gap separating the talented leaders from the others has grown instead of narrowed.[41] Finding talent has become a major concern of businesses and states. Entrepreneurial talent can both increase and reduce inequalities, and it plays a key role in smaller businesses in job creation and start-ups in innovation, but it also plays a critical role in larger organizations and even in public bodies.[42]

According to the GTCI 2020[43] and the six core pillars it considers (enable, attract, grow, retain, vocational and technical skills, and global knowledge skills), Sweden has the highest rank of all EU countries, ranking 4th with the overall score of 75.82. Only Switzerland, the United States, and Singapore are ahead of it. Among the top five EU countries are Sweden, Denmark, the Netherlands, Finland, and Luxembourg. Croatia is ranked 59th in the world (in 2019 it was ranked 56th) with a modest index of 53.53.[44]

---

[38] Ibid.

[39] Ibid.

[40] INSEAD. "The Global Talent Competitiveness Index 2020". Accessed April 19, 2020. https://gtcistudy.com/wp-content/uploads/2020/01/GTCI-2020-Report.pdf

[41] Ibid.

[42] INSEAD. "The Global Talent Competitiveness Index 2020". Accessed April 19, 2020. https://gtcistudy.com/wp-content/uploads/2020/01/GTCI-2020-Report.pdf

[43] Ibid.

[44] Ibid.

Entrepreneurial talent should be seen as a state of mind that can be developed, enhanced, and nurtured with a mix of policies, incentives, and management approaches that need to be tailored to the specific context of individual countries. In particular, it is expected that phenomena such as digitization and globalization will increase its role. As the future of work is expected to be radically affected by the rapid spread of artificial intelligence, the share of paid workers will continue to decline, and the number of free agents will increase. The emergence of new business models will encourage new ways of extracting and sharing value from information. Such an ongoing business and economic context will clearly favour countries and organizations that have the capacity to mobilize relevant entrepreneurial talents.

4. Conclusion

In today's highly dynamic business environment, countries need to strengthen existing comparative advantages and develop new ones to keep up with rapid changes in technology, demand, and global competition. For this purpose, countries optimize their competitive forces and strengthen economic performance and efficiency through innovation[45], which ultimately leads to competitiveness.

This paper identified rather heterogeneous results for European Union member states. Regarding innovation performance, according to the European Innovation Scoreboard (2019), Denmark, Finland, the Netherlands, and Sweden are innovation leaders with results well above the EU average. These results are supported by other methodologies of research, which explains why Sweden achieved the best results in all five methodologies, being placed 1st in the Global Innovation Index (2019) in the overall GII as well as in the Innovation Input and Innovation Output Sub-Index by the Bloomberg Innovation Index (2020), and in R&D intensity (but the 2nd EU country overall) by the EIS (2019) and the Global Talent Competitiveness Index (2020), placing it among the ten top EU countries. Furthermore, the EIS (2019) categorization as innovation leaders correlates to all methodologies since Finland, Denmark, and

[45] Goksoy, Asli, Vayvay, Ozalp, and Nilufer Ergeneli. 2013. "Gaining competitive advantage through innovation strategies: An application in warehouse management processes." *American Journal of Business and Management*, 2, no. 14 (2013): 304–321. http://worldscholars.org/index.php/ajbm/article/view/463/pdf

Netherlands have followed Sweden as countries among the top five EU countries.

On the other hand, according to EIS (2019), there have also been changes in innovation performance. Estonia (formerly a moderate innovator) joined a group of strong innovators; Luxembourg and the United Kingdom (both countries previously innovation leaders) are now among the strong innovators; and Slovenia (formerly a strong innovator) is now a moderate innovator. However, modest innovators (Romania and Bulgaria) and moderate innovators (Cyprus, Malta, and Croatia) have recorded the poorest results among the EU countries, which shows that all findings of this research mostly correlate despite the difference in research methodologies. Moreover, innovation leaders have somewhat different results in competitiveness (the Netherlands 1st, Sweden 3rd, Denmark 5th, and Finland 6th) but are still some of the most competitive EU countries.

The research shows that abolishing administrative procedures, reducing corporate levies, and creating an atmosphere of legal certainty can improve the business and investment climate while fostering scientific and entrepreneurial cooperation can simultaneously strengthen the technological readiness of the economy to apply new knowledge to the creation of innovative products and services, all of which will foster and contribute to innovation and competitiveness performance. However, the European Union member states show highly uneven economic performance and heterogeneous level of competitiveness, meaning that no universal methodology has been implemented to facilitate and strengthen more equal economic development, innovation performance, and competitiveness. For this reason, there are high expectations and perspectives for more convergent, tailored, and sustainable development of European Union member states in the new cohesion policy for the next long-term EU budget 2021–2027, as well as its accompanying financial perspective for the period 2021–2027.

References

Bilas, Vlatka and Sanja Franc. *Innovation and Development*. Zagreb: Notitia d.o.o., 2018.

Bloomberg. 2020. "Bloomberg Innovation Index 2020". Accessed April 16, 2020. https://www.bloomberg.com/news/articles/2020-01-18/germany-breaks-korea-s-six-year-streak-as-most-innovative-nation

Camison, Cesar. "Competitiveness and sustainability in tourist firms and destinations", *Competitiveness, Sustainability and Tourism*, 6, no. 12 (2020): 1–6. file:///C:/Users/Vlatka/Downloads/sustainability-12-02388.pdf

Cornell University, INSEAD, and WIPO. "The Global Innovation Index 2019: Creating Healthy Lives – The Future of Medical Innovation, Ithaca, Fontainebleau, and Geneva". 2019. Accessed April 30, 2020, https://www.wipo.int/publications/en/details.jsp?id=4434.

Dogan, Ebru. "The effect of innovation on competitiveness", *Istanbul University, Faculty of Economics, Department of Business Administration, Istanbul, Ekonometri ve İstatistik Sayı*, 24 (2016): 60–81. http://static.dergipark.org.tr/article-download/e228/6dfc/9d38/587d11a314943.pdf?

Duspara, Lena, Knežević, Sanja, and Mladen Turuk. "Competitiveness and innovation challenge in Croatia", *Poslovna izvrsnost Zagreb*, XI no. 2 (2017): 41–58. https://hrcak.srce.hr/file/284317

European Commission. "Communication from the Commission: Europe 2020. A strategy for smart, sustainable and inclusive growth", 2010. Brussels: European Commission. Accessed April 22, 2020. http://ec.europa.eu/eu2020/pdf/COMPLET%20EN%20BARROSO%20%20%20007%20-%20Europe%202020%20-%20EN%20version.pdf

European Commission. "Eco-innovation the key to Europe's future competitiveness". 2012. Brussels: European Commission. Accessed April 15, 2020. http://ec.europa.eu/environment/pubs/pdf/factsheets/eco_innovation.pdf

European Commission. "Europe 2020 Flagship Initiative Innovation Union". 2011. Brussels: European Commission. Accessed April 30, 2020. https://ec.europa.eu/research/innovation-union/pdf/innovation-union-communication-brochure_en.pdf

European Commission, Joint Research Centre – Research and Innovation Observatory. 2020. "Business enterprise R&D expenditure (BERD) share as a percentage of GDP, 2018". Accessed April 27, 2020. https://rio.jrc.ec.europa.eu/stats/business-enterprise-rd-expenditure-berd-source-funds-value-or-intensity

Eurostat. "Business expenditure on R&D (BERD) by NACE Rev. 2 activity". 2020. Accessed April 22, 2020. http://appsso.eurostat.ec.europa.eu/nui/show.do?dataset=rd_e_berdindr2&lang=en

Eurostat. "Gross domestic expenditure on R&D (GERD)". Accessed April 18, 2020.

https://ec.europa.eu/eurostat/tgm/table.do?tab=table&init=1&plugin=1&language=en&pcode=t2020_20

Eurostat. "HRST by category, sex and age". Accessed April 23, 2020. https://ec.europa.eu/eurostat/web/products-datasets/product?code=hrst_st_ncat

Eurostat. "Intramural R&D expenditure (GERD) by sectors of performance". Accessed April 16, 2020. http://appsso.eurostat.ec.europa.eu/nui/show.do?dataset=rd_e_gerdtot&lang=en

Eurostat. "Research and development expenditure, by sectors of performance". Accessed April 18, 2020. https://ec.europa.eu/eurostat/web/science-technology-innovation/data/main-tables.

Eurostat. "Total R&D personnel by sectors of performance, occupation and sex". Accessed April 19, 2020. http://appsso.eurostat.ec.europa.eu/nui/show.do?wai=true&dataset=rd_p_persocc

Farinha, Luis, Ferreira, Joao J. M., and Sara Nunes. "Linking innovation and entrepreneurship to economic growth". *Competitiveness Review*, 4, no. 28 (2018): 451–475. https://www.researchgate.net/publication/325578655_Linking_innovation_and_entrepreneurship_to_economic_growth

Ferreira, Joao J., Fernandes, Christina I., and Vanessa Ratten. "Entrepreneurship, innovation and competitiveness: What is the connection?", *International Journal of Business and Globalisation* 1, no. 18 (2017): 73–95. https://www.researchgate.net/publication/312117305_Entrepreneurship_innovation_and_competitiveness_What_is_the_connection

Goksoy, Asli, Vayvay, Ozalp, and Nilufer Ergeneli, 2013. "Gaining competitive advantage through innovation strategies: An application in warehouse management processes", *American Journal of Business and Management* 2, no. 14 (2013): 304–321. http://worldscholars.org/index.php/ajbm/article/view/463/pdf.

INSEAD. "The Global Talent Competitiveness Index 2020". Accessed April 19, 2020. https://gtcistudy.com/wp-content/uploads/2020/01/ GTCI-2020-Report.pdf

Maastricht Economic and Social Research Institute on Innovation and Technology (MERIT). 2020. "European Innovation Scoreboard 2019". Accessed April 18, 2020. https://ec.europa.eu/docsroom/documents/38781/attachments/1/translations/en/renditions/native

OECD. "Frascati Manual 2015 – Guidelines for Collecting and Reporting Data on Research and Experimental Development". 2015. Accessed April 26, 2020. https://www.oecd.org/sti/frascati-manual-2015-9789264239012-en.htm

OECD/Eurostat. *Oslo Manual 2018: Guidelines for Collecting, Reporting and Using Data on Innovation, 4th Edition, The Measurement of Scientific, Technological and Innovation Activities*. Luxembourg: OECD Publishing, Paris/Eurostat, 2018.

OECD. "PISA 2018 Results COMBINED EXECUTIVE SUMMARIES VOLUME I, II & III". 2019. Accessed April 27, 2020. https://www.oecd.org/pisa/Combined_Executive_Summaries_PISA_2018.pdf

World Economic Forum. "The Global Competitiveness Report 2019", 2019. Accessed April 16, 2020. http://www3.weforum.org/docs/WEF_TheGlobalCompetitivenessReport2019.pdf

CHAPTER SIX

TOP-DOWN VS BOTTOM-UP DIASPORA ENGAGEMENT: LATVIA VS AUSTRALIA

IEVA BIRKA[1]

Abstract

Developed countries are increasingly realizing the vast potential of their global diasporas; however, few studies of how developed countries are going about engaging their diasporas, to what effect, and what can be learned from their experience exist. This article reviews the diaspora engagement approach literature from the standpoint of developed countries and then applies the theoretical framework to assess Latvia and Australia. The top-down or centralized approach of Latvia and the bottom-up or de-centralized approach of Australia are evaluated and the advantages and disadvantages of both presented. The conclusion reached is that for diaspora engagement strategies to be a success, they cannot be completely top-down or centralized. Likewise, they cannot be totally bottom-up or decentralized. A certain amount of diaspora empowerment and initiative is needed to sustain the diaspora policy, just as the diaspora approach requires a certain amount of government backing and authority to overcome systematic or institutional constraints. However, what the article also shows through the Latvian and Australian case analysis is that diaspora engagement strategies are not static, and they can be developed and adjusted to achieve the desired outcome.

Keywords: *diaspora, migration, economic development, policy implementation, Australia, Latvia*

---

[1] Faculty of Social Sciences, University of Latvia, Ieva.birka@lu.lv

Funding Acknowledgement: This work was supported by the European Regional Development Fund Activity 1.1.1.2. 'Post-doctoral Research Aid', research agreement No. 1.1.1.2/16/I/001, under Grant No. 1.1.1.2/ VIAA/1/16/013 'Harnessing the Economic Potential of the Diaspora'.

1. Introduction

In the academic literature focused on migration and development analysis, the importance of the contribution by the diaspora in the developing world is now an undisputed given. The underlying "migration and development theory asserts that migrant-sending states can gain through the remittances, investments, knowledge transfers, and political influence of their diasporas".[2] As a response, a wide variety of diaspora strategies have emerged to enable countries of origin to preserve and cultivate connections with their populations abroad, and a vast collection of literature outlines how diasporas can aid development and how developing countries should go about formulating and establishing diaspora engagement strategies.[3,4,5,6,7,8,9]. What is relatively new is the eagerness of developed countries to also involve themselves in what Birka and Kļaviņš[10] define as

[2] Gamlen, Alan. "Diasporas." In *Global Migration Governance*, pp. 266–286. Oxford University Press, 2011.

[3] Adams Jr, Richard H., and John Page. "Do international migration and remittances reduce poverty in developing countries?" *World Development* 33, no. 10 (2005): 1645–669.

[4] De Haas, Hein. "International migration, remittances and development: Myths and facts." *Third World Quarterly* 26, no. 8 (2005): 1269–284.

[5] Brinkerhoff, Jennifer M. "Diasporas, skills transfer, and remittances: Evolving perceptions and potential." *Converting Migration Drains into Gains: Harnessing the Resources of Overseas Professionals* (2006): 1–32.

[6] Ionescu, Dina. *Engaging Diasporas as Agents for Development.* Geneva: International Organization for Migration, 2006.

[7]Newland, Kathleen, and Hiroyuki Tanaka. *Mobilizing Diaspora Entrepreneurship for Development*. Washington, DC: Migration Policy Institute, 2010.

[8] Agunias, Dovelyn Rannveig, and Kathleen Newland. *Developing a Road Map for Engaging Diasporas in Development: A Handbook for Policymakers and Practitioners in Home and Host Countries*. International Organization for Migration, 2012.

[9] Newland, Kathleen, and Sonia Plaza. "What we know about diasporas and economic development." *Policy Brief* 5 (2013). Washington, DC: Migration Policy Institute.

[10] Birka, Ieva, and Didzis Kļaviņš. "Diaspora diplomacy: Nordic and Baltic perspective." *Diaspora Studies* 13, no. 2 (2020): 115–132.

diaspora diplomacy, or the involvement of the state in the promotion of a "systematic relationship, for mutual benefit, sustained between the country-of-origin government, diaspora groupings in countries of residence, and the various interest associations in both the country of origin and country of residence". As such, developed countries face the task of establishing diaspora strategies or policies; however, there is little information and few case analyses on best practice approaches to diaspora strategy design and implementation.

The aim of this article is to contribute to filling this knowledge gap by re-examining the diaspora literature from the standpoint of developed countries. First, the possible contributions diasporas can make to their countries of origin will be reviewed and the initiatives that are especially enticing for developed countries will be identified. Then, the available resources for government policy planning and the recognized steps for diaspora engagement strategy development will be reviewed and the possible direction for diaspora engagement strategy focus presented. Once these steps are internalized by the country of origin, they are faced with the task of understanding how best to go about achieving their envisioned goals and engaging the diaspora. Thus, the article will focus on providing a deeper understanding of top-down versus bottom-up policy initiatives by analysing their characteristics, benefits, drawbacks, and alternatives. Finally, the theoretical overview, as it pertains to diaspora engagement for developed countries, will be applied to examine Latvia and Australia, two countries employing very different diaspora engagement initiatives, in order to understand how they function in reality and what lessons can be learned from policy implementation.

2. Diaspora for Developed Countries

Defining diasporas, also for developed countries, is no easy task. The wide array of available definitions is impressive. As Hugo[11] points out, until recently the individuals who are now referred to as diaspora were known as expatriates. Expatriates are "people who are citizens or permanent residents of a nation but who reside abroad on a long-term or permanent

[11] Hugo, Graeme. "Developed country diasporas: The example of Australian expatriates." *Espace Populations Sociétés. Space Populations Societies* 1 (2006): 181–202.

basis".[12] However, due to rapid globalization, the internationalization of labour markets, and the acceptance of transnationalism as a part of modern life, a contemporary discourse on diaspora identity has developed. Agunias and Newland[13] define diaspora broadly as "emigrants and their descendants who live outside the country of their birth or ancestry, either on a temporary or permanent basis, yet still maintain affective and material ties to their countries of origin." Considering that the previously defined systematic relationship between the country of origin and the diaspora groupings envisions mutual benefits, a broader encompassing definition allows for a greater interpretation of who can self-identify, and be recognized, as part of the diaspora.

Diaspora can be utilized in a variety of ways by the country of origin. Brinkerhoff (2012)[14] lists the possible diaspora contributions as economic remittances, homeland economic investments, skills transfers, diaspora philanthropy, and political influence. Ionescu[15] makes specific note of business networks, professional networks, scientific networks, community initiatives, and diaspora-networking platforms, among others. Newland and Tanaka[16] emphasize the potential of networking organizations, mentoring organizations, investment organizations, and venture capital and partnership organizations. Combining the previously mentioned findings and supplementing them with their own observations, Agunias and Newland[17] identify six focus areas for diaspora engagement: remittances, direct investments, transfer of human capital, which involves

---

[12] Hugo, Graeme. "Developed country diasporas: The example of Australian expatriates." *Espace populations sociétés. Space populations societies* 2006/1 (2006): 182.

[13] Agunias, Dovelyn Rannveig, and Kathleen Newland. *Developing a Road Map for Engaging Diasporas in Development: A Handbook for Policymakers and Practitioners in Home and Host Countries*. International Organization for Migration, 2012.

[14] Brinkerhoff, Jennifer M. "Diasporas, skills transfer, and remittances: Evolving perceptions and potential." *Converting Migration Drains into Gains: Harnessing the Resources of Overseas Professionals* (2006): 1–32.

[15] Ionescu, Dina. *Engaging Diasporas as Agents for Development.* Geneva: International Organization for Migration, 2006. p. 27–31.

[16] Newland, Kathleen, and Hiroyuki Tanaka. *Mobilizing Diaspora Entrepreneurship for Development*. Washington, DC: Migration Policy Institute, 2010.

[17] Agunias, Dovelyn Rannveig, and Kathleen Newland. *Developing A Road Map for Engaging Diasporas in Development: A Handbook for Policymakers and Practitioners in Home and Host Countries*. International Organization for Migration, 2012.

return migration and knowledge circulation, philanthropic contributions, capital market investments, and diaspora tourism.

Relatively developed countries view their diasporas as more than just senders of remittances. In these instances, the greatest potential in engaging the diaspora and mobilizing their resources is to be had in the following areas: trade, investment, and skills and knowledge transfer.[18] As such, where developing countries enact diaspora strategies as a "development for poverty reduction" strategy and focus on remittance and investment from the diaspora, developed countries are interested in "advancing development in the knowledge-based economy".[19] The focus of developed-country-diaspora strategies is thus "upon the role of diaspora knowledge networks (DKN) as a source of global competitive advantage and a mechanism for brokering integration into the global economy".[20] The knowledge of the diaspora valued by the country of origin has to do with "foreign market information and contacts that can lower the transaction costs of trade".[21] Furthermore, the diaspora can serve as a point of contact in the country of settlement, and a source of information for investors and in promoting trade, thus facilitating cross-border transactions.[22] According to Hickey,[23] "There has also been a parallel growth in explicit strategies by high-income countries aimed at attracting high-skilled and entrepreneurial talent from around the world." Thus, another facet of developed-country-diaspora strategy is focused on talent retention, attraction, and the promotion of return migration of highly qualified individuals.

---

[18] Newland, Kathleen, and Sonia Plaza. "What we know about diasporas and economic development." *Policy Brief* 5 (2013). Washington, DC: Migration Policy Institute.

[19] Ho, Elaine Lynn-Ee, Maureen Hickey, and Brenda SA Yeoh. "Special issue introduction: New research directions and critical perspectives on diaspora strategies." *Geoforum* 59 (2015): 153.

[20] Ho, Elaine Lynn-Ee, and Mark Boyle. "Migration-as-development repackaged? The globalizing imperative of the Singaporean state's diaspora strategies." *Singapore Journal of Tropical Geography* 36, no. 2 (2015): 165.

[21] Gould, David M. "Immigrant links to the home country: Empirical implications for US bilateral trade flows." *The Review of Economics and Statistics* (1994): 303.

[22] Leblang, David. "Another link in the chain: Migrant networks and international investment." *DIASPORA for* (2011): 79.

[23] Hickey, Maureen. "Diaspora strategies in the sending states of Southeast Asia: Rights, skills and questions of value." *Singapore Journal of Tropical Geography* 36, no. 2 (2015): 150.

For diaspora engagement to be successful, a clear strategy and plan is necessary. As such, Agunias and Newland[24] suggest a four-step plan of action for putting a diaspora engagement strategy into place. The first step in this plan is for the country of origin to understand its goals and capacities and its overall goal for diaspora engagement. The second step involves "serious, comprehensive data collection; mapping the location of the diaspora; compiling inventories of diaspora skills and experiences."[25] This data is a valuable resource for becoming acquainted with the diaspora, its spatial location, and available resources. In the third step, the country of origin builds trust and creates open channels of communication with the diaspora. The fourth and final step involves stakeholder mobilization for putting the actual diaspora engagement strategy into place.[26]Agunias and Newland[27] make clear from the start that their plan cannot be a one-size-fits-all model for government engagement of diaspora as country-specific contexts, historical experiences, structural constraints, and cultural influences are likely to require adjustments and tailor-made solutions. However, this plan does offer a road map for evaluating what implementation stage the diaspora engagement strategy of a country is in.

Alan Gamlen[28,29] offers another useful typology for evaluating the direction taken by the country of origin in formulating a diaspora engagement strategy. He identifies three types of diaspora engagement strategies: remittance capture or tapping, diaspora networking, and diaspora integration. In Gamlen's typology, remittance capture is not just the simple act of encouraging money transfer back home. Besides remittances, the country of origin is materially interested in tapping the resources of the .diaspora and is focused on diaspora "investments,

---

[24] Agunias, Dovelyn Rannveig, and Kathleen Newland. *Developing a Road Map for Engaging Diasporas in Development: A Handbook for Policymakers and Practitioners in Home and Host Countries*. International Organization for Migration, 2012.

[25] Ibid, p. 27.

[26] Ibid, p. 32.

[27] Ibid, p. 25.

[28] Gamlen, Alan John. "Diasporas." In *Global Migration Governance*, pp. 266–286. Oxford University Press, 2011.

[29] Gamlen, Alan John. "The brain drain is dead; long live the New Zealand diaspora." Working Paper No. 10. Oxford: Centre on Migration, Policy and Society University of Oxford, 2005.

connections, skills, and strategic capabilities."[30] The diaspora networking approach is less concerned with material gains and more focused on encouraging the exchange of knowledge and skills. The country of origin acts as an intermediary in facilitating this exchange. The diaspora networking approach foresees opportunities for enhancing career opportunities, granting access to information related to investment opportunities, and enabling information exchange through contact networks, websites, and newsletters. According to Gamlen,[31] face-to-face contact is important to the diaspora networking approach, and networks are developed regionally. Finally, the integration strategy,[32] or embracing approach,[33] is focused on the preservation and development of national identity across international borders. Here, there is an emphasis on recognizing the diaspora as constituencies to whom citizenship and voting rights should be extended, and who are encouraged to take an active part in the social and political life of the country of origin from wherever they may be.

Once the above steps to formulating the focus of the diaspora engagement initiatives have been taken, there is another decision that the country-of-origin policy designers and implementers must make. This decision regards institutional design – whether to approach the engagement process from a centralized approach or to proceed in a more de-centralized manner. The following section will evaluate the theoretical and practical aspects of the top-down, or centralized, policy approach and the de-centralized, or bottom-up, policy approach.

3. Top-down vs Bottom-up Policy Development

The top-down approach to policy development starts with a policy decision made by the government. According to Conyers,[34] there is usually an explicit objective, which has been stated in a policy document or

[30] Gamlen, Alan John. "Diaspora institutions and diaspora governance." *International Migration Review* 48 (2014): 203.

[31] Gamlen, Alan John. "The brain drain is dead; long live the New Zealand diaspora." Working Paper No. 10. Oxford: Centre on Migration, Policy and Society University of Oxford. (2005): 28.

[32] Ibid.

[33] Gamlen, Alan John. "Diaspora institutions and diaspora governance." *International Migration Review* 48 (2014): 189.

[34] Conyers, Diana. "Decentralisation and development: A framework for analysis." *Community Development Journal* 21, no. 2 (1986): 92.

declaration, in which the central government is responding to an issue or a perceived need. Elmore[35] describes the inherent logic of the top-down approach as one of forward mapping, which "begins at the top of the process, with as clear a statement as possible of the policy maker's intent, and proceeds through a sequence of increasingly more specific steps to an outcome against which success or failure can be measured." This can be likened to the bureaucratic process model where there is a policy message at the top which is then passed down the chain for implementation. As such, implementation is straightforward as the "transmission of a blueprint to the operating units because the structures, constraints, (and) priorities have already been delineated."[36] The main problem with this approach is its rigidity. According to Sabatier,[37] the impulse of top-down approaches is to "start from the perspective of (central) decision-makers and thus tend to neglect other actors." This often leads 'top-downers' to overlook or neglect strategic initiatives or alternative approaches that could be substituted or could supplement planned policy initiatives from the private sector.

The bottom-up approach to policy formation does the opposite and looks at "the multitude of actors who interact at the operational level on a particular problem or issue."[38] The bottom-up approach begins with a review of the involved actors, their interests, problems, and adopted strategies for dealing with the identified issue(s). The bottom-up strategies tend not to be tied to one specific goal, and as such are freer to develop in spontaneous ways that can lead to unintended but useful outcomes. Further, the bottom-up approach can involve a multitude of strategic partners that can be interchanged as need be, thus, these approaches are much more flexible in strategic interactions. According to the bottom-up approach, there is also an emphasis on empowering the action of individuals.[39,40,41]

---

[35] Elmore, Richard F. "Backward mapping: Implementation research and policy decisions." *Political Science Quarterly* 94, no. 4 (1979): 602–603.

[36] Dyer, Caroline. "Operation Blackboard: Policy implementation in Indian elementary education." Symposium Books Ltd, (2001): 52.

[37] Sabatier, Paul A. "Top-down and bottom-up approaches to implementation research: A critical analysis and suggested synthesis." *Journal of Public Policy* (1986): 30.

[38] Ibid, p. 22.

[39] Braun, Ann. *Managing Natural Resources for Sustainable Livelihoods: Uniting Science and Participation*. IDRC, 2003.

Community studies literature gives valuable insight into the top-down and bottom-up approaches and offers a hybrid tactic for utilizing the best of both methods. In the community studies literature, the bottom-up approach is also known as the grassroots tactic, and the emphasis is on the participation and empowerment of the community. Nikkhah and Redzuan,[42] in their reformulation of the earlier work of Conyers,[43] offer a useful overview of the three types of community development approaches (See table 6-1). In the government-managed and centralized top-down approach, the intended action is initiated by the government itself. The target group of the action is more or less passive with low empowerment. In the bottom-up approach, governments take the passive role and are simply there in an administrative capacity to assist and enable. Here, the community itself initiates action and is engaged and empowered. There is a third possible approach, the partnership or cooperation approach, in which the government and the community work together in identifying issues and initiating action, with each side taking responsibility for what they know best.

Table 6.1. The summary of the relationship among approaches, participation, and level of empowerment

Approaches	Participation	Empowerment
Top-down	Participation as a mean (static, passive, controllable)	Low empowerment
Partnership (cooperative)	Working together	Moderate empowerment
Bottom-up	Participation as an end (active,dynamic, and self-mobilization)	High empowerment and Sustainable development

Source: Nikkhah Hedayat Allah and Maarof Redzuan

In the early days of academic discourse on transnationalism and diaspora engagement, when the focus was just on developing countries

[40] Chambers, Robert. *Whose Reality Counts*? Vol. 25. London: Intermediate Technology Publications, 1997.
[41] Nikkhah Hedayat Allah, and Maarof Redzuan. "Participation as a medium of empowerment in community development." *European Journal of Social Sciences* 11, no. 1 (2009): 170–176.
[42] Ibid.
[43] Conyers, Diana. "Decentralisation and development: A framework for analysis." *Community Development Journal* 21, no. 2 (1986): 88–100.

and their relationship with the diaspora, Portes[44] wrote that "grass-roots transnationalism is seldom initiated by governments from the sending countries, governments enter the picture as the importance of the phenomenon becomes evident." The assumption here was that as migration rates increase, as migrants became active and self-organized, they would exert pressure on the country of origin for recognition or assistance, and the exerted pressure would prompt a response. Gamlen[45] termed this the reactive hypothesis. However, with diaspora engagement activities becoming more commonplace and expanding to developed countries, Gamlen[46] made the case for a proactive hypothesis of country-of-origin involvement in grassroots transnational activities. This approach sees countries of origin involve themselves in community organization activities, specifically, "Migrant associations are often established with or by consular and diplomatic officers; the officers move on, but organizations mature and become independent and eventually seek new and expanded forms of recognition from new officers."[47]

The most detailed evaluation of top-down and bottom-up policy approaches as they apply to diaspora engagement was carried out by Yevgeny Kuznetsov,[48] who labelled them as centralized versus de-centralized approaches to diaspora engagement. The centralized approach starts at home and works outward. The end-goal is contact with the diaspora as opposed to viewing the diaspora as a means of achieving something. As such, when it comes to pairing diaspora talent with country-of-origin dynamic sectors of industry, the "centralized top-down schemes, particularly those managed by the government, have proven to be of very limited efficacy in terms of reaching this objective."[49] Another negative aspect of simply concentrating on the diaspora as such is that it can lead to burnout. According to Kuznetsov,[50] "many diaspora initiatives fail because they require a lot of participation (conferences, databases, responding to surveys) but yield little by way of practical results." Once the initial

---

[44] Portes, Alejandro. "Conclusion: Towards a new world – the origins and effects of transnational activities." *Ethnic and Racial Studies* 22, no. 2 (1999): 466–467.
[45] Gamlen, Alan John. "Diasporas." In *Global Migration Governance*, Oxford University Press, (2011): 274.
[46] Ibid.
[47] Ibid, p. 275.
[48] Kuznetsov, Yevgeny. *How Can Talent Abroad Induce Development at Home: Towards a Pragmatic Diaspora Agenda*. Migration Policy Institute, 2013.
[49] Ibid, p. 294.
[50] Ibid, p. 313.

enthusiasm of diaspora members fades, scepticism sets in and the networks can no longer be sustained. As Agunias and Newland[51] point out, "All parties must feel that they are deriving value from the relationship." The formal arrangements of a top-down approach can also stifle enthusiasm and creativity. "Diaspora ministries, for instance, which are sometimes proposed as a best-practice solution to design and manage diaspora strategies, have a role to play as an entry point to the diaspora agenda, but they can just as easy stifle and bureaucratize interactions with diasporas."[52]

On the other hand, the de-centralized approach begins its work abroad by identifying where the diaspora is and taking note of what they have to offer. As such, for the bottom-up, decentralized approach, the starting point is identifying "a diverse portfolio of projects and initiatives reflecting local needs and capabilities."[53] The focus is on enabling diaspora to come together, to network amongst themselves in specific regions, and ideally to link with country-of-origin sector representatives to allow for the exchange of knowledge, flourish of new ideas, and supremely form joint initiatives. The drawback of this approach is in the abundance of ideas it can generate. Thus, a "binding constraint remains on the home country's side: its ability to follow up on and implement ideas and projects generated by the diaspora members."[54] "The constraints may be related to the insufficient interest and willingness of home country recipients (i.e., companies) to receive support, or it may have to do with the infrastructure constraints necessary to facilitate matching the supply and demand of project ideas."[55]

However, no diaspora engagement strategy is completely decentralized, and a coordination role must be played by the country of origin's government. "The centralized effort has its role as well, particularly in sharing emerging good practices and in improving the institutional context for diaspora engagement."[56] Agunias and Newland[57] also suggest that a

---

[51] Agunias, Dovelyn Rannveig, and Kathleen Newland. *Developing a Road Map for Engaging Diasporas in Development: A Handbook for Policymakers and Practitioners in Home and Host countries*. International Organization for Migration, (2012): 29.

[52] Kuznetsov, Yevgeny. *How Can Talent Abroad Induce Development at Home: Towards a Pragmatic Diaspora Agenda*. Migration Policy Institute, (2013): 303.

[53] Ibid, p. 313.

[54] Ibid, p. 296.

[55] Ibid, p. 297.

[56] Ibid, p. 303.

completely centralized approach to diaspora engagement may not be the ideal solution as "political credibility and broad commitment may require a grassroots mobilization effort among diaspora members." As such, Kuznetsov[58] points out that the central question becomes: How can governments provide a coherent, centralized framework to assure diverse, bottom-up diaspora initiatives that fit specific local circumstances? His work suggests balancing organizational support and top-down impulses from the government side with individual initiative and creativity through the bottom-up impulses. As such, he presents the framework illustrated below (see figure 6-1).

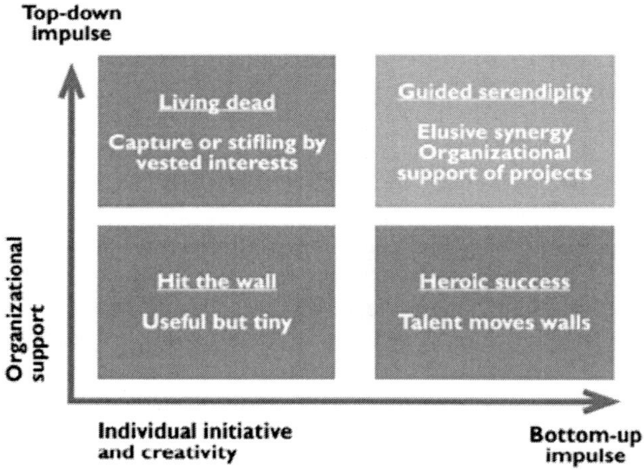

Figure 6-1: Monitoring framework diaspora initiatives
Source: Yevgeny Kuznetsov

The ideal diaspora engagement scenario envisions organizational and financial support from the country of origin with robust participation from the target group and the flourishing of creative ideas. The perfect mix of support and participation is hard to achieve, and if the portions are not just

---

[57] Agunias, Dovelyn Rannveig, and Kathleen Newland. *Developing a Road Map for Engaging Diasporas in Development: A Handbook for Policymakers and Practitioners in Home and Host Countries*. International Organization for Migration, (2012): 155.

[58] Kuznetsov, Yevgeny. *How Can Talent Abroad Induce Development at Home: Towards a Pragmatic Diaspora Agenda*. Migration Policy Institute, (2013): 17.

right, it can result in three undesirable scenarios. The first is the 'hit the wall' scenario where diaspora initiatives are effective when on a small-scale but are resistant to up-scaling or lack the financial and organizational resources required to grow. The 'living dead' situation is where the government invests a disproportionate number of resources but does not achieve the envisioned results, or where top-down bureaucratic assistance stifles creativity so the initiative is unable to grow. And, finally, the 'heroic success' scenario is where there is significant creativity and involvement from the target group, with ideas and initiatives but because of the lack of resources or support, they are unable to make an impact on a grand scale. The desired 'guided serendipity' scenario is achieved "when organizational support is subtle yet effective and facilitates and encourages members' creativity."[59]

The next section of the article will review the real-world examples of the diaspora engagement initiatives of Latvia and Australia. The aim of this analysis is to demonstrate where in the diaspora engagement process these countries are and how closely their actions reflect those suggested by Agunias and Newland[60] in their diaspora engagement road map. The overview will present a portrait of the diaspora of Latvia and Australia and how this background has influenced the direction of the diaspora engagement approach. Finally, the section will illustrate what method of diaspora engagement has been adopted and why, and, according to the Kuznetsov's[61] framework, how balanced the top-down vs bottom-up elements of these diaspora engagement strategies are.

4. Latvia

Latvia is a small country of only about two million inhabitants (Office of Citizenship and Migration Affairs of the Republic of Latvia 2021).[62] The population of Latvia is aging, continuing emigration is leading to rapid

---

[59] Ibid, p. 310.

[60] Agunias, Dovelyn Rannveig, and Kathleen Newland. *Developing a Road Map for Engaging Diasporas in Development: A Handbook for Policymakers and Practitioners in Home and Host Countries*. International Organization for Migration, (2012): 155.

[61] Kuznetsov, Yevgeny. *How Can Talent Abroad Induce Development at Home: Towards a Pragmatic Diaspora Agenda*. Migration Policy Institute, (2013): 17.

[62] Republic of Latvia Saeima. 2018. "Saeima supports a new diaspora law." November 2. Accessed June 1, 2021. http://www.saeima.lv/en/news/saeima-news/27366-saeima-supports-a-newdiaspora-law

depopulation, and, according to United Nations estimates, by 2050 Latvia's population may have shrunk by 22%.[63] However, Latvia has a sizable diaspora population living abroad – an estimated 373,000 individuals (Cabinet of Ministers 2021). Emigration from Latvia is understood to have taken place in two waves, creating the old and new diaspora. The old diaspora, roughly estimated at the time to number 200,000, fled Latvia for the West in the 1940s. The new diaspora, also an estimated 200,000 individuals, if not more, left Latvia between 2000 – 2010.[64]

Latvia has done considerable work in meeting the necessary preconditions for diaspora engagement success suggested in Agunias and Newland's[65] road map for diaspora engagement. Specifically, its efforts to gather information and getting to know the diaspora through various government commissioned surveys and projects must be praised.[66] The most in-depth effort was carried out in 2014 when the project *The Emigrant Communities of Latvia* surveyed 14,068 individuals living abroad. The project established a diaspora population profile, including its main characteristics such as size, the geographic location of target groups, and background information.

The findings shaped the diaspora policy focus. For example, the survey results revealed that a significant segment of the emigrants could be classified as highly qualified.[67] This was further collaborated by a 2016 International Monetary Fund report showing that Latvian emigrants'

---

[63] United Nations Population Division Department of Economic and Social Affairs. 2019. Australia. *World Population Prospects: The 2019 Revision.* Accessed June 1, 2020. https://population.un.org/wpp/

[64] Hazans, Mihalis. "The changing face of Latvian emigration, 2000–2010." In Zepa, B., Kļave, E. (eds.) *Latvia. Human Development Report 2010/2011. National Identity, Mobility and Capability,* (2011): 77–101. Riga: Advanced Social and Political Research Institute of the University of Latvia.

[65] Agunias, Dovelyn Rannveig, and Kathleen Newland. *Developing a Road Map for Engaging Diasporas in Development: A Handbook for Policymakers and Practitioners in Home and Host Countries*. International Organization for Migration, (2012): 155.

[66] Birka, Ieva. "Engaging the diaspora for economic gain: What can Latvia expect?" *Journal of Baltic Studies* 51, no. 4 (2020): 497–511.

[67] Hazans, Mihails. "Smadzeņu aizplūde no Latvijas 21. Gadsimtā" (Brain drain from Latvia in the 21st century). In Mieriņa, I. (ed.) *Latvijas emigrantu kopienas: Cerību diaspora (The Latvian Diaspora of Hope),* (2015): 85–92. Riga: Latvijas Universitātes Filozofijas un socioloģijas institūts.

education levels tend to be higher than that of the general population.[68] Additionally, it was ascertained that 15% had very weak or no Latvian language knowledge, and an additional 11% classified their language knowledge as mediocre.[69] Another interesting finding was that only 11% of the respondents claimed to be involved in diaspora organizations or associations.[70]

The sheer scale of the diaspora, the proportion of the highly qualified abroad, and the lack of bottom-up activity, evident by the low number of diaspora organization memberships, has prompted the government of Latvia to respond to the diaspora issue in a centralized manner. As a result, the Latvian diaspora strategy is a prime example of the top-down approach to diaspora engagement. Most recently, it has won praise from the British Foreign Policy Group Diaspora Report,[71] in which the Latvian approach is listed among the global best practice examples. The centrality of the diaspora and its importance to the future development trajectory of the Latvian state was affirmed in 2018 when Latvia became one of a handful of countries that implements a separate diaspora legislative framework in the form of a Diaspora Law.[72] The Diaspora Law aims to establish a methodical framework for the implementation of diaspora policy and assigns the main management task to the Ministry of Foreign Affairs. The Diaspora Law envisions five focus areas:

(1) maintaining and strengthening diaspora's ties with Latvia and its national identity

---

[68] Atoyan, Mr Ruben V., Lone Engbo Christiansen, Allan Dizioli, Mr Christian H. Ebeke, Mr Nadeem Ilahi, Ms Anna Ilyina, Mr Gil Mehrez et al. *Emigration and its Economic Impact on Eastern Europe*. International Monetary Fund, 2016.

[69] Koroļeva, Ilze. and Mieriņa, Inta. 2015. Uzticama informācija par Latvijas emigrantiem un remigrantiem iegūšanas pētnieciskiem risinājumiem (Reliable information about Latvian emigrants and remigrants acquisition for research). *Akadēmiskā dzīve (Academic Life)* (51) 2014/2015, 6–23.

[70] Mieriņa, Inta, Ose, Liesma and Agnese Lāce. *Vienojošās nacionālās identitātes un Latvijas kultūrtelpas nostiprināšana (Unifying national identities and strengthening the cultural space of Latvia).* Riga: University of Latvia Diaspora and Migration Research Centre. (2017): 56.

[71] Gaston, Sophia and Aspinall, Evie. 2021. *Harnessing our Global Footprint Transforming the UK Government's Engagement with the UK Diaspora.* London: British Foreign Policy Group.

[72] Republic of Latvia Saeima. 2018. "Saeima supports a new diaspora law." November 2. Accessed June 1, 2021. http://www.saeima.lv/en/news/saeima-news/27366-saeima-supports-a-newdiaspora-law

(2) protecting the rights and freedoms of diaspora abroad
(3) promoting cooperation with and participation of the diaspora in the fields of economy, science, and culture
(4) facilitating the civic and political participation of the diaspora
(5) supporting those who wish to return to Latvia

As a result, the diaspora policy of Latvia is multifaceted and corresponds to the three categories suggested by Gamlen.[73,74] The policy ensures that individuals of Latvian origin residing abroad can maintain and expand their ties with Latvia; promotes the Latvian language, culture, and sense of belonging to Latvia in the diaspora; extends civic and political rights; and strives to facilitate favorable conditions for cooperation and remigration.

The wide array of aims and focuses asserted in the Diaspora Law is the cumulative result of various diaspora engagement approaches Latvia has been implementing since 2004 when the first *Diaspora Support Program 2004-2009* was introduced and headed by the Secretariat of the Special Assignment Minister for Society Integration Affairs.[75] Since then, various government initiatives focusing on different aspects of the diaspora have been inaugurated by a variety of state actors. Table 6-2 presents the major government policy documents that have been crafted to address diaspora issues or which have included specific provisions dealing with the diaspora. What is evident is that the centralized, or top-down policy approach, pervades with various government institutions developing and then implementing initiatives.

---

[73] Gamlen, Alan John. "The brain drain is dead; long live the New Zealand diaspora." (2005). Working Paper No. 10. Oxford: Centre on Migration, Policy and Society University of Oxford.

[74] Gamlen, Alan John. "Diasporas." In *Global Migration Governance*, pp. 266–286. Oxford University Press, 2011.

[75] Republic of Latvia. 2004. *Par Latviešu diasporas atbalsta programmu 2004.–2009.gadam (Diaspora Support Programme 2004-2009).* Cabinet of Ministers Order No. 738.

Table 6-2: Diaspora Policy Documents and Initiatives of Latvia

Year(s)	Document	Responsible Institution
2004–2009	Diaspora Support Programme 2004-2009	Secretariat of Special Assignment Minister for Society Integration Affairs
2012–2018	National Identity, Civil Society and Integration 2012–2018 Policy Guidelines	Ministry of Culture
2013–2016	Return Migration Support Action Plan 2013–2016	Ministry of Economics
2015–2017	Action Plan on Cooperation with the Diaspora for 2015–2017	Ministry of Foreign Affairs
2019–	Diaspora Law	Ministry of Foreign Affairs
2021–2023	Action Plan on Cooperation with the Diaspora for 2021–2023	Ministry of Foreign Affairs

With the passing of the Diaspora Law, the centralized policy planning role, as well as the coordination and implementation role, has been assigned to the Ministry of Foreign Affairs of Latvia (MFA). In accordance with the new law, the diaspora itself has a right to co-participate in the development and implementation of the diaspora policy. As such, the MFA is tasked with channelling the bottom-up input through the establishment of a Diaspora Advisory Council "which is a consultative institution established with a view to promote coordinated development of diaspora policy and annual priorities, as well as implementation and assessment of diaspora policy."[76] Thus, as of late, there are initiatives, safeguarded in law, that attempt to incorporate the bottom-up signals in the

[76] Republic of Latvia Saeima. 2018. Saeima Supports a New Diaspora Law. November 2. Accessed June 1, 2021. http://www.saeima.lv/en/news/saeima-news/27366-saeima-supports-a-newdiaspora-law

top-down centralized policy planning process in Latvia. As such, the Latvian government is now actively returning to the diaspora engagement road map step of trust building and mobilizing stakeholders, as outlined by Agunias and Newland.[77]

The data suggests that this approach is working as diaspora organization membership has grown and now stands at 18%.[78] The number is still not very high, but the achieved growth in a few short years gives reason to hope that with stable financing of the diaspora policy, now entrenched in law, the diaspora organizations will receive the assistance necessary to expand their self-organizing capacities. One such example of a diaspora organization that has recently began work is #EsiLV, or Economic Cooperation and Investment for Latvia, whose goal is to promote diaspora networking and idea sharing. Initiatives like #EsiLV are supplementing the government's work, with the bottom-up involvement of the diaspora aiding the effort to achieve Kuznetsov's[79] outlined guided serendipity scenario, in which there is a robust participation of the diaspora and a flourishing of creative ideas with the organizational and financial support of the country of origin. According to the Gaston and Aspinall report,[80] it is specifically the Latvian achievements in institutionalizing diaspora policy and guaranteeing stable financing that create certainty for the diaspora population and promote the flourishing potential of diaspora engagement.

Finally, one drawback to the centralized approach to diaspora engagement taken by Latvia must be mentioned: the lack of a one-stop website or agency for clear and concise information to the diaspora. As already outlined, the Latvian diaspora policy focus areas are many; there is an emphasis on language and culture, extending rights and opportunities

---

[77] Agunias, Dovelyn Rannveig and Kathleen Newland. *Developing a Road Map for Engaging Diasporas in Development: A Handbook for Policymakers and Practitioners in Home and Host Countries*. International Organization for Migration, 2012.

[78] Mieriņa, Inta and Rasa Jansone. *Diasporas satīklošana: Iesaistīšanās prakse un sadarbības iespējas (Diaspora networking: Engagement practice and cooperation opportunities).* Riga: University of Latvia Diaspora and Migration Research Centre, 2019.

[79] Kuznetsov, Yevgeny. *How can Talent Abroad Induce Development at Home: Towards a Pragmatic Diaspora Agenda*. Migration Policy Institute, 2013: 310.

[80] Gaston, Sophia and Aspinall, Evie. *Harnessing our Global Footprint Transforming the UK Government's Engagement with the UK Diaspora.* London: British Foreign Policy Group, 2021.

for civic participation, promoting cooperation and the transfer of knowledge, and facilitating return migration. There is even the stated goal, which aims to support diaspora organizations in their capacity to self-organize. What is missing is an easily accessible information platform that outlines all these focus areas, the corresponding actions being taken, and how one can get involved in a language that is easy to read and understand. The lack of such a website or agency has been mentioned again and again by a variety of migration and diaspora experts.[81,82,83,84] Such an information source would make it easier for the Latvian diaspora to understand what they can expect from the diaspora policy of Latvia and how they can begin to contribute and engage.

5. Australia

Australia is a vast country in both size and population. The current population is estimated to be around 23.6 million people.[85] According to the United Nations population analysis, it is also one of the countries that can expect healthy population growth in the next century, and a country that has a stable and growing population of a working age.[86] In trying to understand the diaspora engagement strategy of Australia, it is also worth noting that Australia is a federation comprised of six self-governing states.

---

[81] Birka, Ieva. Can return migration revitalize the Baltics? Estonia, Latvia, and Lithuania engage their diasporas, with mixed results. *Migration Information Source*, May 8, 2019. Washington, D.C.: Migration Policy Institute.

[82] Mieriņa, Inta and Rasa Jansone. *Diasporas satīklošana: Iesaistīšanās prakse un sadarbības iespējas (Diaspora networking: Engagement practice and cooperation opportunities).* Riga: University of Latvia Diaspora and Migration Research Centre, 2019.

[83] Mieriņa, Inta., Evija Zača, Jānis Buholcs, 2018. *Diasporas politikas attīstība (Development of Diaspora Policy).* Riga: University of Latvia Diaspora and Migration Research Centre.

[84] Krapāne, A. 2017. *Diaspora kā Latvijas ārpolitikas prioritāte (Diaspora as foreign policy priority).* January 11, 2017. Riga: Latvian Institute of International Affairs.

[85] Australian Government. 2014. *Department of Foreign Affairs and Trade Public Diplomacy Strategy 2014–2016.* Accessed June 1, 2021. https://www.dfat.gov.au/people-to-people/public-diplomacy/Pages/public-diplomacy-strategy

[86] United Nations Population Division Department of Economic and Social Affairs. 2019. Latvia. *World Population Prospects: The 2019 Revision.* Accessed June 1, 2021. https://population.un.org/wpp/

Individual states can, therefore, develop, implement, and oversee their own diaspora engagement strategies as part of their international engagement approaches.[87] However, this paper will analyse, the overarching approach of the federal government.

In the early 2000s, several academic investigations were carried out to ascertain emigration rates and emigration destinations as well as glean an understanding of the expatriate profile.[88,89,90] The studies were conducted in cooperation with the Australian government or with the aim of drawing its attention to the diaspora topic. The Hugo, Rudd, and Harris[91] project also included an *Emigration Survey* of a total of 2070 expatriates, which at the time was the largest survey of Australians overseas. As already discussed, information gathering is a vital step in the Agunias and Newland[92] road map for diaspora engagement in order to map the location of the diaspora and understand its skills and potential contribution.

What emerged from these reports was that in the 1990s, the rate of permanent departure had increased by 146%, and long-term departure had increased by 41%.[93] This had resulted in "approximately one million Australians outside Australia, perhaps three-quarters of whom live offshore on a permanent or long-term basis".[94] Even more startling was the

---

[87] Australian Council of Learned Academies. 2016. *Australia's Diaspora Advantage.* Accessed June 1, 2021. https://apo.org.au/sites/default/files/ resource-files/2016-05/apo-nid64904.pdf

[88] Commonwealth of Australia. 2005. *They Still Call Australia Home: Inquiry into Australian Expatriates.* The Senate, Legal and Constitutional References Committee.

[89] Hugo, Graeme, Kevin R. Harris, and Dianne M. Rudd. *Emigration from Australia: Economic Implications*. Melbourne: Committee for Economic Development of Australia, 2001.

[90] Hugo, Graeme John, Dianne M. Rudd, and Kevin R. Harris. *Australia's Diaspora: Its Size, Nature and Policy Implications*. Committee for Economic Development of Australia, 2003.

[91] Ibid.

[92] Agunias, Dovelyn Rannveig, and Kathleen Newland. *Developing a Road Map for Engaging Diasporas in Development: A Handbook for Policymakers and Practitioners in Home and Host Countries*. International Organization for Migration, 2012.

[93] Hugo, Graeme John, Dianne M. Rudd, and Kevin R. Harris. *Australia's Diaspora: Its Size, Nature and Policy Implications*. Committee for Economic Development of Australia, (2003):10–11.

[94] Fullilove, Michael, and Chlöe Flutter. *Diaspora: The World Wide Web of Australians*. Longueville Media, 2004.

fact that "Over two-thirds of all Australia-born permanent departures and Australian resident long-term departures are managers, administrators, professionals and para-professionals".[95] These professionals chose to migrate to the European Union, specifically to the United Kingdom, to the United States, and more and more to Hong Kong and other developed parts of Asia.[96] Thus, the Australian diaspora is an elite category of diaspora, situated in the business hubs of the world, it is relatively young, highly educated and skilled, well connected and positioned and positively disposed to Australia.

Almost simultaneously to these academic studies being carried out, the new Australian consul-general in New York in 2002 was laying the groundwork for the Young Australian Professionals Association (YAPA), which would go on to become one of the most successful diaspora organizations in the world Advance – Australia's Global Community.[97] The aim of the diaspora group founded in New York was to promote what Gamlen[98] calls diaspora networking. The Consul-General himself had enjoyed a long career in international banking and was aware of the importance of networks and contacts for career development. Additionally, he wanted "to leverage the talent pool of Australian professionals resident in New York."[99]

The diaspora engagement approach of the Australian consulate general was very much bottom-up or de-centralized, with minimal organizational assistance and financial support, and a high level of empowerment of the diaspora members themselves. This is a prime example of Gamlen's[100] grassroots proactive hypothesis where the country of origin, through the consulate, helps to establish a diaspora association. After the initial support from the consulate, YAPA grew and scaled up quite quickly and

---

[95] Hugo, Graeme John, Dianne M. Rudd, and Kevin R. Harris. *Australia's Diaspora: Its Size, Nature and Policy Implications*. Committee for Economic Development of Australia, (2003):10–11.

[96] Ibid.

[97] Stone, Diane, and Elena Douglas. "Advance diaspora diplomacy in a networked world." *International Journal of Cultural Policy* 24, no. 6 (2018): 710–723.

[98] Gamlen, Alan John. "The brain drain is dead; long live the New Zealand diaspora." (2005). Working Paper No. 10. Oxford: Centre on Migration, Policy and Society University of Oxford.

[99] Stone, Diane, and Elena Douglas. "Advance diaspora diplomacy in a networked world." *International Journal of Cultural Policy* 24, no. 6 (2018): 710–723.

[100] Gamlen, Alan John. "Diasporas." In *Global Migration Governance*, pp. 266–286. Oxford University Press, 2011.

on its own accord. The draw of the organization became the opportunity for individuals to make contacts and progress in their career paths because of them. The organization's slogan became "Mentors, jobs and deals."[101] As such, the network was less about diaspora and more about professional growth. "YAPA was able to build a large network not so much by bringing Australians together around being Australian, but with a focus on their industry sector and professional interests."[102] In 2004, the organization changed its name to Advance – Young Australian Professionals in America, sought to open city-based chapters in the United States, and began helping Australian companies to enter the United States market. Then, in 2006, it outgrew the United States and was rebranded as Advance – Global Australian Professionals, with chapters in the business hubs of the world.[103]

Only after this self-organizing and up-scaling process did Advance re-enter a formal relationship with the Australian government. Since then, it has received half of its funding from the Commonwealth government with contributions by the Department of Foreign Affairs and Trade and the Department of Industry, Science, Energy and Resources.[104] Subsequently, Advance has also enjoyed the patronage of the prime minister of Australia and has more actively taken on the role of providing "a bridge for skills and knowledge acquired overseas to be leveraged for Australia's benefit."[105] From 2006 onward, Advance has organized events and awards to recognize influential Australians working around the world, hosted regional networking events, coordinated mentoring partnerships, implemented rapid-growth entrepreneurships programs, assisted Australian companies to enter global markets, and has informed Australian diaspora about opportunities to return home.

Although Advance has formally partnered with the Australian government for some time now, the diaspora engagement strategy of Australia remains very much de-centralized. Advance is left to operate remotely, rarely showing up as a government partner in government documents. This can best be attested by the 2019–2020 *Australian Government Department of Foreign Affairs and Trade Annual Report*, which makes no mention of the diaspora or the Advance organization in the 134 pages of text. The *Public*

---

[101] Stone, Diane, and Elena Douglas. "Advance diaspora diplomacy in a networked world." *International Journal of Cultural Policy* 24, no. 6 (2018): 710–723.
[102] Ibid.
[103] Ibid.
[104] Advance.org. 2021. *About.* Accessed June 1, 2021. https://advance.org/support/
[105] Advance.org. 2021. *About.* Accessed June 1, 2021. https://advance.org/support/

Diplomacy Strategy 2014–2016 of the DFTA also makes no mention of Advance as a partner in public and diaspora diplomacy. Back in 2005, there was an attempt by the Senate Legal and Constitutional References Committee to ascertain how best to meet the needs of the expatriate population and move towards a more centralized diaspora strategy. Various recommendations were made, including the creation of a diaspora web-portal, a policy unit at DFTA, a more advanced data-collection strategy, and the recognition of various formal rights of the diaspora and the implementation of those rights through policy.[106] In 2013 there was another report by the Joint Standing Committee on Migration of the Parliament of the Commonwealth of Australia. Again, the relevant diaspora chapter concluded that there was indeed an "underutilization of the diaspora by the Australian Government."[107] However, not much came of the reports and recommendations and the diaspora engagement strategy of Australia remains decentralized.

As of late, there have been renewed calls for the government of Australia to involve itself more directly in diaspora relations with a strategic national approach, including working with diaspora communities not only outside of Australia but in Australia in order to fully utilize their talent, knowledge, networks, and good will towards Australia in economic growth and development.[108] [109] Not only is this decentralized strategy failing to fully utilize the highly qualified and elite diaspora of Australia abroad but as of late there are also indications that a centralized diaspora strategy is needed to help overcome some serious issues related to return migration that diaspora organizations, such as Advance, cannot resolve by themselves. A 2019 report and survey carried out by Advance and the recruitment firm Indeed, titled *They Still Call Australia Home,* disclosed that, the Australians who chose to return after years abroad were facing

---

[106] Commonwealth of Australia. 2005. *They Still Call Australia Home: Inquiry into Australian Expatriates.* The Senate, Legal and Constitutional References Committee.
[107] Parliament of the Commonwealth of Australia. 2013. *Inquiry into Migration and Multiculturalism in Australia.* Accessed June 1, 2021.
https://www.aph.gov.au/parliamentary_business/committees/house_of_representatives_committees?url=mig/multiculturalism/report/fullreport.pdf
[108] Asia Taskforce Sub-Committee on Asian-Australian and Diaspora. 2020. *A Forgotten Advantage.* Asia Taskforce Discussion Paper No. 6. June 1, 2021.
https://asiasociety.org/sites/default/files/inline-files/Asia_Taskforce_Discussion_Paper_3_Asian-Australian_Diaspora.pdf
[109] PWC. 2016. *Our Diaspora's Got Talent.* Accessed June 1, 2021.
https://www.pwc.com.au/pdf/our-diasporas-got-talent.pdf

alarming problems finding suitable employment in Australia. Recruiters prioritize candidates with Australian-only work experience and businesses are aiding in creating an environment that discourages Australians from working overseas. This unfavourable environment leads to many returnees regretting their decision to return to Australia and drives them to emigrate once more.

What the Australian example illustrates is that a completely decentralized diaspora strategy, where the country of origin is involved only through financing and almost no organizational support, is also not the best solution. This approach, leaving everything in the hands of diaspora organizations themselves, fails to fully utilize the potential of the diaspora as they are not fully integrated in the national strategy and engaged as partners. Further, a diaspora organization approach cannot address structural and institutional shortcomings by itself; government policy design and implementation are also necessary. The diaspora might be highly engaged and empowered in this type of approach but there is also a need for political credibility and strong signals from above that, in this case, returning diaspora is welcome and appreciated.

Conclusion

For diaspora engagement to be a success, especially for developed countries that are interested in more than simply encouraging and receiving remittances, the approach cannot be completely top-down, or centralized. A certain amount of diaspora engagement, through diaspora organizations, consultative councils, and the like, is necessary. Otherwise, the lack of involvement from the diaspora themselves will result in a lack of legitimacy of the initiated diaspora actions and is likely to end in what Kuznetsov[110] termed the living dead outcome of diaspora engagement. Likewise, the diaspora engagement approach cannot be totally bottom-up, leaving the diaspora organizations completely in charge of harnessing the potential of the diaspora through whatever initiatives they see fit, with the country of origin only involved through financing or patronage. At some point, for the initiatives to have wide-reaching impact, government involvement is needed to put resolutions or policy into action. Further, government support and involvement are needed to overcome systematic

---

[110] Kuznetsov, Yevgeny. *How Can Talent Abroad Induce Development at Home: Towards a Pragmatic Diaspora Agenda*. Migration Policy Institute, 2013.

or institutional constraints that diaspora organizations or investigative reports identify.

Such a strategy, where there is involvement from both sides, is in line with the partnership or cooperative approach advocated by community studies theory. This is also the conclusion reached by Kuznetsov[111] in his analysis of centralized versus decentralized approaches to diaspora engagement. Both approaches suggest that a mutually reinforcing relationship between the government, which provides organizational support, financing and authority, and the diaspora, which provides ideas and actual involvement, is necessary for success.

This article has demonstrated the above-mentioned conclusions in practice by carrying out an analysis of the diaspora engagement approach of Latvia and Australia. Latvia, which is facing a demographic decline, does not have time to wait for bottom-up diaspora action and, therefore, took a more centralized approach to diaspora engagement. Australia, a large country with stable growth, had time to wait for diaspora organizations to gain clout, self-organize, and develop, and has since taken a very decentralized approach to diaspora engagement. However, what the analysis has also shown is that the approach to diaspora engagement can start out one way or the other and then evolve over time. Latvia has shown that the centralized approach it took at the beginning, with institutionalized action, guaranteed funding, and organizational support for the diaspora, has paid off with increased diaspora organization membership and involvement. The diaspora organizations are now aiding in furthering the intentions of government policy by promoting networking, skills, and knowledge transfer between Latvia and the diaspora from a bottom-up approach. On the other hand, the Australian approach has shown that the bottom-up strategy can also be highly effective in terms of aiding in creating a powerful diaspora organization with minimal involvement from the government and with highly empowered and engaged diaspora members. However, for years the Australian approach has been open to criticism from within and outside the government for failing to fully utilize the potential of its diaspora through this decentralized approach. Further, the diaspora organization itself has now identified significant roadblocks in the potential utilization of its diaspora, which are likely to require government assistance and authority to overcome. Thus, the Australian approach is now facing the question of how to develop further. Will the government increase its involvement with top-down impulses to put into

[111] Ibid.

practice initiatives and resolve roadblocks identified by the diaspora organizations themselves, or will the approach remain decentralized in the hands of diaspora organizations with the Australian government only involved through funding and patronages? Time will tell.

References

Advance.org. 2021. *About.* Accessed June 1, 2021. https://advance.org/support/

Adams Jr, Richard H., and John Page. "Do international migration and remittances reduce poverty in developing countries?" *World Development* 33, no. 10 (2005): 1645–669.

Agunias, Dovelyn Rannveig, and Kathleen Newland. *Developing a Road Map for Engaging Diasporas in Development: A Handbook for Policymakers and Practitioners in Home and Host Countries*. International Organization for Migration, 2012.

Australian Council of Learned Academies. 2016. *Australia's Diaspora Advantage.* Accessed June 1, 2021. https://apo.org.au/sites/default/files/resource-files/2016-05/apo-nid64904.pdf

Australian Government, 2021. *Our Country.* Accessed June 1, 2021. https://info.australia.gov.au/about-australia/our-country

Australian Government, 2020. *Department of Foreign Affairs and Trade 2019-2020 Annual Report.* Accessed June 1, 2021. https://www.dfat.gov.au/sites/default/files/dfat-annual-report-2019-20.pdf

Australian Government, 2014. *Department of Foreign Affairs and Trade Public Diplomacy Strategy 2014–2016.* Accessed June 1, 2021. https://www.dfat.gov.au/people-to-people/public-diplomacy/Pages/public-diplomacy-strategy

Asia Taskforce Sub-Committee on Asian-Australian and Diaspora, 2020. *A Forgotten Advantage.* Asia Taskforce Discussion Paper No. 6. June 1, 2021. https://asiasociety.org/sites/default/files/inline-files/Asia_Taskforce_Discussion_Paper_3_Asian-Australian_Diaspora.pdf

Atoyan, Mr Ruben V., Lone Engbo Christiansen, Allan Dizioli, Mr Christian H. Ebeke, Mr Nadeem Ilahi, Ms Anna Ilyina, Mr Gil Mehrez et al. *Emigration and its Economic Impact on Eastern Europe*. International Monetary Fund, 2016.

Birka, Ieva. "Engaging the diaspora for economic gain: What can Latvia expect?" *Journal of Baltic Studies* 51, no. 4 (2020): 497–511.

Birka, Ieva. "Can return migration revitalize the Baltics? Estonia, Latvia, and Lithuania engage their diasporas, with mixed results." *Migration Information Source*, May 8, 2019. Washington, D.C.: Migration Policy Institute.

Birka, Ieva, and Didzis Kļaviņš. "Diaspora diplomacy: Nordic and Baltic perspective." *Diaspora Studies* 13, no. 2 (2020): 115–132.

Braun, Ann. *Managing Natural Resources for Sustainable Livelihoods: Uniting Science and Participation*. IDRC, 2003.

Brinkerhoff, Jennifer M. "Diasporas, skills transfer, and remittances: Evolving perceptions and potential." *Converting Migration Drains into Gains: Harnessing the Resources of Overseas Professionals* (2006): 1–32.

Cabinet of Ministers of the Republic of Latvia. 2021. *Par Plānu darbam ar diasporu 2021–2023. Gadam (Plan for Work with the Diaspora 2021–2023).* Accessed June 1, 2021. https://likumi.lv/ta/id/320368-par-planu-darbam-ar-diasporu-20212023-gadam

Chambers, Robert. *Whose Reality Counts*. Vol. 25. London: Intermediate Technology Publications, 1997.

Commonwealth of Australia. 2005. *They Still Call Australia Home: Inquiry into Australian Expatriates.* The Senate, Legal and Constitutional References Committee.

Conyers, Diana. "Decentralisation and Development: A Framework for Analysis." *Community Development Journal* 21, no. 2 (1986): 88–100.

De Haas, Hein. "International migration, remittances and development: Myths and facts." *Third World Quarterly* 26, no. 8 (2005): 1269–284.

Dyer, Caroline. *Operation Blackboard: Policy Implementation in Indian Elementary Education*. Symposium Books Ltd, 2001.

Elmore, Richard F. "Backward mapping: Implementation research and policy decisions." *Political Science Quarterly* 94, no. 4 (1979): 601–616.

Esi.LV. 2021. *Ekonomiskā sadarbība un investīcijas Latvijai (Economic cooperation and investments for Latvia).* Accessed June 1, 2021. https://www.facebook.com/esiLVkopiena

Fullilove, Michael, and Chlöe Flutter. *Diaspora: The World Wide Web of Australians*. Longueville Media, 2004.

Hazans, Mihails. Smadzeņu aizplūde no Latvijas 21. gadsimtā (Brain drain from Latvia in the 21st century). In Mieriņa, I. (ed.) *Latvijas emigrantu kopienas: Cerību diaspora (The Latvian Diaspora of Hope),* (2015): 85–92. Riga: Latvijas Universitātes Filozofijas un socioloģijas institūts.

Hazans, Mihalis. The Changing Face of Latvian Emigration, 2000–2010. In Zepa, B., Kļave, E. (eds.) *Latvia. Human Development Report*

2010/2011. National Identity, Mobility and Capability, (2011): 77–101. Riga: Advanced Social and Political Research Institute of the University of Latvia.

Hugo, Graeme John, Dianne M. Rudd, and Kevin R. Harris. *Australia's Diaspora: Its Size, Nature and Policy Implications*. Committee for Economic Development of Australia, 2003.

Hugo, Graeme, Kevin R. Harris, and Dianne M. Rudd. *Emigration from Australia: Economic Implications*. Melbourne: Committee for Economic Development of Australia, 2001.

Indeed, and Advance.org. 2019. *They Still Call Australia Home.* Accessed June 1, 2021. https://advance.org/app/uploads/2020/11/Indeed_Advance-TheyStillCallAustraliaHomeReport-1.pdf

International Organization for Migration, 2005. *Results of the Survey "Engaging Diasporas as Agents of Development."* Geneva: International Organization for Migration.

Gamlen, Alan John. "Diaspora institutions and diaspora governance." *International Migration Review* 48 (2014): 180–217.

Gamlen, Alan John. "Diasporas." In *Global Migration Governance*, Oxford University Press, (2011): 266–286.

Gamlen, Alan John. "The brain drain is dead; long live the New Zealand diaspora." Working Paper No. 10. Oxford: Centre on Migration, Policy and Society University of Oxford, 2005

Gaston, Sophia and Aspinall, Evie, 2021. *Harnessing our Global Footprint Transforming the UK Government's Engagement with the UK Diaspora.* London: British Foreign Policy Group.

Gould, David M. "Immigrant links to the home country: Empirical implications for US bilateral trade flows." *The Review of Economics and Statistics* (1994): 302–316.

Hickey, Maureen. "Diaspora strategies in the sending states of Southeast Asia: Rights, skills and questions of value." *Singapore Journal of Tropical Geography* 36, no. 2 (2015): 147–163.

Ho, Elaine Lynn‐Ee, and Mark Boyle. "Migration‐as‐development repackaged? The globalizing imperative of the Singaporean state's diaspora strategies." *Singapore Journal of Tropical Geography* 36, no. 2 (2015): 164–182.

Ho, Elaine Lynn-Ee, Maureen Hickey, and Brenda S. A. Yeoh. "Special issue introduction: New research directions and critical perspectives on diaspora strategies." *Geoforum* 59 (2015): 153-158.

Hugo, Graeme. "Developed country diasporas: The example of Australian expatriates." *Espace Populations Sociétés. Space Populations Societies* 1 (2006): 181-202.

Ionescu, Dina. *Engaging Diasporas as Agents for Development.* Geneva: International Organization for Migration, 2006.

Koroļeva, Ilze, and Mieriņa, Inta. 2015. Uzticama informācija par Latvijas emigrantiem un remigrantiem iegūšanas pētnieciskiem risinājumiem (Reliable information about Latvian emigrants and remigrants acquisition for research). *Akadēmiskā dzīve (Academic Life)* (51) 2014/2015, 6–23.

Krapāne, A. 2017. *Diaspora kā Latvijas ārpolitikas prioritāte (Diaspora as Foreign Policy Priority).* January 11, 2017. Riga: Latvian Institute of International Affairs.

Kuznetsov, Yevgeny. *How Can Talent Abroad Induce Development at Home: Towards a Pragmatic Diaspora Agenda*. Migration Policy Institute, 2013.

Leblang, David. "Another link in the chain: Migrant networks and international investment." *DIASPORA for* (2011): 79.

Mieriņa, Inta and Rasa Jansone. *Diasporas satīklošana: Iesaistīšanās prakse un sadarbības iespējas (Diaspora networking: Engagement practice and cooperation opportunities).* Riga: University of Latvia Diaspora and Migration Research Centre, 2019.

Mieriņa, Inta, Evija Zača, Jānis Buholcs, 2018. *Diasporas politikas attīstība (Development of Diaspora Policy).* Riga: University of Latvia Diaspora and Migration Research Centre.

Mieriņa, Inta, Ose, Liesma and Agnese Lāce, 2017. *Vienojošās nacionālās identitātes un Latvijas kultūrtelpas nostiprināšana (Unifying National Identities and Strengthening the Cultural Space of Latvia).* Riga: University of Latvia Diaspora and Migration Research Centre.

Newland, Kathleen, and Sonia Plaza. "What we know about diasporas and economic development." *Policy Brief* 5 (2013). Washington, DC: Migration Policy Institute.

Newland, Kathleen, and Hiroyuki Tanaka. *Mobilizing Diaspora Entrepreneurship for Development*. Washington, DC: Migration Policy Institute, 2010.

Nikkhah Hedayat Allah, and Maarof Redzuan. "Participation as a medium of empowerment in community development." *European Journal of Social Sciences* 11, no. 1 (2009): 170–176.

Office of Citizenship and Migration Affairs of the Republic of Latvia (2021). *Iedzīvotāju reģistra statistika 2021. Gadā (Statistics of the Residents of Latvia 2021).* Accessed June 1, 2021.

https://www.pmlp.gov.lv/lv/iedzivotaju-registra-statistika-2021-gada

Parliament of the Commonwealth of Australia. 2013. *Inquiry into Migration and Multiculturalism in Australia.* Accessed June 1, 2021. https://www.aph.gov.au/parliamentary_business/committees/house_of_representatives_committees?url=mig/multiculturalism/report/fullreport.pdf

Portes, Alejandro. "Conclusion: Towards a new world – the origins and effects of transnational activities." *Ethnic and Racial Studies* 22, no. 2 (1999): 463–477.

PWC. 2016. *Our Diaspora's Got Talent*. Accessed June 1, 2021. https://www.pwc.com.au/pdf/our-diasporas-got-talent.pdf

Republic of Latvia. 2018. Diasporas Likums (Diaspora Law). *Latvijas Vēstnesis* 225 (6311). 14 November.

Republic of Latvia Saeima. 2018. Saeima Supports a New Diaspora Law. November 2. Accessed June 1, 2021. http://www.saeima.lv/en/news/saeima-news/27366-saeima-supports-a-newdiaspora-law

Republic of Latvia. 2004. *Par Latviešu diasporas atbalsta programmu 2004–2009 gadam (Diaspora Support Programme 2004–2009).* Cabinet of Ministers Order No. 738.

Sabatier, Paul A. "Top-down and bottom-up approaches to implementation research: A critical analysis and suggested synthesis." *Journal of Public Policy* (1986): 21–48.

Stone, Diane, and Elena Douglas. "Advance diaspora diplomacy in a networked world." *International Journal of Cultural Policy* 24, no. 6 (2018): 710–723.

United Nations Population Division Department of Economic and Social Affairs. 2019. Australia. *World Population Prospects: The 2019 Revision.* Accessed June 1, 2020. https://population.un.org/wpp/

United Nations Population Division Department of Economic and Social Affairs. 2019. Latvia. *World Population Prospects: The 2019 Revision.* Accessed June 1, 2021. https://population.un.org/wpp/

CHAPTER SEVEN

MANIPULATION DETECTION IN FINANCIAL STATEMENTS

STEFAN MILOJEVIĆ[1]
IVANA ČOVIĆ[2]

Abstract

Financial statements, as the end product of the accounting information system, represent a structural presentation of the financial condition and financial success of an entity's operations during a specific time. Lately, financial fraudulent behaviour is on the increase, with financial fraud being detected. There has been a significant increase in academic research in the field of accounting manipulation over the last decades. This paper aims to explore the modalities and patterns of fraud in financial statements and to point out the key determinants in the emergence of fraudulent financial statements. The paper uses the method of content analysis.

Key words: *financial reports, corporations, fraud, red flags*

Introduction

The main financial statements include the statement of financial position, the statement of profit or loss and other comprehensive income, the cash flow statement, and the statement of changes in equity. Protecting

[1] Director of Sector "Fraud Prevention and Fraud Investigations", Audit, Accounting, Financial and Consulting Services Company "Moody's Standards", Belgrade, Republic of Serbia
[2] Serbia

investors from fraud is a significant concern for both standard setters and policy makers. Bankruptcy, corporate fraud, and earnings manipulation are serious challenges for stakeholders in recent years. The Association of Certified Fraud Examiners (ACFE) argues that fraud in financial statements is the intentional misrepresentation of the financial information about a company, done by intentionally misrepresenting or materially omitting amounts or disclosing false and misleading information in financial statements, in order to convey it to interested users.[3] "Fraudulent financial reports can have a substantial negative impact on a company's existence as well as market value."[4]

Fraud, in any context, has been an integral fact of the business world for thousands of years; it was recognized by the very first legislators, who fought against it. In Hammurabi's Babylonian law, which dates back to 1800 BC, the problem of deception of the people was openly confronted; "If a shepherd, entrusted with sheep and cattle, is guilty of fraud and false reporting of increase in natural yield or if he sells it, then he will be condemned and forced to pay the owner an amount that is ten times higher than that caused by the loss."[5]

All parts of this fraud can be classified into four basic elements:

1. Misrepresentation of a material nature
2. Expertise – knowledge that the representation is false or a reckless disregard for the truth
3. Reliability – a person who agrees to make a presentation, justifiably relying on it
4. Damages – financial damage caused by all of the above

People react negatively to fraud, primarily due to the misuse of their expectations by other people. One of the main outcomes of fraud is financial loss. Accounting and auditing are two professions that are inextricably linked to fraud detection, investigation, and prevention. Many elements of modern society are focused on maintaining a fair environment.

---

[3] Egbunike, Patrick Amaechi, and Ikponmwosa Michael Igbinovia. "Threat of bankruptcy and earnings management in Nigerian listed banks." *Acta Universitatis Danubius. OEconomica* 14, no. 3 (2018): 238–250.

[4] Kassem, Rasha, and Mohamed A. Hegazy. "Fraudulent financial reporting: Do red flags really help?" *International Journal of Academic Research: Economics and Engineering* 4 (2010): 69–79.

[5] *Hammurabi's Code of Laws* (1780 bce), L. W. King, trans, https://sourcebooks.fordham.edu/ancient/hamcode.asp, accessed on 25.5.2020.

For that purpose, laws are passed, agencies are established for their implementation, the police are engaged, ethics and morals are taught in schools, and perpetrators of fraud are punished by deprivation of liberty or acquired property, all with the aim of detecting, punishing, and deterring fraud.[6]

1. The Main Causes of Fraud

Considering the way society evolved, followed by trade, starting from barter all the way to e-commerce, so has fraud developed from simple to increasingly complex forms, and fraud defined by Hammurabi can be considered only the beginning. Until a few years ago, companies in the developed world took the position that their business risk was highest in relation to "third world" companies and those companies located in emerging countries, with foreign business cultures and less developed regulatory environments considered as creating a greater risk.

Fraud includes a set of irregularities and illegal actions a characteristic of which is intentional deception. The five elements of fraud are:[7]

- a misrepresentation of a material fact, making it false,
- which is made intentionally, knowingly, or recklessly,
- which is believed by the victim,
- acted upon by the victim,
- which is to the victim's damage.

The increasing chance to access and operate in emerging markets, or less developed markets, provides an opportunity to start business practices that are not otherwise allowed in domestic markets. As such, the regulatory bodies in the major industrialized countries enacted laws to combat potential corruption. However, as society evolved, so did the ways of thinking, markets, and fraud, and such laws as a way to fight corruption and fraud were no longer adequate. Fraud risk factors are numerous and borderless, and fraud initiates concerns about a company's operations; financial pressures including access to finance, market entry, and dominance of competition; legal requirements and exposures; personal needs; and so

---

[6] Golden, Thomas W. *A Guide to Forensic Accounting Investigation*. John Wiley & Sons, 2011: 1–3.

[7] https://www.osc.state.ny.us/sites/default/files/local-government/documents/pdf/2019-01/red_flags_fraud.pdf, accessed on 26.5.2020.

on. In the last few years, the events that have befallen several European multinational companies show that mass fraud knows no borders.

Auditing standards define fraud as an intentional act resulting in a material misrepresentation in the financial statements. Research shows that fraud is more likely to occur if three conditions are present – pressures, opportunities, and attitudes, i.e., rationalization. These three conditions are recognized as the triangle of fraud.

It is worth noting that auditors use the fraud triangle as a tool to help identify areas of risk during the fraud brainstorming process. The first step of the fraud triangle is incentives or pressures – this condition is present when managers or employees have incentives or are under pressure to commit fraud. The second step is opportunities – this condition is present when circumstances allow management or employees to commit and conceal false reporting. The final step of the triangle of fraud is attitude; that is, rationalization. This condition is present when management or employees show an attitude, character, or set of ethical values that allow an unfair act to be committed, or when the environment creates pressure on management or employees to induce good people to join in on the act of fraud.[8]

Certain examples of the top ten red flags of fraud were included in the ACFE's report on occupational fraud and abuse published in 2008. Some of them are:[9]

1) living beyond the person's means
2) financial difficulties
3) control issues and unwillingness to share duties
4) divorce/family issues
5) unusually close association with vendor/customer
6) irritability
7) suspiciousness or defensiveness
8) addiction problems
9) past legal problems, and past employment problems

After 12 years according to ACFE's report,[10] the seven most-common red flags were:

---

[8] Hess, Megan F., and Lindsay M. Andiola. "Fraud risk brainstorming at Tesla motors." *Issues in Accounting Education* 33, no. 2 (2018): 24–25.

[9] ACFE report, 2008. https://www.acfe.com/, accessed on 23.4.2020.

[10] ACFE report to the nation, https://www.acfe.com/report-to-the-nations/2020/, accessed on 26.6.2020.

(1) living beyond means
(2) financial difficulties
(3) unusually close association with a vendor or customer
(4) excessive control issues or unwillingness to share duties
(5) unusual irritability, suspiciousness, or defensiveness
(6) a general "wheeler-dealer" attitude involving shrewd or unscrupulous behaviour
(7) recent divorce or family problems

It is interesting to note that at least one of these seven red flags had been identified before the perpetrator was caught in 76% of all cases (ACFE report, 2020).

Fraud in financial statements is deliberate action committed by an employee or manager such as: fictitious income, report on understated expenses, etc. The results of fraud detection research by Bishop (2004) for 450 companies that were victims of fraud in 2004, according to the ACFE report, suggest that there are several ways to detect fraud. Some of them are internal audit, employees in the form of advice, internal control, external audit, advice from customers, suppliers, anonymous advice, and notifications from the police. Bishop (2004) states that most fraud was detected by internal audit (23.8%) and then by employees (23.6%). However, if the data of employees, suppliers, consumers, and anonymous advisors are taken into account as a category of information, it is concluded that this is the most common method of detecting fraud (39.6%).[11]

The analysis of financial statements is a very important tool for assessing the financial position of a company. The results are used by internal and external users, in an adequate manner, in order to make good managerial, investment, and other decisions. The key areas that include the analysis of financial statements are revenues, inventories, capital structure, liquidity, profitability, indebtedness, and cash flows from operating and financing activities.[12]

---

[11] Herawati, Nurul. "Application of Beneish M-Score models and data mining to detect financial fraud." *Procedia-Social and Behavioral Sciences* 211 (2015): 925.
[12] Kulchev, Krasimir. "The interpretation of financial statements in terms of contemporary financial analysis." *Accounting and Audit* (2017): 74.

2. Red Flags as Warning Indicators for the Detection of Manipulative Actions

The undesirable situations or conditions that consistently contribute to fraud, waste, and misuse of resources are referred to as fraud red flags. When reviewing a company's stocks or financial statements, some undesirable characteristics may be pointed out as red flags – contributors to fraud or circumstances indicating the presence of fraud.[13]

Numerous fraud researchers and professional investigators have emphasized the need for the early detection of fraud. Although there are many ways in which fraud can be detected, a particularly effective and inexpensive way is to identify the fraudster by examining the behaviour of the employees because of the characteristics typical of fraudsters.[14]

Researchers who deal with the detection of manipulative actions and the factors influencing them replaced rationalization with honesty because they thought that a good person would most likely not commit fraudulent actions. They based their research on previous cases and the individual analyses of each perpetrator of fraud and concluded that dissatisfaction and disappointment are some of the factors that influenced the occurrence of manipulative actions in an individual, particularly if they considered their rights had been denied. They set the hypothesis that factors related to the size and bureaucratization of the organization provide many opportunities that could lead to fraud but also disinterest, and even to a situation they called the Robin Hood Syndrome.[15] They tested 65 red flags by looking at historical data on fraudulent activities and concluded that red flags occur in a large number of cases, mostly in the areas of accounting and auditing. They stated that some of the red flags contain personal characteristics that characterize manipulators, some of which are the lack of ethics, the desire to beat the already established system, the lack of stability, and the like. Also, high debts and financial losses, insufficient income for a normal life, excessive alcohol use, resentment, and mobbing

---

[13] https://corporatefinanceinstitute.com/resources/knowledge/other/fraud-red-flags/, accessed on 12.3.2020.

[14] Sandhu, Namrata. "Behavioural red flags of fraud: An ex-post assessment of types and frequencies." *Global Business Review* 21, no. 2 (2020): 507.

[15] The Robin Hood syndrome is an economic phenomenon in which earnings are distributed in such a way as to reduce economic inequality. The effect is named after Robin Hood, the mythical character famous for taking from the rich to give to the poor.

by superiors and associates are other factors that influence the occurrence of manipulative actions.[16]

Many of the respondents who participated in the research said that professional relationships had a strong impact on internal audits and the red flag of manipulative actions. The research involved 82 respondents – internal auditors, of whom 99% were exposed to red flags, 85% of them used red flags, and 82% discovered manipulative actions. In parallel, the researchers used data from 82 organizations employing the aforementioned internal auditors; 62% of these organizations discovered manipulative actions, and 61% of them believe that red flags are very effective when it comes to detecting fraud. *Sas no. 99*[17] (*AICPA* classified 42 red flags into three groups –opportunities, incentives, and rationalization, i.e., attitudes – in order to analyse, their effectiveness (as we mentioned earlier, the tringle of fraud). In the first group, called opportunities by the researchers, 14 red flags were classified; in the second group, called incentives, 16 red flags were classified; and in the third group, called rationalization 12 red flags were classified. Within the third group, the group average related to the detection of manipulative acts is 4.32, which shows the degree of efficiency of red flags in detecting fraud. In second place in terms of the efficiency of red flags detecting fraud is the first group, i.e., opportunities, with 14 red flags and an average of 4.12; and in third place is the group that researchers called incentives with an average of 3.47.

Directors and executive managers have as a task, and the goal as well, to prevent such situations, but in a situation where the line of delegation of authority and responsibility is clearly defined, it is harder for employees to commit fraud. Employees are more likely to commit fraud if the internal control system is not well developed; if there is an inefficient accounting system, and if the audit committee has not implemented a correction of reporting issued by internal and external auditors. Fraud can occur as a result of excessive pressure coming from the manager, board of directors, investors, creditors, or analysts. It can also be linked to managerial

---

[16] Sheridan, Terry A. *Managerial Fraud: Executive Impression Management, Beyond Red Flags*. Routledge, 2016: 25–26.

[17] SAS No. 99 – Statement on Auditing Standards No. 99: Consideration of Fraud in a Financial Statement Audit – defines fraud as an intentional act that results in significant misinterpretation in financial statements. Two types of fraud are most commonly analysed – misleading statements about false financial reporting (e.g., falsification of accounting records) and false statements about embezzlement (theft of property or false expenses). This standard also defines the fraud triangle.

compensation or to performance appraisal depending on pre-set financial goals.[18]

Associated with different types of fraudulent actions are certain balance sheet accounts. For example, fraud involving related-party transactions is associated with high other receivables, prepaid expenses, other currents, short-term loans, notes payable, other short-term liabilities, long-term debt, long-term payables, deferred tax liabilities, and other non-current liabilities. The effective prediction of each different type of fraud is enabled by the pattern of accounts identified.[19] In the income statement, these are usually sales revenues, provisions, certain types of costs, and so on.

3. Conclusion

Fraud risk management is becoming more important to companies. Accounting fraud has always existed and will continue to exist. Financial statements are an important part of a company. They are the primary source of data for studying the financial position and performance of companies as well as cash flows. Fraudulent financial reporting refers to the intentional overestimation or underestimation of balance sheets in financial statements and is an increasingly important issue in the accounting profession. Numerous academic studies and signals from practice have pointed to the need to find ways to detect fraud early in order to prevent the negative effects that may arise for decision-makers.

References

"ACFE Report to The Nations | 2020 Global Fraud Study." 2020. *Acfe.Com*. https://www.acfe.com/report-to-the-nations/2020/

"ACFE report, 2008." 2020. *Acfe.Com*. https://www.acfe.com/

---

[18] Moyes, Glen D., Ping Lin, Raymond M. Landry, and Handan Vicdan. "Internal auditors' perceptions of the effectiveness of red flags to detect fraudulent financial reporting." *Available at SSRN 961457* (2006).

[19] Yi Wei, Jianguo Chen, Carolyn Wirth. *Detecting Fraud in Chinese Listed Company Balance Sheets.* https://mro.massey.ac.nz/bitstream/handle/10179/8746/SSRN-id2777949%20Detecting%20Fraud%20in%20Chinese%20Listed%20Company%20Balance%20Sheets.pdf, Accessed on 26.6.2020.

Egbunike, Patrick Amaechi, and Ikponmwosa Michael Igbinovia. "Threat of bankruptcy and earnings management in Nigerian listed banks." *Acta Universitatis Danubius. OEconomica* 14, no. 3 (2018).

Golden, Thomas W. *A Guide to Forensic Accounting Investigation*. John Wiley & Sons, 2011.

"Hammurabi's Code of Laws (1780 BCE)". 2020. Sourcebooks.Fordham.Edu. https://sourcebooks.fordham.edu/ancient/hamcode.asp.

Herawati, Nurul. "Application of Beneish M-Score models and data mining to detect financial fraud." *Procedia-Social and Behavioral Sciences* 211 (2015): 924–930.

Hess, Megan F., and Lindsay M. Andiola. "Fraud risk brainstorming at Tesla motors." *Issues in Accounting Education* 33, no. 2 (2018): 19–34.

"Fraud Red Flags – Learn to Identify Internal Indicators of Fraud." 2020. *Corporate Finance Institute*. https://corporatefinanceinstitute.com/resources/knowledge/other/fraud-red-flags/.

"AICPA". 2020. *AICPA*. https://www.aicpa.org/.

Red Flags Fraud. 2020. *Osc.State.Ny.Us*. https://www.osc.state.ny.us/files/local-government/publications/pdf/red_flags_fraud.pdf.

Kassem, Rasha, and Mohamed A. Hegazy. "Fraudulent financial reporting: Do red flags really help?" *International Journal of Academic Research: Economics and Engineering* 4 (2010).

Kulchev, Krasimir. "The Interpretation of Financial Statements in Terms of Contemporary Financial Analysis." (2017).

Moyes, Glen D., Ping Lin, Raymond M. Landry, and Handan Vicdan. "Internal auditors' perceptions of the effectiveness of red flags to detect fraudulent financial reporting." *Available at SSRN 961457* (2006).

Sandhu, Namrata. "Behavioural red flags of fraud: An ex-post assessment of types and frequencies." *Global Business Review* 21, no. 2 (2020): 507–525.

Sheridan, Terry A. *Managerial Fraud: Executive Impression Management, Beyond Red Flags*. Routledge, 2016.

Yi Wei, Jianguo Chen, Carolyn Wirth, *Detecting Fraud in Chinese Listed Company Balance Sheets*. https://mro.massey.ac.nz/bitstream/handle/10179/8746/SSRN-id2777949%20Detecting%20Fraud%20in%20Chinese%20Listed%20Company%20Balance%20Sheets.pdf, accessed on 26.6.2020

CHAPTER EIGHT

CONVERGENCE IN PRIMARY ENERGY CONSUMPTION PER CAPITA AMONG EUROPEAN COUNTRIES: EVIDENCE FROM FOURIER UNIT ROOT TESTS

AYCAN HEPSAG[1]

Abstract

The present paper aims to investigate the convergence of primary energy consumption per capita among European countries, which are Austria, Belgium, Bulgaria, Cyprus, Czech Republic, Denmark, Finland, France, Germany, Greece, Hungary, Iceland, Ireland, Italy, Luxembourg, the Netherlands, Norway, Poland, Portugal, Romania, Slovakia, Spain, Sweden, Switzerland, Turkey, and the United Kingdom, by employing the Fourier unit root tests of Becker et al. (2006) and Enders and Lee (2012). The data set involves the annual per capita primary energy consumption of European countries for the period from 1965 to 2018. The differential series per capita primary energy consumption of each country is calculated to test the convergence hypothesis of per capita primary energy consumption among European countries. The empirical results suggest that per capita primary energy use in Belgium, Bulgaria, Cyprus, Czech Republic, Denmark, France, Germany, Greece, Hungary, Iceland, Ireland, Italy, Luxembourg, the Netherlands, Poland, Portugal, Romania, Slovakia, Spain, Sweden, Turkey, and the United Kingdom has a divergent pattern. The results indicate that per capita primary energy consumption has diverged from the Europe average, implying that shocks to series are

[1] Associate Professor, Istanbul University, Faculty of Economics, Department of Econometrics, Beyazıt, Istanbul, Turkey

permanent. On the other hand, only four European countries, i.e., Austria, Finland, Norway, and Switzerland, are found to be converging. It is suggested that the European countries that are diverging need to pursue policies to make their primary energy supply more stable. Thus, these countries may also move from being diverging to converging.

***Keywords**: convergence, divergence, primary energy consumption per capita, Fourier unit root test, European countries.*

1. Introduction

It is well known that energy sources have a key role in the economic development of countries, and energy is essential but not a free input in the production of goods and services. The convergence of energy sources emerges if countries with low energy consumption are catching up with countries with higher energy consumption. If the per capita energy consumption is converging, deviations therefrom are transitory and will eventually diminish. On the other hand, if the movements of per capita energy consumption have characteristics of hysteresis, deviations therefrom caused by exogenous shock/innovation in the energy markets will have a permanent effect thereon[2]. The knowledge of whether the movements in per capita energy consumption have a transitory or a permanent effect is of great importance to policymakers to determine effective energy policies.

The present paper aims to investigate the convergence of primary energy consumption per capita among European countries by employing the Fourier unit root tests of Becker et al.[3] and Enders and Lee[4]. In the existing literature, many papers examine whether the primary energy consumption per capita is convergent or divergent. Meng et al.,[5] the first study among the others, investigated the convergence of primary energy consumption per capita among OECD countries and reported they have a

---

[2] Borozan, Djula. "Testing for convergence in electricity consumption across Croatian regions at the consumer's sectoral level." *Energy Policy* 102 (2017): 145.

[3] Becker, Ralf, Walter Enders, and Junsoo Lee. "A stationarity test in the presence of an unknown number of smooth breaks." *Journal of Time Series Analysis* 27, no. 3 (2006): 381–409.

[4] Enders, Walter, and Junsoo Lee. "The flexible Fourier form and Dickey–Fuller type unit root tests." *Economics Letters* 117, no. 1 (2012): 196–199.

[5] Meng, Ming, James E. Payne, and Junsoo Lee. "Convergence in per capita energy use among OECD countries." *Energy Economics* 36 (2013): 536–545.

convergent pattern in terms of primary energy consumption per capita. Anoruo and DiPietro[6] examined the validity of convergence of primary energy consumption per capita for 22 African countries and found they are converging. Mishra and Smyth (2014) documented the same situation for ASEAN countries. Fallahi and Voia[7] also investigated the convergence of primary energy consumption per capita among OECD countries and reported that 13 out of OECD countries are converging.

The rest of the paper is as follows: We present the econometric methodology in the second section. The data and empirical results are discussed in the third section. The fourth section concludes the paper.

2. Methodology

In this paper, we employ the Fourier unit root tests of Becker et al.[8] and Enders and Lee[9]. The main advantage of the Fourier unit root test is that it considers the gradual shifts rather than sudden changes by means of Fourier functions. Therefore, the numbers and forms of breaks are not important.

Becker et al. (2006) consider the following auxiliary regression models to test the null of stationarity against the alternative of unit root:

$$y_t = \alpha + \gamma_1 \sin\left(\frac{2\pi kt}{T}\right) + \gamma_2 \cos\left(\frac{2\pi kt}{T}\right) + \varepsilon_t$$

$$y_t = \alpha + \beta t + \gamma_1 \sin\left(\frac{2\pi kt}{T}\right) + \gamma_2 \cos\left(\frac{2\pi kt}{T}\right) + \varepsilon_t \quad , \qquad (1)$$

---

[6] Anoruo, Emmanuel, and William R. DiPietro. "Convergence in per capita energy consumption among African countries: Evidence from sequential panel selection method." *International Journal of Energy Economics and Policy* 4, no. 4 (2014): 568.

[7] Fallahi, Firouz, and Marcel-Cristian Voia. "Convergence and persistence in per capita energy use among OECD countries: revisited using confidence intervals." *Energy Economics* 52 (2015): 246–253.

[8] Becker, Ralf, Walter Enders, and Junsoo Lee. "A stationarity test in the presence of an unknown number of smooth breaks." *Journal of Time Series Analysis* 27, no. 3 (2006): 381–409.

[9] Enders, Walter, and Junsoo Lee. "The flexible Fourier form and Dickey–Fuller type unit root tests." *Economics Letters* 117, no. 1 (2012): 196–199.

where t is the time trend, k is the number of frequencies, sin and cos are the trigonometric terms. In Becker et al.'s unit root test, we estimate the auxiliary regression by OLS and obtain the residuals. Then, the KPSS test is employed the OLS residuals. The estimation procedure is based on the choice of optimal k, and we focus on the regression results which minimize the sum of squared residuals for the optimal k. The test statistic is calculated for the model with intercept and with intercept and trend, respectively, as follows:

$$\tau_{\mu}(k) \; or \; \tau_{\tau}(k) = \frac{1}{T^2} \frac{\sum_{t=1}^{T} S_t(k)^2}{\tilde{\sigma}^2} \tag{2}$$

where $\tau_{\mu}(k)$ is the test statistic for the model with intercept and $\tau_{\tau}(k)$ is the test statistic for the model with intercept and trend. If the $\tau_{\mu}(k)$ and $\tau_{\tau}(k)$ test statistics are smaller than the critical values obtained by Becker et al. (2006), the null hypothesis of stationarity cannot be rejected. On the other hand, if the test statistics are greater than the critical values, the null of stationarity is rejected.

Becker et al. (2006) stated that if the null hypothesis of stationarity cannot be rejected, the significance of the trigonometric terms should be checked. If the trigonometric terms are not statistically significant, it is implied that we do not need to employ Becker et al.'s unit root test (2006). In this case, it is appropriate to employ the KPSS test. We use the F statistic to test the null hypothesis $(\gamma_1 = \gamma_2 = 0)$ against the alternative hypothesis $(\gamma_1 \neq \gamma_2 \neq 0)$. The F test statistic is obtained as follows:

$$F(k) = \left(\frac{SSR_0 - SSR_1(k)/2}{SSR_1(k)/(T-k)} \right), \tag{3}$$

where SSR_0 and SSR_1 are the sum of squared residuals obtained from the specification with and without imposing $\gamma_1 = \gamma_2 = 0$ in (1), respectively.

Enders and Lee [10] proposed another new strategy to test the null of unit root against the stationary by considering the following auxiliary regression models, which are similar to models in the ADF unit root test:

$$\Delta y_t = \alpha + \gamma_1 \sin\left(\frac{2\pi kt}{T}\right) + \gamma_2 \cos\left(\frac{2\pi kt}{T}\right) + \delta y_{t-1} + \varepsilon_t$$

$$\Delta y_t = \alpha + \beta t + \gamma_1 \sin\left(\frac{2\pi kt}{T}\right) + \gamma_2 \cos\left(\frac{2\pi kt}{T}\right) + \delta y_{t-1} + \varepsilon_t \quad , \qquad (4)$$

where t is the time trend, k is the number of frequencies, sin and cos are the trigonometric terms. Enders and Lee (2012) suggest estimating the models in (4) by OLS and testing the null hypothesis of unit root $(\delta = 0)$ against the alternative hypothesis of stationarity $(\delta < 0)$.

Enders and Lee[11] also mentioned the necessity of checking the significance of the trigonometric terms after the rejection of the unit root hypothesis. If the trigonometric terms are not statistically significant, it is implied that we do not need to employ the unit root test of Enders and Lee. In this case, it is appropriate to employ the ADF unit root test.

3. Data and Empirical Results

The data set involves the annual primary energy consumption per capita (kg of oil equivalent) of 26 European countries between 1965 and 2018 – Austria, Belgium, Bulgaria, Cyprus, Czech Republic, Denmark, Finland, France, Germany, Greece, Hungary, Iceland, Ireland, Italy, Luxembourg, the Netherlands, Norway, Poland, Portugal, Romania, Slovakia, Spain, Sweden, Switzerland, Turkey, and the United Kingdom. Then we calculated the natural logarithm of the ratio of energy consumption per capita relative to the average of 26 European countries in the sample, as follows:

---

[10] Enders, Walter, and Junsoo Lee. "The flexible Fourier form and Dickey–Fuller type unit root tests." *Economics Letters* 117, no. 1 (2012): 196–199.

[11] Ibid.

$$x_{i,t} = \ln\left(\frac{energy\ consumption\ per\ capita_{i,t}}{energy\ consumption\ per\ capita_{AVERAGE,t}}\right), \quad (5)$$

where ln denotes the natural logarithm. If the $x_{i,t}$ follows a unit root process, it means that i. country is not convergent. We employ the unit root tests of Becker et al.[12] and Lee and Enders[13] on $x_{i,t}$ for 26 European countries and present the results in table 8-1.

According to the results of Becker et al.'s Fourier unit root test(2006), presented in table 8-1, the null hypothesis of stationarity is rejected for Austria, Belgium, Bulgaria, Cyprus, Czech Republic, Finland, France, Germany, Greece, Hungary, Iceland, Ireland, Italy, Luxembourg, the Netherlands, Norway, Poland, Portugal, Romania, Slovakia, Spain, Sweden, Switzerland, Turkey, and the United Kingdom, and the null hypothesis of stationary cannot be rejected for Denmark at the 5% level. The results support the validity convergence of primary energy consumption per capita only for Denmark among the European countries.

On the other hand, when we interpret the results of Enders and Lee's Fourier unit root test,[14] we determine that the null hypothesis of unit root is rejected for Belgium, Bulgaria, Cyprus, Czech Republic, Denmark, France, Germany, Greece, Hungary, Iceland, Ireland, Italy, Luxembourg, the Netherlands, Poland, Portugal, Romania, Slovakia, Spain, Sweden, Turkey, and the United Kingdom, and cannot be rejected for Austria, Finland, Norway, and Switzerland at the 5% level. We find empirical evidence for the validity of convergence of primary energy consumption per capita in Austria, Finland, Norway, and Switzerland among the European countries.

[12] Becker, Ralf, Walter Enders, and Junsoo Lee. "A stationarity test in the presence of an unknown number of smooth breaks." *Journal of Time Series Analysis* 27, no. 3 (2006): 381–409.
[13] Enders, Walter, and Junsoo Lee. "The flexible Fourier form and Dickey–Fuller type unit root tests." *Economics Letters* 117, no. 1 (2012): 196–199.
[14] Ibid.

Table 8-1. The Results of Fourier Unit Root Tests

Countries	$F-KPSS$	k^*	$F-stat$	$F-ADF$	k^*	$F-stat$
Austria	0.09058*	1	-	-4.86554** (0)	1	4.99436
Belgium	0.28759*	2	-	-3.57817 (0)	2	-
Bulgaria	0.09466*	1	-	-3.13267 (0)	1	-
Cyprus	0.09936*	1	-	-3.48629 (0)	1	-
Czech Republic	0.31876*	2	-	-1.57944 (0)	2	-
Denmark	0.09419	2	24.16217***	-3.88914 (0)	2	-
Finland	0.14584*	1	-	-5.54146** (0)	1	11.73985***
France	0.15739*	1	-	-2.85701 (0)	1	-
Germany	0.16837*	1	-	-4.07754 (0)	1	-
Greece	0.20976*	1	-	-1.63670 (0)	4	-
Hungary	0.13387*	1	-	-3.40514 (0)	1	-
Iceland	0.06705*	1	-	-3.18523 (0)	1	-
Ireland	0.09415*	1	-	-2.87973 (0)	1	-
Italy	0.90493*	2	-	-4.14130 (0)	1	-
Luxembourg	0.09207*	1	-	-2.21213 (0)	3	-
Netherlands	0.36168*	3	-	-3.40342 (0)	3	-
Norway	0.05957*	1	-	-5.61519** (0)	1	9.67847***
Poland	0.13274*	1	-	-3.11470 (0)	1	-
Portugal	0.16434*	1	-	-3.16408 (0)	1	-
Romania	0.13438*	1	-	-2.41015 (0)	1	-
Slovakia	0.15567*	1	-	-3.01400 (0)	1	-
Spain	0.26735*	1	-	-1.40082 (0)	2	-
Sweden	0.11424*	1	-	-3.58365 (0)	1	-
Switzerland	0.05172*	1	-	-5.12534** (0)	1	8.79106
Turkey	0.30908*	3	-	-3.62626 (0)	3	-
United Kingdom	0.20881*	1	-	-2.34698 (0)	1	-

Notes: $F-KPSS$ and $F-ADF$ represent the test statistics of Becker et al. (2006) and Enders and Lee (2012), respectively. * denotes that the null of stationary is rejected at the 5% significance level. ** denotes that the null of unit root is rejected at the 5% significance level. *** denotes the significance of trigonometric terms. The optimal lag lengths are determined through Akaike Info Criterion (AIC) and are given in parentheses. k^* is the optimal frequency.

4. Conclusions

The present paper aims to investigate the convergence of primary energy consumption per capita among European countries employing the Fourier unit root tests of Becker et al.[15] and Enders and Lee.[16] The data set involves the annual primary energy consumption per capita (kg of oil equivalent) of 26 European countries for the period from 1965 to 2018 – Austria, Belgium, Bulgaria, Cyprus, Czech Republic, Denmark, Finland, France, Germany, Greece, Hungary, Iceland, Ireland, Italy, Luxembourg, the Netherlands, Norway, Poland, Portugal, Romania, Slovakia, Spain, Sweden, Switzerland, Turkey, and the United Kingdom. The empirical results suggest that primary energy use per capita in Belgium, Bulgaria, Cyprus, Czech Republic, France, Germany, Greece, Hungary, Iceland, Ireland, Italy, Luxembourg, the Netherlands, Poland, Portugal, Romania, Slovakia, Spain, Sweden, Turkey, and the United Kingdom has a divergent pattern. The results indicate that primary energy consumption per capita has diverged from the Europe average, implying that shocks to the series are permanent. On the other hand, only five European countries, i.e., Austria, Denmark, Finland, Norway, and Switzerland, are found to be converging. It is suggested that the European countries that are diverging need to pursue policies to make their primary energy supply more stable. Thus, these countries may also move from being diverging to converging.

References

Anoruo, Emmanuel, and William R. DiPietro. "Convergence in per capita energy consumption among African countries: Evidence from sequential panel selection method." *International Journal of Energy Economics and Policy* 4, no. 4 (2014): 568.

[15] Becker, Ralf, Walter Enders, and Junsoo Lee. "A stationarity test in the presence of an unknown number of smooth breaks." *Journal of Time Series Analysis* 27, no. 3 (2006): 381–409.

[16] Enders, Walter, and Junsoo Lee. "The flexible Fourier form and Dickey–Fuller type unit root tests." *Economics Letters* 117, no. 1 (2012): 196–199.

Becker, Ralf, Walter Enders, and Junsoo Lee. "A stationarity test in the presence of an unknown number of smooth breaks." *Journal of Time Series Analysis* 27, no. 3 (2006): 381–409.

Borozan, Djula. "Testing for convergence in electricity consumption across Croatian regions at the consumer's sectoral level." *Energy Policy* 102 (2017): 145–153.

Enders, Walter, and Junsoo Lee. "The flexible Fourier form and Dickey–Fuller type unit root tests." *Economics Letters* 117, no. 1 (2012): 196–199.

Fallahi, Firouz, and Marcel-Cristian Voia. "Convergence and persistence in per capita energy use among OECD countries: Revisited using confidence intervals." *Energy Economics* 52 (2015): 246–253.

Meng, Ming, James E. Payne, and Junsoo Lee. "Convergence in per capita energy use among OECD countries." *Energy Economics* 36 (2013): 536–545.

Mishra, Vinod, and Russell Smyth. "Convergence in energy consumption per capita among ASEAN countries." *Energy Policy* 73 (2014): 180–185.

CHAPTER NINE

STRATEGIC APPROACH TO THE SUSTAINABLE DEVELOPMENT OF SPA TOURISM IN SERBIA

BOSILJKA SREBRO[1]
TAMARA VUJIC[2]
MILAN VUJIC[3]
MARKO MILASINOVIC[4]
SRDJAN NIKOLOVSKI[5]

Abstract

One of the most important managerial issues in the tourism industry is how to use the process of strategic management in planning, developing, and managing tourism resources. It is emphasized that for a tourist organization to make better assessments of the future and thus make sound management decisions, the organization should officially include the strategic planning process in the structure of its business and thus force its management to engage in long-term thinking and planning. The research concludes with the necessity to apply the concept of sustainable development, which will include all relevant aspects important for the

---

[1] MSc PhD candidate, University of Belgrade, Faculty of Organizational Sciences, Belgrade, Serbia
[2] MSc, UTD Narcis Divcibare, Valjevo, Serbia
[3] MSc PhD candidate University of Kragujevac, Faculty of Hotel Management and Tourism in Vrnjacka Banja, Vrnjacka Banja, Serbia
[4] MSc, University of Kragujevac, Faculty of Hotel Management and Tourism in Vrnjacka Banja, Vrnjacka Banja, Serbia
[5] MD CRA PhD candidate, University of Belgrade School of Medicine, Belgrade, Serbia

development of sustainable spa tourism; namely, innovation in order to increase competitiveness, the application of modern technologies, and the continuous application of strategic management techniques that should shape the whole process.

Keywords: *strategic approach, strategic management, sustainable development, spa treatment, spa tourism*

1. Introduction – Spa treatment

Spa treatment is well known for its benefits on every organ system, mostly by its numerous non-pharmacological treatments. However, despite its long history and popularity, the role of spa treatment in modern medicine is still not clear.[6]

A wide variety of therapeutic modalities are used in spa therapy, including hydrotherapy, balneotherapy, mud-pack therapy, physiotherapy, and exercise.[7] Spa care usually consists of a wellness holiday lasting two to three weeks and produces a unique therapeutic atmosphere that can contribute to the placebo effect. Minimizing discomfort and enhancing the overall well-being of the patient play a significant role,[8] Balneotherapy uses natural thermal mineral water, the concept of which is based on sodium, potassium, calcium, and magnesium cations as well as sulphide, chloride, and bicarbonate anions. Most of these mineral ingredients are believed to be adsorbed through the skin, which is an active immune organ and may play an important role in the mechanism, but this has not been proven to date.[9] A mudpack is described as a natural product consisting of a mixture of mineral or mineral-medicinal water with organic or inorganic matter obtained from biological or geological processes and used as a therapeutic treatment in the form of a mud wrap applied locally or throughout the body. The key use of the therapy is to alleviate musculoskeletal rheumatic pain. Different systematic reviews and meta-analyses have recently been conducted on spa therapy for rheumatic

---

[6] Verhagen, Arianne P., Sita M.A. Bierma-Zeinstra, Maarten Boers, Jefferson Rosa Cardoso, Johan Lambeck, Rob de Bie, and Henrica C.W. de Vet. "Balneotherapy for osteoarthritis." *Cochrane Database of Systematic Reviews* 4 (2007).

[7] Ibid.

[8] Bender, Tamos, Zeki Karagulle, Geza P. Balint, Christoph Gutenbrunner, Peter V. Balint, and Shaul Sukenik. 2004. "Hydrotherapy, balneotherapy, and spa treatment in pain management". *Rheumatology International* 25 (3): 220–224.

[9] Ibid.

diseases.[10]

2. Spa tourism – A literature review

According to Sharpley,[11] definitions of sustainable tourism are approached from two angles: sustainable tourism as an economic activity and sustainable tourism as a broader element of sustainable development.

Globalization, environmental variability, volatile economic values, and market instability cause numerous changes in all aspects of life. In conditions of rapidly emerging changes, Brdar et al.[12] state that innovation is a key element for all participants in the tourist field in order to achieve competitiveness. The same authors point out that the provision of quality services is the goal of every tourist company because this ensures the loyalty of service users and emphasize that two-way communication based on the exchange of ideas, information, and experiences, in which all factors should participate in the tourist offering, is important. The continuous search for responsible and sustainable practices in the tourism industry paves the way for alternative approaches to tourism development. Local communities are often at the forefront of innovative tourism entrepreneurship and development strategies.[13] Generally speaking, innovation, sustainability (financial and developmental), and providing high quality services are the three pillars on which the strategy of tourism organizations should be based.

A significant sector of the international tourism industry focuses on the natural and cultural attributes of targets, destinations, and places. According

---

[10] Verhagen, Arianne P., Sita M.A. Bierma-Zeinstra, Maarten Boers, Jefferson Rosa Cardoso, Johan Lambeck, Rob de Bie, and Henrica C.W. de Vet. "Balneotherapy for osteoarthritis." *Cochrane Database of Systematic Reviews* 4 (2007); Sharpley, Richard. "Tourism and sustainable development: Exploring the theoretical divide." *Journal of Sustainable Tourism* 8, no. 1 (2000): 1–19.

[11] Sharpley, Richard. "Tourism and sustainable development: Exploring the theoretical divide." *Journal of Sustainable Tourism* 8, no. 1 (2000): 1–19.

[12] Brdar, Ivana, Radmila Zivkovic, Jelena Gajic, Jelena Stankovic, and Natasa Kilibarda. "Smart tourism – The possibility of applying the Internet of Things in modern tourism business," Sinteza 2018 International Scientific Conference on Information Technology and Data Related Research. (2018): 166–122.

[13] Aquino, Richard S., Michael Lück, and Heike A. Schänzel. "A conceptual framework of tourism social entrepreneurship for sustainable community development". *Journal of Hospitality and Tourism Management* 37(2018): 23–32.

to Pavlovic et al.,[14] the simplest definition of sustainable tourism is "any type of tourism that contributes to the protection of the environment, social and economic integrity and the promotion of natural, created and cultural values on a permanent basis." Rebollo and Baidal[15] point out that the debate on sustainable tourism development usually focuses on small tourism practices, such as rural tourism or ecotourism, which are inappropriately called "alternative" tourism judging by the problems they are beginning to create. The authors also emphasize that mature destinations in the Mediterranean are a classic example of inappropriate environmental practices and disrespect for the principles of sustainability present in scientific discourse long before the 1992 Rio summit. What is crucial, however, is that the restructuring processes in traditional destinations have led to a more complex reality in which sustainability has become an inevitable reference as a factor of competitiveness and because of growing social demand.

Butler[16] states that it is necessary to understand that tourist destination areas develop and change over time and react to changes in tourism that change them; they are not a static environment and need responsible and proactive planning and management. In particular, his research implies that policy coordination, proactive planning, acceptance of growth constraints, the education of all parties involved, and commitment to a long-term perspective are prerequisites for successfully linking tourism and sustainable development.

Today, many people travel abroad to receive medical, dental, and surgical care while on holiday. Medical tourism is one of the most promising industries because it has significant economic potential, includes trade in services, and represents a union of at least two segments: medicine and tourism.[17] Medical tourism, which includes dental, medical, and surgical intervention, goes beyond the usual relaxation, exercise, and spa visits that could be included in rest/recovery.

---

[14] Pavlovic, Marija, Nikola Radivojevic, and Jelena Lazic. "Održivi razvoj banjskog turizma u Srbiji". *Industrija* 37 (2) (2009): 37–57.

[15] Rebollo, J. Fernando Vera, and Josep A. Ivars-Baidal. "Measuring sustainability in a mass tourist destination: Pressures, perceptions and policy responses in Torrevieja, Spain." *Journal of Sustainable Tourism* 11 (2003): 181–203.

[16] Butler, W. Richard. "Tourism, environment, and sustainable development." *Environmental Conservation* 18 (1991): 201–209.

[17] Wang, Hsiu-Yuan. "Value as a medical tourism driver." *Managing Service Quality: An International Journal* (2012): 465–491.

Further research shows different models concerning strategies related to sustainable spa tourism. As a result, a model has been proposed that includes key factors to be taken into account when it comes to the development of sustainable spa tourism.

3. Strategic management and today's tourist environment

In developed countries, tourism is one of the potential generators of economic growth and development.[18] Today's tourist environment is becoming more competitive and complex, so every tourist organization needs to intensify its promotional efforts with the aim of earning money. The continuing nature of the tourist business requires that tourist organizations at the national, state, and local levels provide assessments of what is likely to happen in the future and decide how to adapt to future events.[19] Applying the principle of sustainability is the best way to protect tourist destinations from degradation in a social, cultural, and environmental way.[20] For sound managerial decisions, the formal incorporation of a strategic planning process into the structure of the activities of the tourism organization is of special importance, especially from the aspect of sustainable tourism.

Brutland's definition of sustainable development implies standards of behaviour that must be respected as the human community strives to meet the needs of survival and well-being. The model of sustainable development is a normative concept that includes the economic, social, and environmental sustainability components as its building blocks. According to the World Tourism Organization, sustainable tourism means respecting and meeting the needs of tourists, who are on the demand side of tourist services, as well as the tourist areas that are the suppliers in the tourism market. Tourism management, taking into account today's socio-economic, cultural,

---

[18] Vojinovic, Zeljko, and Sanja Zivkovic. "The competitiveness of tourism in Serbia and the role of insurance in tourism." 3rd International Scientific Conference, "Tourism in function development of the Republic of Serbia: Tourism in the era of digital transformation." Thematic proceedings I, University of Kragujevac, Faculty of hotel management and tourism in Vrnjacka Banja (2018): 673–691.

[19] Chon, Kye-Sung, and Michael D. Olsen. 1990. "Applying the strategic management process in the management of tourism organizations." *Tourism Management* 11 (1990): 206–213.

[20] Niedziółka, Iwona. "Sustainable tourism development." *Regional Formation and Development Studies* 8, no. 3 (2014): 157–166.

and natural conditions, should include the concept of sustainable development that should enable the achievement of economic, social, and aesthetic goals while preserving cultural values, social integrity, key environmental assessments, and biological diversity.[21]

The intention, as Fuchs et al. point out, is that tourists increasingly discover new leisure purposes and styles with an emphasis on health and skills development as they relate to cultural and social valuation.[22] Thus, destination managers increasingly measure success not only through the number of tourists but also through "yield" per user, which includes economic, social, and environmental dimensions. This ranges from focus on growth to a special role in generating sustainable yield.

Szromek and Naramski[23] point out that in the case of modern health activities, it seems justified to use two main criteria to divide the business strategy and business model for sustainable tourism:

(a) Perspective I is focused on creating value for the enterprise, which uses the criterion of dividing the model based on the type of recipient of services, with two dominant groups of recipients:
- insurers (financing the stay of patients in the spa from insurance funds),
- individual and business recipients (self-financing of stay).

(b) Perspective II focuses on customer value creation, which uses the criterion of model division based on the type of health product dominated by:
- traditional form of spa product (spa treatment), and
- modern form of spa products (mixed).

Trends in the development of spa tourism in Bulgaria are presented taking into account the Strategy for Sustainable Tourism Development, Horizon 2030. Kazandzhieva[24] states that one of the main drivers of the future growth of health and wellness tourism in Bulgaria in the coming

---

[21] Environment and tourism in the context of sustainable development. Environmental Resources Management, London, 1992.

[22] Fuchs, Matthias, Peter Fredman, and Dimitri Ioannides. "Tourism PhD studies." *Tourism Education: Global Issues and Trends*, 2015: 61–79.

[23] Szromek, Adam R., and Mateusz Naramski. "A business model in spa tourism enterprises: Case study from Poland." *Sustainability* 11, no. 10 (2019): 2880.

[24] Kazandzhieva, Velina. "Trends in the development of spa and wellness tourism." In *International Tourism Forum Spa and Wine*, 2014, pp. 1–8.

years will be the categorization of local spa hotels in accordance with adopted international standards. It should be noted that Bulgaria has seven spa hotel complexes that are certified (EuropeSpa Wellness) by the European SPA Association (European SPA Association – ESPA) for the quality of their services, the same number of certified restaurants as the Czech Republic, which is the most popular spa destination in Europe. These are important facts to keep in mind when creating a sustainable spa tourism strategy. Thermal (spa) tourism in Greece has been developing since the beginning of the 19th century thanks to a number of significant thermal springs spread throughout the country. After an era of prosperity from the mid-20th century to the 1970s, spa tourism entered a period of recession and decline.[25] For the last 20 years, Greek spas and especially their infrastructure (thermal installations) have suffered from abandonment and degradation. In parallel with this development and as a result of wider socio-economic and cultural changes, some new categories of visitors/clients of thermal springs have emerged.

The social role of spa companies and their sustainable development are important issues at the national level. One study concluded that in order to find a balance between expanding business activities and their permitted interference in spas, activities aimed at sustainable development should be included in modern business models.[26] However, out of 5,000 relevant publications, very few attempts have been made to assess the entire global tourism sector in a sense that reflects global research on sustainable development. The industry is not yet close to sustainability.[27] Mihalic et al.[28] state that the literature used in their research shows the gap between the conceptual understanding of sustainable tourism development and the implementation of tourism sustainability.

---

[25] Beriatos, Elias, and Marilena Papageorgiou. "Towards sustainable spa tourism activities in Greece." *WTEE* 120 (2009): 773–781.

[26] Szromek, Adam R., and Mateusz Naramski. "A business model in spa tourism enterprises: Case study from Poland." *Sustainability* 11, no. 10 (2019): 2880.

[27] Buckley, Ralf. 2012. "Sustainable tourism: Research and reality." *Annals of Tourism Research* 39 no. 2 (2012): 528–546.

[28] Mihalič, Tanja, Tina Šegota, Ljubica Knežević Cvelbar, and Kir Kuščer. "The influence of the political environment and destination governance on sustainable tourism development: A study of Bled, Slovenia." *Journal of Sustainable Tourism* 24 no.11 (2016): 1489–505.

4. Strategic development of sustainable spa tourism in the Republic of Serbia

Looking at the geographical and geological characteristics of the territory of Serbia, our country has excellent preconditions for a quality model of sustainable tourism. However, due to its long absence from the international tourist market (sanctions, wars of the 90s), long-term decline in the quality of tourist services, lack of infrastructure, and irresponsible attitude towards environmental protection, the concept of sustainable development in tourism has been delayed. "Despite the significant attention that tourism academics and practitioners have paid to the sustainable development of tourism in recent years, there has been a failure in the tourism literature to link this concept to the theory of its parental paradigm, sustainable development."[29] As the authors further point out, the applicability of sustainable development to the specific context of tourism is rarely questioned as a result so this paper elaborates on this omission in the literature. Liu[30] dealt with this issue with almost the same attitude. She pointed out that sustainable tourism has become an increasingly popular field of research since the late 1980s but the debate on sustainable tourism is vague, divided, and often off target because of the assumptions and arguments. According to Xu et al.,[31] research in the field of sustainable tourism is increasingly important due to the significant growth of the tourism industry and the resulting unsustainable impacts. In addition, the importance of innovations in sustainable tourism studies is emphasized in the sense that they are useful for facing several challenges, including socio-environmental impacts; a critical turn in tourism research; and the growth of ICT, mobile technologies, and big data analytics, and it is logical to state that these changes especially are transforming this field and creating new research opportunities.

---

[29] Sharpley, Richard. "Tourism and sustainable development: Exploring the theoretical divide." *Journal of Sustainable Tourism* 8, no. 1 (2000): 1–19.

[30] Liu, Zhenhua. "Sustainable tourism development: A critique." *Journal of Sustainable Tourism* 11, no. 6 (2003): 459–475.

[31] Xu, Feifei, Nicholas Nash, and Lorraine Whitmarsh. "Big data or small data? A methodological review of sustainable tourism." *Journal of Sustainable Tourism* 28 no. 2 (2019): 144–163.

Puczkó and Rátz[32] investigated the characteristics of tourism development on Lake Balaton in Hungary and discussed how the perception of residents and tourists about the physical impacts of tourism development affects the sustainability of tourism in the region. The results of this research showed that due to the characteristics of tourism development in the region, only a certain form of mass tourism can be maintained, although in a better way, and that residents and tourists have recognized both positive and negative impacts on tourism development. At the same time, the economic benefit for residents is considered to be the most significant impact of tourism. This should certainly be taken as a relevant factor when designing the concept of sustainable tourism development in our country because Hungary is a country in the immediate environment. Another research-based recommendation in this paper that should be considered is that regional organizations must address the impact of tourism and change the local population's short-term approach.

The paper by Mihalic et al.[33] focuses on a comparative discussion of tourism sustainability in the context of mountain tourism destinations. Using a three-dimensional model, the authors analysed Austrian, Slovenian, and Swiss mountain destinations where they were comparable in terms of their environment, level of innovation, and development stages. The results of the research showed that the Swiss and Austrian mountain destinations surpassed the Slovenian ones in almost all aspects except for the protection and quality of the natural environment and the inherited socio-cultural attraction, where significant differences were not determined. These findings would undoubtedly benefit the authorities in development and tourism policy in terms of improving the factors that determine the sustainable development of a tourist destination.

Lozano-Oyola et al.[34] applied the differential dynamic index (which generates values indicating the sustainability of the destination from a social, economic, and environmental point of view on the one hand, and

---

[32] Puczkó, László, and Tamara Rátz. "Tourist and resident perceptions of the physical impacts of tourism at Lake Balaton, Hungary: Issues for sustainable tourism management." *Journal of Sustainable Tourism* 8 no. 6 (2000): 458–478.

[33] Mihalič, Tanja, Tina Šegota, Ljubica Knežević Cvelbar, and Kir Kuščer. "The influence of the political environment and destination governance on sustainable tourism development: A study of Bled, Slovenia." *Journal of Sustainable Tourism* 24 no. 11 (2016): 1489–505.

[34] Lozano-Oyola, M., Blancas, F. J., Gonzalez, M. and Caballero, R., Sustainable tourism tags to reward destination management. *Journal of Environmental Management*, 250 (2019): 109–458.

management assessments by policy makers on the other), which assigned the label of sustainable tourism to urban areas of Andalusia. Sustainable tourism labels are awarded to those places that have made progress to motivate local managers to be more efficient, committed, and objective in evaluating the results of their work. The authors state that it is possible to adapt to the needs of individual places.

Ristic et al.[35] used SWOT analysis in the context of sustainable rural development in their research. The paper gives recommendations in the form of research results as a basis for developing a strategy for the future development of tourism in the observed area. They point out that tourism is sustainable when it can generate development compatible with the economic and social needs of the protected area and its environmental constraints. This is what should be kept in mind when defining the strategy of sustainable development of spa tourism.

One of the important segments in considering the issue of sustainable tourism is the research of sustainable market sectors. So far, only a few studies have systematically searched for and described "eco-segments" or sustainable tourism groups. Dolnicar[36] reviews the usefulness of such approaches, examines previous studies that explore potential target segments, and describes a group of summer tourists in Austria who care about maintaining the natural environment. This is an important issue for considering the sustainability of the natural environment in spa tourism.

Hall's research[37] deals with the geographical, political, and transformational contexts of sustainable tourism development in Central and Eastern Europe. He also talks about the potential and some key issues in such development and its management in the region.

Spa tourism in Serbia also has great potential for development in the coming period, but in order to escape the category of missed opportunities, structural changes in the management of spa tourism are necessary. It is necessary to create a stable legal and institutional environment so that the results of a strategic approach in tourism management are recognized and valorized. Serbia needs a new law on spas because the last one was passed

---

[35] Ristić, Dušan, Danijela Vukoičić, and Miroljub Milinčić. "Tourism and sustainable development of rural settlements in protected areas – Example NP Kopaonik (Serbia)." *Land Use Policy* 89 (2019): 104–231.

[36] Dolnicar, Sara. "Insights into sustainable tourists in Austria: A data-based a priori segmentation approach." *Journal of Sustainable Tourism* 12 no. 3 (2004): 209–218.

[37] Hall, Derek. "Sustainable tourism development and transformation in Central and Eastern Europe." *Journal of Sustainable Tourism* 8 no. 6 (2000): 441–457.

in 1992, which would put spa tourism, taking into account its tendencies and novelties, within a legal framework that the outdated law does not recognize. In order to implement a successful tourism strategy, it is first necessary to define the actual ownership of Serbian spas. The privatization of Serbian spas was announced in 2008 but due to a dispute between the state and the health insurance fund over property and legal issues, was abandoned until 2019 when two spas, Kursumlijska Banja and Vranjska Banja, were privatized. In order for the privatization process not to leave doubts in the professional public, it is necessary to be transparent and to unambiguously define what the subject of privatization is. Common economic logic dictates that thermal springs, as a natural good, would remain in state ownership and the future owner would pay a fee for their use; the facilities, however, could be privatized.

The future development of spa tourism in Serbia must be based on the already mentioned strategic approach. The most important component of the strategy is its dynamism and ability to adapt to changes, so the spa tourism development strategy must respect the complexity of changes in the environment, firmly demanding the implementation of the strategy; more precisely, the consistent behaviour of all factors involved in tourism in spas. Quality strategy implies defining target segments on the demand side for tourist services; in the case of Serbian spas, it is necessary to target more foreign tourists because, as shown in table 9-1 below, during the period January – July 2019, 64,198 foreign tourists visited spas, which is 18% of the total number of visits to spas in Serbia. The remaining 82% were domestic tourists. In order for Serbian spas to be competitive, it is necessary to compose a diverse tourist offer because some people prefer an active vacation and others a passive one. The multidimensional connection between the tourist-recreational and health function of spas is confirmed by the wellness program, which was developed in spas throughout Europe, and which is just beginning in the spas of Serbia. Designing a diverse tourist offer is of great importance because it adjusts to the seasonal tourist traffic imminent in the spa centres of Serbia. The introduction of various events throughout the year – cultural and entertainment events, fairs, congresses (Vrnjacka Banja is in the lead) – would reduce the impact of the season in Serbian spas, which begins in June and lasts until September, and generate about 55% of the total income from overnight stays, which would enable the stabilization of financial inflows throughout the year and create opportunities for new investments in spas. A diversified tourist offer would enable the local population to be employed in the off season, relieving the increased presence of guests in the season, which can have negative implications for the ecological system of spa centres. European Union experts estimate a seasonal concentration of traffic of about 40% during the three most intensive months as an ideal sustainable development.

The general public usually views health and medical tourism as the same but there are important differences between them. Due to their similarities, they are often researched together. Health tourism means organized trips outside one's local environment in order to maintain, improve, and renew one's psycho-physical condition. Medical tourism is treated as a subset of health tourism and refers to organized travel outside one's jurisdiction in order to improve health through medical interventions.[38] Medical tourism, alternatively called health and wellness tourism, is a term that originated from the rapid growth in the number of people from all over the world travelling to other countries for medical, dental, and surgical care while visiting, resting, and fully experiencing the attractions of the countries they were visiting.[39]

According to a report on a global spa summit,[40] about 67% of respondents from the global spa industry observed the importance of *wellness* tourism for the tourism sector. Spas are categorized on the following basis:[41]

(1) Destination spa: The main goal is to develop healthy habits among travellers, which includes *wellness* education, ayurvedic cuisine, and the acquisition and maintenance of physical fitness.
(2) Medical spa: It is characterized by licensed physicians and the provision of *wellness* care.
(3) Spa centre of mineral springs: Offers hydro treatments with the help of thermal or natural spring waters.
(4) Resort or Spa hotel: A hotel that provides spa treatments such as fitness and *wellness*.

Medical tourism is evolving as a multibillion-dollar industry. It must be noted here that the main goal of medical tourists is to obtain quality

---

[38] Carrera, Percivil M., and John F.P. Bridges. "Globalization and healthcare: Understanding health and medical tourism." *Expert Review of Pharmacoeconomics & Outcomes Research* 6, no. 4 (2006): 447–454.

[39] George, Babu P., and Alexandru Nedelea. "Medical Tourism: The Next Big Thing to Come." *Available at SSRN 1264925* (2008).

[40] Clarke, Alan. "Wellness Tourism and Medical Tourism: Where do Spas Fit?. Global Spa Summit." *International Journal of Spa and Wellness* 2 no.1 (2019): 1–2.

[41] International Spa Association. 2020. https://experienceispa.com/

medical treatment at a reasonable price.[42] Table 9-1 includes the average stay of foreign tourists in spas in the Republic of Serbia.

Table 9-1. Information on the average stay of foreign tourists in spas in the Republic of Serbia

	2014	2015	2016	2017	2018	2019			
	Total	Total	Total	Total	Total	Total	Geom mean	**Minimum**	**Maximum**
Spas total	3,21	2,92	**2,95**	3,01	2,88	**2,88**	2,97	2,88	3,21
Vrnjačka Banja	2,82	2,82	**2,69**	2,66	2,59	**2,54**	2,68	2,54	2,82
Sokobanja	3,88	2,4	**2,2**	2,56	2,82	**2,84**	2,74	2,2	3,88
Aranđelovac- Bukovička Banja	2,24	2,06	**2,35**	2,53	2,49	**2,46**	2,35	2,06	2,53
Mataruška Banja	2,82	10,33	**9,55**	8,26	8,15	**7,9**	7,27	2,82	10,33
Banja Koviljača	5,07	5,39	**5,56**	5,67	5,3	**5,49**	5,41	5,07	5,67
Prolom Banja	3,1	2,82	**3,21**	3,16	3,04	**2,94**	3,04	2,82	3,21
Gornja Trepča	**12,73**	**12,62**	**12,43**	**12,39**	**12,28**	**12,92**	**12,56**	**12,28**	**12,92**
Vranjska Banja	2,39	5,04	**6,08**	5,22	5,47	**6,49**	4,88	2,39	6,49
Banja Kanjiža	4,06	1,97	**2,46**	3,18	2,44	**2,61**	2,71	1,97	4,06
Banja Junaković	3,39	3,99	**3,59**	3,27	3,34	**4,01**	3,59	3,27	4,01
Banja Vrdnik	3,01	2,73	**2,31**	2,45	2,29	**2,37**	2,51	2,29	3,01
Banja Rusanda	10,08	8,23	**9,96**	8,46	10	**10,08**	9,43	8,23	10,08
Banja Palić	**1,53**	**1,63**	**1,55**	**1,49**	**1,54**	**1,58**	**1,55**	**1,49**	**1,63**
Selters Banja	6,84	8,96	**5,92**	7,82	6,73	**9,2**	7,48	5,92	9,2
Lukovska Banja	4,59	3,66	**4,13**	3,65	3,83	**4,48**	4,04	3,65	4,59
Gamzigradska Banja	2,23	3,82	**4,35**	5,95	3,43	**14,09**	4,69	2,23	14,09
Ribarska Banja	4,57	4,11	**3,54**	9,75	6,45	**5,34**	5,31	3,54	9,75
Sirajinska Banja	3,87	5,38	**4,9**	3,96	4,49	**4,25**	4,44	3,87	5,38
Banja Vrujci	3,78	3,22	**3,54**	3,31	3,81	**4,69**	3,70	3,22	4,69
Niška Banja	2,51	2,81	**3,08**	3,26	3,25	**4,76**	3,21	2,51	4,76
Minimum	**1,53**	**1,63**	**1,55**	**1,49**	**1,54**	**1,58**	**1,55**	**1,49**	**1,63**
Maximum	**12,73**	**12,62**	**12,43**	**12,39**	**12,28**	**14,09**	**12,56**	**12,28**	**14,09**

On average, foreign tourists stayed in Gornja Trepca spa for 12 days. It was also the spa most visited by foreign tourists, while the Palic spa had the lowest number of visitors. Selters spa had an average attendance of about 9 days. In all spas, the trend is steady, i.e., there are no significant changes. The question is why do foreign tourists spend most of their time in the Gornja Trepca spa? More detailed research should be done at the level of local self-government on the possibilities for attracting investments.

[42] Singh, Siddharth. "Medical Tourism in India". Conference Proceedings – 3rd International Conference on Booming Service Sector from Achievements to Growth Prospects organized by Sri Guru Gobind Singh College of Commerce, University of Delhi, India (2016).

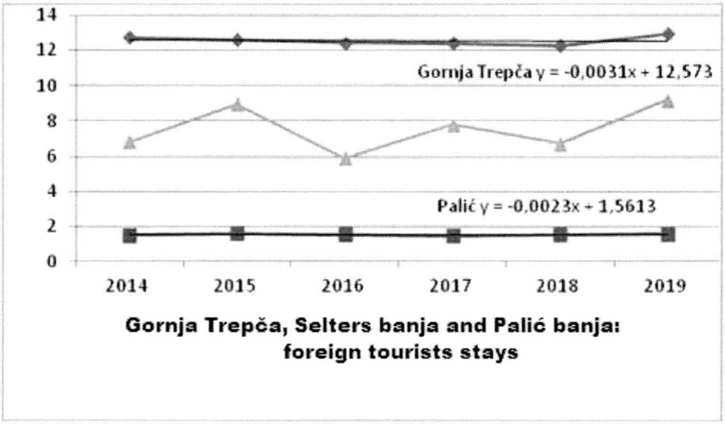

Figure 9-1. The average time foreign tourists stay in Gornja Trepca, Selters Spa, and Palic Spa

As can be seen in figure 9, for the period from 2014 to 2019, Gornja Trepca and Palic Spa both have a linear trend, with the first being the most visited and the second the least visited. For Selters Spa, there are variations from year to year, from six nights to ten, resulting in an irregular trend line.

Table 9-2 covers the average number of domestic tourists in the spas of the Republic of Serbia.

From the data shown in table 9-2, it can be noticed that domestic tourists stayed in Selters Spa for an average of about 21 days for the observed period from 2014–2019. It was also the spa most visited by domestic tourists, while the Palic Spa had the lowest number of visitors. Selters Spa had the highest attendance on average because the state finances the stay of clients. For the observed period, the trend is stable in all spas, i.e., there are no significant changes, except at Selters Spa, which had the highest attendance in 2016. Figure 9.2 shows the number of overnight stays by domestic tourists in Selters Spa for the period 2014–2019.

Table 9-2. Information on the average stay of domestic tourists in spas in the Republic of Serbia

Domestic	2014	2015	2016	2017	2018	2019			
	Domestic	Domestic	Domestic	Domestic	Domestic	Domestic	Geom.rate	minimum	maximum
Spas total	5,1	4,66	4,68	4,56	4,57	4,44	4,66	4,44	5,1
Vrnjačka Banja	3,5	3,29	3,5	3,42	3,47	3,35	3,42	3,29	3,5
Sokobanja	5,27	4,95	4,97	4,98	5,24	5	5,07	4,95	5,27
Arandelovac- Bukovička Banja	2,38	2,37	2,57	2,77	2,67	2,67	2,57	2,37	2,77
Mataruška Banja	9,52	10,95	10,04	9,5	10,28	9,5	9,95	9,5	10,95
Banja Koviljača	9,78	7,33	6,67	6,25	5,74	5,35	6,72	5,35	9,78
Prolom Banja	5,44	5,75	6,02	6,08	5,49	5,39	5,69	5,39	6,08
Gornja Trepča	10,08	10,14	9,86	9,96	10	9,61	9,94	9,61	10,14
Vranjska Banja	5,84	8,4	9,12	8,79	9,31	6,77	7,93	5,84	9,31
Banja Kaniža	4,83	5,2	4,67	4,65	4,8	4,8	4,82	4,65	5,2
Banja Junakovič	8,43	7,61	8,42	7,04	6,52	6,92	7,45	6,52	8,43
Banja Vrdnik	4,33	3,73	4,62	3,86	3,98	3,96	4,07	3,73	4,62
Banja Rusanda	9,06	9,39	9,94	11,22	10,88	10,88	10,20	9,06	11,22
Banja Palić	**2,01**	**1,75**	**1,77**	**1,74**	**1,79**	**2,04**	**1,85**	**1,74**	**2,04**
Selters Banja	**20,33**	**21,3**	**23,21**	**21,76**	**20,86**	**21,24**	**21,43**	**20,33**	**23,21**
Lukovska Banja	7,01	6,98	6,81	6,87	6,81	7,43	6,98	6,81	7,43
Gamzigradska Banja	11,06	10,83	12,25	9,64	8,99	9,81	10,38	8,99	12,25
Ribarska Banja	7,48	6,96	6,86	6,41	6,85	6,77	6,88	6,41	7,48
Sirajinska Banja	8,89	8,19	8,07	7,23	6,43	7,99	7,76	6,43	8,89
Banja Vrujci	3,84	4,16	4,63	4,43	4,91	5,32	4,52	3,84	5,32
Niška Banja	9,05	9,44	8,33	8,5	7,59	7,88	8,44	7,59	9,44
Minimum	**2,01**	**1,75**	**1,77**	**1,74**	**1,79**	**2,04**	**1,85**	**1,74**	**2,04**
Maximum	**20,33**	**21,30**	**23,21**	**21,76**	**20,86**	**21,24**	**21,43**	**20,33**	**23,21**

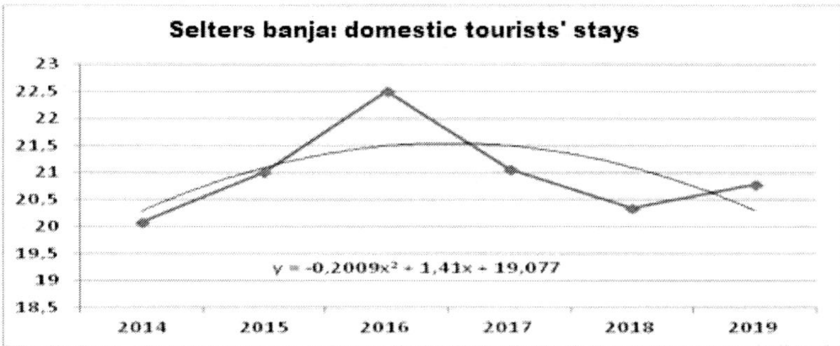

Figure 9-2. The number of overnight stays of domestic tourists in Selters Spa

Based on the presented figure, the maximum participation of domestic tourists is in Selters Spa. The reason for this is that the state financed the stays, on average about 20 days. Table 9-3 shows the ratio of the average stay of domestic tourists to foreign tourists in the spa resorts of the Republic of Serbia.

Table 9-3. The ratio of average stays of domestic tourists to foreign tourists in spas of the Republic of Serbia

	Comparison of domestic versus foreign tourists' overnights							
	2014	2015	2016	2017	2018	2019	minimum	maximum
Spas total	158,88	159,59	158,64	151,50	158,68	154,17	151,50	159,59
Vrnjačka Banja	124,11	116,67	130,11	128,57	133,98	131,89	116,67	133,98
Sokobanja	135,82	206,25	225,91	194,53	185,82	176,06	135,82	225,91
Aranđelovac- Bukovička Banja	106,25	115,05	109,36	109,49	107,23	108,54	106,25	115,05
Mataruška Banja	337,59	106,00	105,13	115,01	126,13	120,25	105,13	337,59
Banja Koviljača	192,90	135,99	119,96	110,23	108,30	97,45	97,45	192,90
Prolom Banja	175,48	203,90	187,54	192,41	180,59	183,33	175,48	203,90
Gornja Trepča	**79,18**	**80,35**	**79,32**	**80,39**	**81,43**	**74,38**	74,38	81,43
Vranjska Banja	244,35	166,67	150,00	168,39	170,20	104,31	104,31	244,35
Banja Kanjiža	118,97	263,96	189,84	146,23	196,72	183,91	118,97	263,96
Banja Junaković	248,67	190,73	234,54	215,29	195,21	172,57	172,57	248,67
Banja Vrdnik	143,85	136,63	200,00	157,55	173,80	167,09	136,63	200,00
Banja Rusanda	89,88	114,09	99,80	132,62	108,80	107,94	89,88	132,62
Banja Palić	131,37	107,36	114,19	116,78	116,23	129,11	107,36	131,37
Selters Banja	**297,22**	**237,72**	**392,06**	**278,26**	**309,96**	**230,87**	230,87	392,06
Lukovska Banja	152,72	190,71	164,89	188,22	177,81	165,85	152,72	190,71
Gamzigradska Banja	**495,96**	283,51	281,61	162,02	262,10	**69,62**	69,62	495,96
Ribarska Banja	163,68	169,34	193,79	**65,74**	106,20	126,78	65,74	193,79
Sirajinska Banja	229,72	152,23	164,69	182,58	143,21	188,00	143,21	229,72
Banja Vrujci	101,59	129,19	130,79	133,84	128,87	113,43	101,59	133,84
Niška Banja	360,56	335,94	270,45	260,74	233,54	165,55	165,55	360,56
Minimum	**79,18**	**80,35**	**79,32**	**65,74**	**81,43**	**69,62**	**65,74**	**81,43**
Maximum	**495,96**	**335,94**	**392,06**	**278,26**	**309,96**	**230,87**	**230,87**	**495,96**

The data shown in table 9-3 indicate that there were 20.82% more foreign tourists in Gornja Trepca than domestic ones (100 – 79.18 = 20.82%). It was also the spa most visited by foreign tourists, while the Palic Spa had the least number of visitors. Selters Spa had an average attendance of about 9 days. More research should be done in terms of identifying the factors that affect the attraction of domestic and foreign tourists. Figure 9-3 shows the ratio of domestic to foreign tourists for the period 2014–2019.

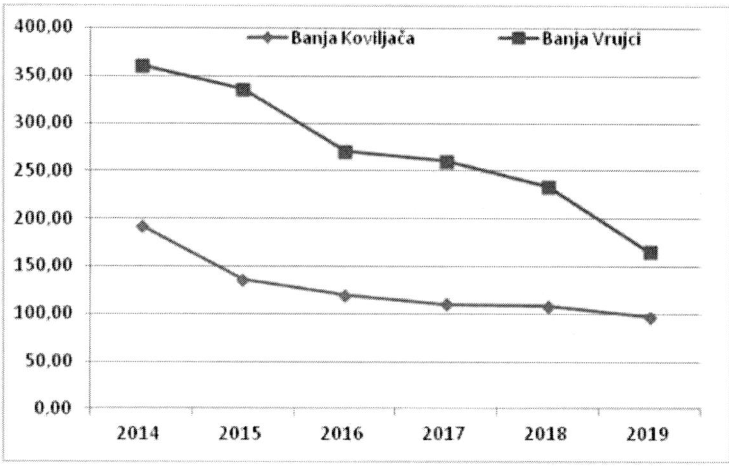

Figure 9-3. The ratio of domestic tourists to foreign tourists

For the observed period, 2014–2019, the number of domestic tourists in Koviljaca and Vrujci markedly decreased, while the participation of foreign tourists showed slight variations (table 9-3, figure 9-3).

The trend of domestic tourists compared to that of foreign tourists for Banja Koviljaca and Mataruska Banja is presented below.

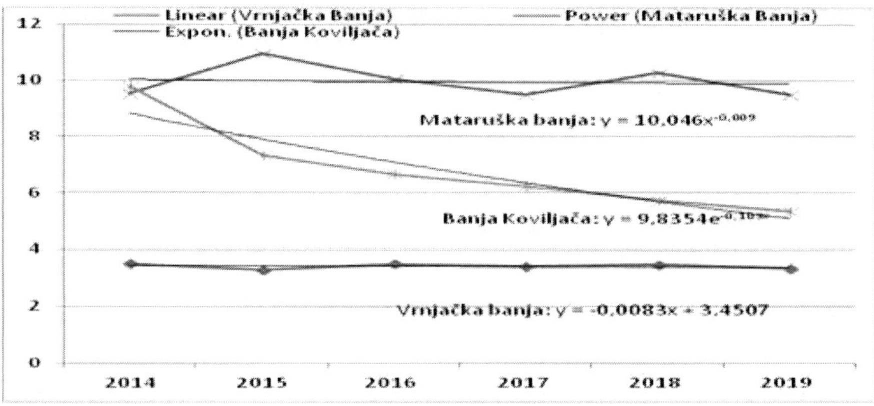

Figure 9-4. The ratio of domestic tourists to foreign tourists: Banja Koviljaca and Mataruska Banja

It can be seen that Banja Koviljaca and Mataruska Banja have a similar trend – a slight exponential decline. These two spas warrant a deeper analysis because the number of overnight stays at Mataruska Banja is on average about 10 days, while at Banja Koviljaca there is a decrease of 7 to 8 days. Vrnjacka Banja has a linear trend for the entire observed period – about 3.5 days. The question arises, considering that the Mataruska and Vrnjacka spas are very close (29.4 km), whether tourists combine their stay in these two spas. Vrnjacka Banja is infrastructurally strong – there are free sources of medicinal water that are of interest for the increasing so-called weekend tourists, and the people who are being treated stay in well-equipped hospitals and hotels. We should not ignore the fact that mineral waters and other natural healing factors are profitable for the development of spa tourism. Mataruska Banja does not have as many arranged and adapted facilities for tourists, as is the case with Vrnjacka Banja, and that certainly affects the number of tourists who visit it.

In order to choose a quality strategy, it is necessary to consider the investment in the tourist offer of spa centres. The strategy could be a model of strategic choice in spa tourism management in Serbia. The focus should be on attracting foreign tourists, primarily from Germany, France, and Sweden. Due to the liberalization of health services within the European Union and the high cost of medical treatment in these countries, it is logical to expect that residents of these countries will seek new places for their medical recovery. Further, it is important to significantly raise the technological level of spa equipment. Special attention should be paid to the development of supporting infrastructure and activities in the development of medical tourism in spas. An important place should be given to the development of the so-called dental tourism.

5. Conclusion

This paper draws attention to the importance of the need to modernize the way of business of tourist spa companies by popularizing the business model and providing an indication of a business model based on the principles of sustainable spa development.

It is necessary to increase the formal literature by forming research tasks identifying the incentive factors for dealing with spa tourism in the Republic of Serbia. Further research should be focused on the possibility of forming alliances between different industries such as employers in spas, insurance companies, and health care providers.

References

Aquino, Richard S., Michael Lück, and Heike A. Schänzel. "A conceptual framework of tourism social entrepreneurship for sustainable community development". *Journal of Hospitality and Tourism Management* 37 (2018): 23–32.

Bender, Tamás, Zeki Karagülle, Géza P. Bálint, Christoph Gutenbrunner, Péter V. Bálint, and Shaul Sukenik. "Hydrotherapy, balneotherapy, and spa treatment in pain management." *Rheumatology International* 25, no. 3 (2005): 220–224.

Beriatos, Elias, and Marilena Papageorgiou. "Towards sustainable spa tourism activities in Greece". *WTEE* 120 (2009): 773–781.

Buckley, Ralf. 2012. "Sustainable tourism: Research and reality." *Annals of Tourism Research* 39, no. 2 (2012): 528–546.

Brdar, Ivana, Radmila Zivkovic, Jelena Gajic, Jelena Stankovic, and Natasa Kilibarda. 2018. "Smart tourism – The possibility of applying the Internet of Things in modern tourism business." Sinteza 2018 International Scientific Conference on Information Technology and Data Related Research: 166–122.

Butler, W. Richard. "Tourism, environment, and sustainable development." *Environmental Conservation* 18 (1991): 201–209.

Carrera, Percivil M., and John F.P. Bridges. "Globalization and healthcare: Understanding health and medical tourism." *Expert Review of Pharmacoeconomics & Outcomes Research* 6, no. 4 (2006): 447–454.

Chon, Kye-Sung, and Michael D. Olsen. "Applying the strategic management process in the management of tourism organizations." *Tourism Management* 11 (1990): 206–213.

Clarke, Alan. "Wellness tourism and medical tourism: Where do spas fit? Global Spa Summit". *International Journal of Spa and Wellness* 2 no.1 (2019): 1-2.

Dolnicar, Sara. "Insights into Sustainable Tourists in Austria: A Data-Based A Priori Segmentation Approach". *Journal of Sustainable Tourism* 12, no. 3 (2004): 209–218.

Ernst, E., and M. H. Pittler. "Wie effektiv ist die Kur? Eine systematische Übersicht randomisierter Studien." *DMW-Deutsche Medizinische Wochenschrift* 123, no. 10 (1998): 273–277.

Fuchs, Matthias, Peter Fredman, and Dimitri Ioannides. "Tourism PhD studies." *Tourism education: Global issues and trends*, 2015: 61–79.

George, Babu P., and Alexandru Nedelea. "Medical tourism: The next big thing to come." *Available at SSRN 1264925*(2008).

Hall, Derek. “Sustainable tourism development and transformation in Central and Eastern Europe.” *Journal of Sustainable Tourism* 8, no. 6 (2000): 441–457.

Harzy, Taoufik, Najoua Ghani, Nessrine Akasbi, Wafaa Bono, and Chakib Nejjari. “Short- and long-term therapeutic effects of thermal mineral waters in knee osteoarthritis: A systematic review of randomized controlled trials”. *Clinical Rheumatology* 28, no. 5 (2009): 501–507.

International Spa Association. 2020. https://experienceispa.com/

Kazandzhieva, Velina. “Trends in the development of spa and wellness tourism.” In *International Tourism Forum Spa and Wine*, pp. 1–8. 2014.

Kotenko, K.V., L. S. Kruglova, N. B. Korchazhkina, E. A. Shatokhina, and V. E. Marionov. “Physical therapy methods for treatment and rehabilitation of oncologic patients (review of literature).” *Meditsina truda i promyshlennaia ekologiia* 11 (2016): 24–29.

Korchazhkina, N. B., L. S. Kruglova, S. N. Turbovskaya, and M. A. Elfimov. “Prophylaxis and rehabilitation of patients with chronic dermatosis (review of literature).” *Meditsina truda i promyshlennaia ekologiia* 11 (2006): 33–38.

Liu, Zhenhua. “Sustainable tourism development: A critique.” *Journal of Sustainable Tourism* 11, no. 6 (2003): 459–475.

Lozano-Oyola, M., Blancas, F. J., Gonzalez, M. and Caballero, R., 2019. Sustainable tourism tags to reward destination management. *Journal of Environmental Management*, 250, p. 109–458.

Mihalič, Tanja, Tina Šegota, Ljubica Knežević Cvelbar, and Kir Kuščer. “The influence of the political environment and destination governance on sustainable tourism development: A study Of Bled, Slovenia.” *Journal of Sustainable Tourism* 24, no. 11 (2016): 1489–505.

Niedziółka, Iwona. “Sustainable tourism development.” *Regional Formation and Development Studies* 8, no. 3 (2014): 157–166.

Pavlovic, Marija, Nikola Radivojevic, and Jelena Lazic. “Održivi razvoj banjskog turizma u Srbiji.” *Industrija* 37 (2009): 37–57.

Palazzi, Carlo, Salvatore D’Angelo, Michele Gilio, Pietro Leccese, Angela Padula, and Ignazio Olivieri. “Pharmacological therapy of spondyloarthritis.” *Expert Opinion on Pharmacotherapy* 16. no. 10 (2015): 1495–504.

Puczkó, László, and Tamara Rátz. “Tourist and resident perceptions of the physical impacts of tourism at Lake Balaton, Hungary: Issues for sustainable tourism management.” *Journal of Sustainable Tourism* 8, no. 6 (2000): 458–478.

Rebollo, J. Fernando Vera, and Josep A. Ivars-Baidal. "Measuring sustainability in a mass tourist destination: Pressures, perceptions and policy responses in Torrevieja, Spain." *Journal of Sustainable Tourism* 11 (2003): 181–203.

Ristić, Dušan, Danijela Vukoičić, and Miroljub Milinčić. "Tourism and sustainable development of rural settlements in protected areas – Example NP Kopaonik (Serbia)." *Land Use Policy* 89 (2019): 104–231.

Sharpley, Richard. "Tourism and sustainable development: Exploring the theoretical divide." *Journal of Sustainable tourism* 8, no. 1 (2000): 1–19.

Singh, Siddharth. "Medical tourism in India." Conference Proceedings – 3rd International Conference on Booming Service Sector from Achievements to Growth Prospects organized by Sri Guru Gobind Singh College of Commerce, University of Delhi, India (2016).

Stier-Jarmer, Marita, Sandra Kus, Dieter Frisch, Carla Sabariego, and Angela Schuh. "Health resort medicine in non-musculoskeletal disorders: Is there evidence of its effectiveness?" *International Journal of Biometeorology* 59, no.10 (2015): 1523–544.

Szromek, Adam R., and Mateusz Naramski. "A business model in spa tourism enterprises: Case study from Poland." *Sustainability* 11, no. 10 (2019): 29-80.

Tenti, Sara, Sara Cheleschi, Mauro Galeazzi, and Antonella Fioravanti. "Spa therapy: Can be a valid option for treating knee osteoarthritis?" *International Journal of Biometeorology* 59, no. 8 (2014): 1133–143.

Tłustochowicz, Witold. "Rational therapeutic approach in rheumatoid arthritis." *Ann Acad Med Stetin* 52 Suppl. 2 (2006): 5–10.

Varga, Csaba. "Balneoprevention: New approaches." *International Journal of Biometeorology* 56, no. 1 (2012): 195–197.

Verhagen, Arianne P., Sita MA Bierma-Zeinstra, Maarten Boers, Jefferson Rosa Cardoso, Johan Lambeck, Rob de Bie, and Henrica C.W. de Vet. "Balneotherapy for osteoarthritis." *Cochrane Database of Systematic Reviews* 4 (2007).

Vojinovic, Zeljko, and Sanja Zivkovic. "The competitiveness of tourism in Serbia and the role of insurance in tourism". 3rd International Scientific Conference, "Tourism in function development of the Republic of Serbia: Tourism in the era of digital transformation." Thematic proceedings I, University of Kragujevac, Faculty of Hotel Management and Tourism in Vrnjacka Banja. 2018: 673–691.

Xu, Feifei, Nicholas Nash, and Lorraine Whitmarsh. "Big data or small data? A methodological review of sustainable tourism". *Journal of Sustainable Tourism* 28 no. 2 (2019): 144–163.

Wang, Hsiu-Yuan. "Value as a medical tourism driver." *Managing Service Quality: An International Journal* (2012): 465–491.

CHAPTER TEN

ANALYSIS OF KEY FINANCIAL PERFORMANCE INDICATORS OF PRIVATE LABORATORIES

SNEŽANA KNEŽEVIĆ[1]
MARIJA MILOJIČIĆ[2]
SRĐAN NIKOLOVSKI[3]
STEFAN MILOJEVIĆ[4]
JOVAN TRAVICA[5]

Abstract

The assessment of financial performance plays a particularly important role in improving the quality of decision-making in profit-oriented organizations. Ratio analysis is one of the most commonly used management techniques. It is widely used by including the assessment of a company's ability to pay its obligations as well as its business and managerial success. The aim of this study is to analyse the key financial performance indicators of private laboratories.

---

[1] Associate Professor Snežana Knežević PhD; Faculty of Organisational Sciences, University of Belgrade, Republic of Serbia.

[2] MSc, PhD Student, University of Belgrade, Faculty of Organisational Sciences, Belgrade, Republic of Serbia

[3] MD CRA, PhD Student, University of Belgrade School of Medicine, Belgrade, Republic of Serbia

[4] MSc, Director of Sector "Fraud Prevention and Fraud Investigations" at Audit, accounting, financial and consulting services company MOODYS STANDARDS, Belgrade, Republic of Serbia.

[5] MSc, National Centre for Corporative Education, Belgrade, Republic of Serbia.

Keywords: *analysis, financial statements, financial performance indicators, private laboratories.*

1. Introduction

The growing need for diagnostic procedures and testing has stressed the capacity of public hospitals, which has resulted in the need for private diagnostic enterprises. Biomedical laboratories are certainly one of the most important links in the chain of diagnostic health care. In-vitro diagnostics, the main group of tests performed in biomedical laboratories, is a necessary tool in clinical practice for the diagnosis, monitoring, and prognosis of disease as well as for predicting the response to applied therapeutic options. Additionally, over the past few decades, there has been an increase in the number of available laboratory tests.

One of the first studies describing the differences between public and private laboratories was published by Hill in 1909.[6] He discussed social as well as medical aspects, emphasizing the importance of both public and private laboratories. However, the importance of public laboratories is still not recognized properly even though these institutions are essential components of the health care industry.[7] Some authors argue that the private sector should take the lead in laboratory testing when it is important for the care and management of patients.[8]

During the last decades, there has been an increasing need in the healthcare industry for the best value at the lowest cost possible. In this period of value-based healthcare, where improving the proportion of patient outcomes to costs is essential, laboratories have a very important role. As a matter of fact, improving laboratory performance is increasingly attracting interest. Ideally, top-notch testing is performed both quickly and economically. In laboratories containing expensive equipment, even small shortcomings can prove costly. Improved productivity can be accomplished by reducing error rates or by improving the already

---

[6] Hill, H. W. "Public laboratories vs. private laboratories." *American Journal of Public Hygiene* 19, no. 4 (1909): 705.

[7] Dowdle W. R. "The future of the public health laboratory." *Annual Review of Public Health*, no. 14 (1993): 649–664; and Dowdle W. R. "The public health laboratory: Does it have a role in the future?" *Curr Issues Public Health* 1 (1995): 25–29.

[8] McDade, Joseph E., and William J. Hausler. "Modernization of public health laboratories in a privatization atmosphere." *Journal of Clinical Microbiology* 36, no. 3 (1998): 609–613.

established functionalities of laboratories. The importance of several key indicators has been described and they can be utilized to survey laboratory performance.[9,10,11,12,13] The majority of them are disease- and condition-related, originating from clinical guidelines. On the other hand, there is a scarcity of studies on indicators of the financial performance of these important parts of the health care system.

The first part of this paper is dedicated to an analysis of the financial performance indicators of companies. The utilization of financial analysis in measuring the financial performance of laboratories is included in the second section, followed by the concluding remarks and list of literature used. The study used the methods of content analysis and ratio analysis of firms' financial statements.

2. Analysis of financial performance indicators of companies

In strategic decision making, finance is often overlooked because it requires short-term investment and funding. In addition, since it does not lead to a return on equity, it also serves as a constraint on financial

---

[9] College of American Pathologists 2019-QTracks [cited 2019 Aug]. Available from: https://estore.cap.org/OA_HTML/ibeCCtpSctDspRte.jsp?section=10498&sitex=10020:22372:US; IFCC: Quality indicators in laboratory medicine [cited 2020 Sep]. Available from: http://217.148.121.44/MqiWeb/Page_QualityIndicators.jsf.

[10] Shahangian, Shahram, and Susan R. Snyder. "Laboratory medicine quality indicators: A review of the literature." *American Journal of Clinical Pathology* 131, no. 3 (2009): 418–431.

[11] Shcolnik, Wilson, Carla Albuquerque de Oliveira, Adriana Sá de São José, César Alex de Oliveira Galoro, Mario Plebani, and David Burnett. "Brazilian laboratory indicators program." *Clinical Chemistry and Laboratory Medicine (CCLM)* 50, no. 11 (2012): 1923–934.

[12] The Royal College of Pathologist. Key performance indicators for laboratory services: Recommendations from the Royal College of Pathologists 2013 [cited 2019 Sep]. Available from: https://www.rcpath.org/uploads/assets/uploaded/131d8206-d7be-4d9b-a29e4f90a35eba15.pdf

[13] Morer, Rosa Ruiz, Mercè Ibarz, M. Antonia Llopis, Alicia Martínez-Iribarren, Carmen Biosca, Núria Serrat Orús, Ma Isabel Llovet, et al. "Quality indicators for extra-analytical processes in clinical laboratory: Ten years' experience." *Revista del Laboratorio Clínico* 9, no. 4 (2016): 147–158.

results.[14] A well-designed and executed financial management is expected to make a positive contribution to the valuation of a business.[15] The financial management dilemma is the achievement of optimal liquidity, solvency, and profitability.[16] For a sound financial recital, working capital management in terms of liquidity and profitability management is important as it has a direct effect on a company's profitability.[17] In order to ensure its smooth operation and fulfill its duty, it is important that a company preserves its liquidity in day-to-day operations as an important part of managing working capital.[18] Through the successful utilization of capital, the ultimate objective of profitability can be achieved. It deals with the maximization of capital for shareholders or owners[19] and can be obtained by evaluating financial results. Financial results imply the cumulative financial stability of the organization for a given period.

One of the most accurate definitions states that financial performance analysis is "the process of determining the operating and financial characteristics of a firm from financial statements and the goal of such analysis are to determine the efficiency and performance of the firm's management, as reflected in the financial reports."[20] Financial performance analysis is the process of determining the operating and financial characteristics of a firm with the goal of determining the firm's efficiency

---

[14] Rafuse, Maynard E. "Working capital management: An urgent need to refocus." *Management Decision* (1996).

[15] Padachi, Kesseven. "Trends in working capital management and its impact on firms' performance: An analysis of Mauritian small manufacturing firms." *International Review of Business Research Papers* 2, no. 2 (2006): 45–58.

[16] Lazaridis, Ioannis, and Dimitrios Tryfonidis. "Relationship between working capital management and profitability of listed companies in the Athens stock exchange." *Journal of Financial Management and Analysis* 19, no. 1 (2006): 26–35.

[17] Rajesh, M., and V. Reddy. "Impact of working capital management on firm's profitability." *Global Journal of Finance and Management* 3, no. 1 (2011): 151–158.

[18] Eljelly, Abuzar. "Liquidity-profitability tradeoff: An empirical investigation in an emerging market." *International Journal of Commerce and Management* 14, no. 2 (2004): 48–58.

[19] Panwala, Manisha. "Dimensions of liquidity management – A case study of the Surat Textile Traders Co-Operative Bank Ltd., Surat." *National Journal of System and Information Technology* 2, no. 1 (2009): 69–78.

[20] Bhunia A., Chand F., Harbour D. "Financial performance analysis – A case study." *Current Research Journal of Social Science*, no. 3 (2011): 269–275.

and performance by analysing its liquidity, profitability, and other indicators.

The ability of a company to analyse its financial position is crucial for improving its competitive position within the marketplace. By carefully analysing its financial performance, the organization can identify opportunities to boost its performance on various levels, which is crucial to its success. Financial performance analysis is an assessment of a company's, sub-business's, or mission's sustainability, solvency, and earnings.

Financial analysts also analyse the short-term and long-term liquidity, solvency, performance, profitability, operating efficiency, and financial stability of the business. Ratio analysis offers relative output metrics of the company and may indicate clues to the underlying financial situation. Reasonable levels of financial performance metrics for which comparisons can be made are needed for the calculation of financial condition and financial quality. In general, the liquid ratio, the debt-equity ratio, the interest coverage ratio, the inventory turnover ratio, the return-on-investment ratio, and the debt-to-net worth ratio are of great benefit in assessing financial status, financial efficiency, and financial stability.

The analysis of the efficiency ratio will determine how well and effectively the organization is running. This ratio tests the company's productivity and the allocation of funds to increase profits. In order to determine the efficacy of the use of company assets, the tables present a set of ratio values, which include assets turnover ratio, fixed assets turnover ratio, current assets turnover ratio, trade receivables collection period, days payable outstanding, and days sales of inventory. Financial statement analysis using ratios is one of the key models for assessing the success of an organization over years and comparing it with the other players in the industry.

The focus of financial statement analysis is the determination and evaluation of key performance indicators (KPIs), which illustrate the strengths, weaknesses, and aberrations that form the basis for comparisons and valuations[21]. This is especially important due to the fact that indicators of financial performance, with financial ratio analysis in particular, have become "important financial decision-support information used by firm management and other stakeholders to assess financial stability and growth potential."[22]

---

[21] Penman, S. *Financial Statement Analysis and Security Valuation*, McGraw-Hill Irwin New York (2001).

[22] Myšková, Renáta, and Petr Hájek. "Comprehensive assessment of firm financial performance using financial ratios and linguistic analysis of annual reports." *Journal of International Studies* 10, no. 4 (2017): 96–108.

3. Utilization of financial analysis in measuring financial performance of private laboratories

In this study, we analysed the financial performance of five private laboratory companies located in Belgrade, Serbia during the period 2016–2019. Official financial reports of analyzed companies were used in this study.[23] Key financial indicators of the analysed business entities are shown in tables 10: 1–4.

Table 10-1. Financial indicators of the analysed business entities for 2016

Name of the indicator	Belladonna	Paster Zavod	Konzilijum	Beo Lab	Bio Medica
Liquidity ratios					
Net Working capital	330	-6,765	26,727	-5,294	73.24
Current Liquidity	2.39	0.54	1.87	0.23	3.74
Quick Ratio	2.39	0.54	1.44	0.19	3.74
Cash Ratio	0.63	0.003	0.29	0.15	0.68
Efficiency ratios					
Total Asset Turnover Ratio	28.00	2.47	1.08	18.57	3.43
Fixed Asset Turnover Ratio	79.17	6.91	1.24	50.18	8.74
Current Asset Turnover Ratio	43.34	3.84	8.64	29.49	5.68
Days Sales in Receivables	5.99	88.10	20.75	2.40	48.21
Days Payable Outstanding	3.79	285.08	14.66	109.87	29.52
Days Inventory Outstanding	0	0	11.38	3.78	0.02

[23] Business Registers Agency. Available at: www.apr.gov.rs.

Profitability					
Gross Profit Margin (%)	56.52	58.03	38.86	46.25	43.75
Operating Margin (ROS) (%)	1.86	0.67	13.28	-3.76	23.69
Return on Assets (ROA) (%)	52.11	1.67	14.36	-69.93	81.37
Return on Equity (ROE) (%)	59.78	n/a	20.43	n/a	111.01
EBIT	1.051	27	65.02	-1.271	151.156
EBITDA	1.281	733	76.689	-1.066	157.481
Solvency ratios					
Debt Ratio	0.27	1	0.28	1	0.22
Financial Leverage Ratio	1.15	n/a	1.42	n/a	1.36
Employees ratios					
Operating Income per employee	2,343.33	1,927	9,189.19	4,999.63	11,175.42
Total Assets per Employee	59.80	834	8,847.90	302.63	3,481.44

Source: Authors' calculation

Table 10-2. Financial indicators of the analysed business entities for 2017

Name of the indicator	Belladonna	Paster Zavod	Konzilijum	Beo Lab	Bio Medica
Liquidity ratios					
Net Working Capital	656	12,070	30,848	792	43,182
Current Liquidity	17	0.30	1.15	2.39	1.95
Quick Ratio	17	0.30	1.08	2.04	1.94
Cash Ratio	7.46	0.006	0.94	1.48	0.44
Efficiency ratios					
Total Asset Turnover Ratio	35.92	2.49	1.02	17.45	3.41
Fixed Asset Turnover Ratio	136.21	7.56	1.44	54.33	7.30
Current Asset Turnover Ratio	48.78	3.71	3.53	25.72	6.44
Days Sales in Receivables	4.51	89.96	18.72	2.67	38.86
Days Payable Outstanding	3.41	240.68	11.33	71.73	28.10
Days Inventory Outstanding	0	0	9.02	2.41	0

Profitability					
Gross Profit Margin (%)	51.65	49.81	34.05	52.76	36.66
Operating Margin (ROS) (%)	2.53	-24.06	11.58	19.16	14.74
Return on Assets (ROA) (%)	90.80	-59.95	11.83	334.38	50.29
Return on Equity (ROE) (%)	108.41	n/a	19.22	2.422.73	67.64
EBIT	1.63	-2.514	67.153	7.636	137.851
EBITDA	1.835	-1.878	80.466	7.87	145.077
Solvency ratios					
Debt Ratio	0.05	1	0.46	0.69	0.29
Financial Leverage Ratio	1.19	n/a	1.62	7.25	1.34
Employees ratios					
Operating Income per Employee	2,056.80	2,058.42	11,011.85	4,797.88	12,613.77
Total Assets per Employee	54.73	678.83	12,913.70	247.13	3,930.94

Source: Authors' calculation

Table 10-3. Financial indicators of the analysed business entities for 2018

Name of the indicator	**Belladonna**	**Paster Zavod**	**Konzilijum**	**Beo Lab**	**Bio Medica**
Liquidity ratios					
Net Working Capital	277	-3,181	52,758	2,847	55,254
Current Liquidity	3.35	0.71	2.08	5.13	2.31
Quick Ratio	3.35	0.42	1.61	4.35	2.30
Cash Ratio	2.07	0.01	0.59	3.77	1.17
Efficiency ratios					
Total Asset Turnover Ratio	52.53	2.65	1.18	11.36	3.86
Fixed Asset Turnover Ratio	468.20	9.14	1.76	38.63	7.47
Current Asset Turnover Ratio	59.17	3.73	3.58	16.09	8.01
Days Sales in Receivables	2.97	64.58	22.18	3.29	23.29
Days Payable Outstanding	1.20	260.19	6.82	3.95	25.91
Days Inventory Outstanding	0	0.13	10.65	3.44	0
Profitability					
Gross Profit Margin (%)	51.82	48.17	32.70	37.24	31.76
Operating Margin (ROS) (%)	0.89	0.15	30.46	7.88	15.95
Return on Assets	46.50	0.39	35.81	89.45	61.54

(ROA) (%)					
Return on Equity (ROE) (%)	53.41	n/a	56.64	152.14	86.04
EBIT	1.03	-700	81.291	3.186	148.63
EBITDA	1.14	-148	97.74	3.376	156.778
Solvency ratios					
Debt Ratio	0.29	1	0.24	0.30	0.28
Financial Leverage Ratio	1.15	-350	1.58	1.70	1.40
Employees ratios					
Operating Income per Employee	2,153.73	1,879.54	12,632.31	5,628.86	15,495.58
Total Assets per Employee	27.26	792.46	9,139.60	708.71	4,122.52

Source: Authors' calculation

Table 10-4. Financial indicators of the analysed business entities for 2019

Name of the indicator	Belladonna	Paster Zavod	Konzilijum	Beo Lab	Bio Medica
Liquidity ratios					
Net Working Capital	886	597	65,303	3,101	31,135
Current Liquidity	12.66	1.05	2.06	1.76	1.29
Quick Ratio	12.66	0.59	1.67	1.66	1.01
Cash Ratio	10.39	0.04	0.75	1.46	0.25
Efficiency ratios					
Total Asset Turnover Ratio	45.35	2.21	1.73	5.88	3.81
Fixed Asset Turnover Ratio	558.15	12.14	2.35	21.11	7.99
Current Asset Turnover Ratio	49.36	2.70	6.71	8.14	7.32
Days Sales in Receivables	1.59	67.46	25.19	3.24	22.35
Days Payable Outstanding	1.77	269.47	15.57	27.32	33.77
Days Inventory Outstanding	0	0.25	10.81	4.20	0
Profitability					
Gross Profit Margin (%)	57.80	48.58	30.04	39.14	19.88
Operating Margin (ROS) (%)	2.96	8.06	8.83	10.10	7.15
Return on Assets (ROA) (%)	134.19	17.80	15.29	59.36	27.25
Return on Equity (ROE) (%)	154.48	n/a	19.96	103.95	44.67
EBIT	3.284	2.129	99.888	4.5	81.548
EBITDA	3.311	2.594	118.367	4.766	93.003

Solvency ratios					
Debt Ratio	0.07	1	0.23	0.49	0.48
Financial Leverage Ratio	1.15	n/a	1.31	1.75	1.64
Employees ratios					
Operating Income per Employee	2,232.60	2,386.82	15,834.31	5,457.37	18,450.94
Total Assets per Employee	71.20	1,227.36	9,329.10	1,236.75	5,490.23

Source: Authors' calculation

During the observed period 2016–2019, most of the analysed companies had a satisfying net working capital part of their long-term capital that finances working assets, and normal approximated stock levels. The positive net working capital indicates that Belladonna, Konzilijum, and BioMedica had sufficient capacity during the period 2016–2019 to meet their short-term liabilities from current assets. The negative net working capital indicates that there was a surplus of short-term liabilities in relation to current assets, which negatively affected the financing of operating business, as was the case with Paster Zavod in the period 2016–2018 and Beo Lab in 2016.

Liquidity ratios indicate the company's ability to meet its short-term liabilities. In this study, we evaluated current liquidity ratio, reduced liquidity ratio, and cash liquidity ratio. The current liquidity ratio shows whether companies have sufficient current assets to cover current liabilities. Analysing the current liquidity ratio in the observed period 2016–2019, we can conclude that the analysed companies finance current assets from long-term sources, and in the future, it can be expected that the companies will remain liquid. Figure 10-1 shows the values of the current liquidity ratio.

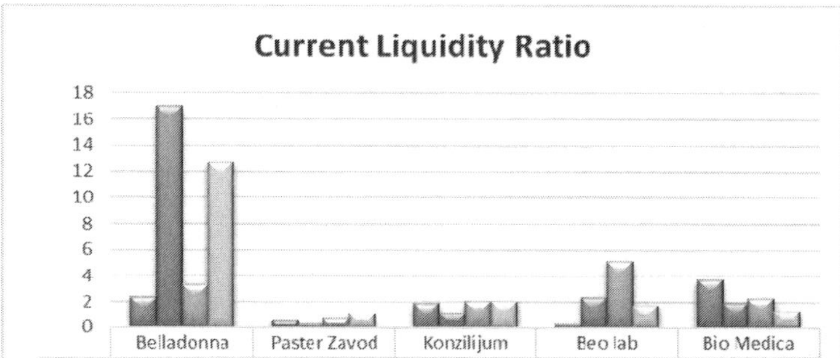

	Belladonna	Paster Zavod	Konzilijum	Beo lab	Bio Medica
2016	2.39	0.54	1.87	0.23	3.74
2017	17	0.3	1.15	2.39	1.95
2018	3.35	0.71	2.08	5.13	2.31
2019	12.66	1.05	2.06	1.76	1.29

Figure 10-1. Values of current liquidity ratio
Source: Tables 10: 1–4

Compared to the other companies, Belladonna recorded the highest level of liquidity in 2017 with a ratio value of 17, which may indicate that the company needs to manage liquidity better in terms of investing cash in the best possible alternatives. As the current liquidity ratio for Belladonna in 2019 is 12.66, the author's recommendation would be to invest the excess liquid assets in less liquid assets that can generate a higher cash flow or distribute the funds to owners. On the other hand, Paster Zavod has the weakest liquidity, and the current liquidity ratio during 2016 was 0.54, which means that the company has twice as many short-term liabilities as current assets. During 2019, Paster Zavod improved its liquidity, and a ratio value of 1.05 means that the company had 5% more current assets than short-term liabilities.

The quick ratio is a measure of short-term liquidity after eliminating the impact of inventories as the least liquid working capital of the company. This ratio assesses a company's ability to settle debts using the most liquid assets within a short period of time. In 2017, Belladonna achieved the highest ratio of reduced liquidity, with a value of 17, which means that each monetary unit of short-term liabilities was covered with 17 monetary units of liquid assets. This implies that the company achieved financial security in a short period of time. Paster Zavod recorded the lowest acid test ratio during the observed period 2016–2019, which indicates a liquidity problem.

How well and efficiently a company is managed can be determined by an analysis of the efficiency ratio. This ratio measures the productivity of the company and the utilization of funds in order to maximize profits. The tables show the set of ratio values in order to assess the efficiency of the use of the company's assets. This set of ratios includes assets turnover ratio, fixed assets turnover ratio, current assets turnover ratio, trade receivables collection period, days payable outstanding, and days sales of inventory.

The asset turnover ratio shows how efficiently the total assets of the analysed companies generate sales revenues. The highest values for 2016 were recorded at Belladonna (28.00) and Beo Lab (18.57), for 2017 at Belladonna (35.92) and Beo Lab (17.45), for 2018 at Belladonna (52.53) and Beo Lab (11.36), and for 2019 at Belladonna (45.35) and Beo Lab (5.88). Thus, these companies, compared to the others analysed in the observed period, used their assets better and more efficiently to generate sales revenue.

The fixed asset turnover ratio shows how efficiently the analysed companies use fixed assets to generate sales revenues. The highest values of this ratio were recorded for 2016 at Belladonna (79.17) and Beo Lab (50.18), for 2017 at Belladonna (136.21) and Beo Lab (54.33), for 2018 at Belladonna (468.20) and Beo Lab (38.63), and for 2019 at Belladonna (558.15) and Beo Lab (21.11). Therefore, these companies, compared to the others analysed in the observed period, used fixed assets better and more efficiently to generate sales revenue. Fixed assets, such as facilities and equipment, are expensive to purchase and maintain so they must be used as much as possible to generate sales revenue.

The current asset turnover ratio shows how many times current assets are turned over during the year through sales revenues. The highest values of this ratio were recorded for 2016 at Belladonna (43.34) and Beo Lab (29.49), for 2017 at Belladonna (48.78) and Beo Lab (25.72), for 2018 at Belladonna (59.17) and Beo Lab (16.09), and for 2019 at Belladonna (49.36) and Beo Lab (8.14), which indicates a higher efficacy level of current asset use.

The highest trade receivables collection period was recorded at Paster Zavod (88.10 days) and Bio Medica (48.21 days) in 2016, in 2017 Paster Zavod (89.96 days) and Bio Medica (38.86 days), in 2018 Paster Zavod (64.58 days) and Bio Medica (23.29 days), and in 2019 Paster Zavod (67.46 days) and Konzilijum (25.19 days). These values may indicate that the analysed companies did not pay enough attention to collection activities. However, the analysed trade receivables collection period shows decreases in the observed period of analysis, which indicates changes in the ability of the company to collect trade receivables.

The days payable outstanding shows the time in days it takes a company to pay off its creditors. The highest days payable outstanding was observed at Paster Zavod (285.08 days) and Beo Lab (109.87 days) in 2016, Paster Zavod (240.68 days) and Beo Lab (71.73 days) in 2017, Paster Zavod (260.19 days) and Bio Medica (25.91 days), in 2018, and Paster Zavod (269.47 days) and Bio Medica company (33.77 days) in 2019. Although Paster Zavod needs the most time to settle its liabilities to creditors, the analysis of the trade receivables collection period for this company concludes that the average number of days of collection of receivables is lower than the average number of days of trade payables settlement in shorter collection deadlines than the deadlines for settling obligations to suppliers. In the observed period 2016–2019, the analysed companies did not face a longer period of time in which they sold their stocks.

Profitability is the most commonly used measure of business performance assessment. It can be defined as the ability of a company to achieve a certain level of profit (preferably maximum) in relation to the engaged funds and capital. Here we will consider the rate of gross profit, ROA, ROE, EBITDA, and EBIT.

The gross profit rate is the percentage of each monetary unit after the seller has calculated the cost of the service provided to the buyer. In the observed period 2016–2019, the analysed companies had approximately equal gross profit rates which did not deviate significantly. This indicates that the analysed companies had uniform returns in the observed period, which represents a good state of stability.

Return on total assets relates to the total assets engaged in business and monitors the effects of those investments. The rate of return on operating assets (ROA) indicates the amount of realized earnings per unit of engaging assets (Figure10-2).

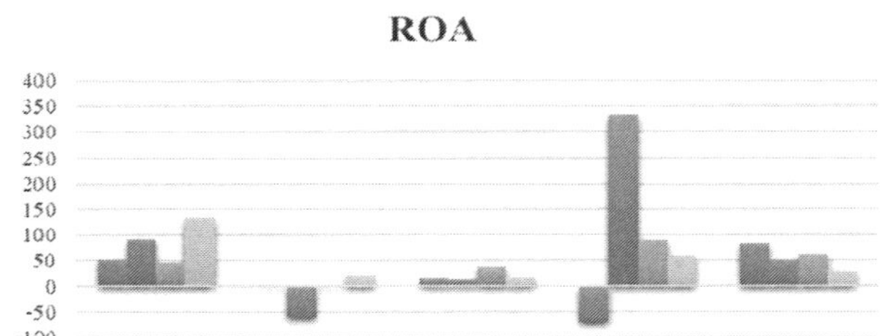

	Belladonna	Paster Zavod	Konzilijum	Beo lab	Bio Medica
2016	52.11	1.67	14.36	-69.93	81.37
2017	90.8	-59.95	11.83	334.38	50.29
2018	46.5	0.39	35.81	89.45	61.54
2019	134.19	17.8	15.29	59.36	27.25

Figure 10-2. Values of return on operating assets
Source: Tables 10:1–4

In the observed period 2016–2019, the highest ROA in 2019 was achieved by Belladonna, which realized 134.19 monetary units of net profit per 100 monetary units of average engaged business assets. Comparing the realized ROA of Belladonna with the previous period, a positive tendency is stated, which is important for investors and creditors in that it indicates the company's achievement of a better financial performance. Beo Lab achieved the highest ROA in 2018 and 2017 (89.45 and 334.38, respectively). Thus, per 100 monetary units of average engaged business assets, Beo Lab realized 89.45 monetary units of net profit in 2018 and 334.38 monetary units of net profit in 2017. The highest ROA in 2016 was achieved by Bio Medica, which generated 81.37 monetary units of net profit per 100 monetary units of average engaged business assets. The lowest ROA was achieved by Beo Lab in 2016 (-69.93), which is unexpected since the company was founded in 2015.

Return on equity (ROE) shows the profit per unit of invested capital. ROE is also a good indicator of a company's growth rate because it is believed that total revenue cannot grow at a rate higher than the current amount of ROE. Within the observed period 2016–2019, the highest value of ROE in 2019 was achieved by Belladonna, which realized 154.48 monetary units of net profit per 100 monetary units of equity. Comparing this to the previous period, a positive tendency is stated, which is important for the owners as it shows how well the management of the company "multiplies" its own capital (Figure 10-3).

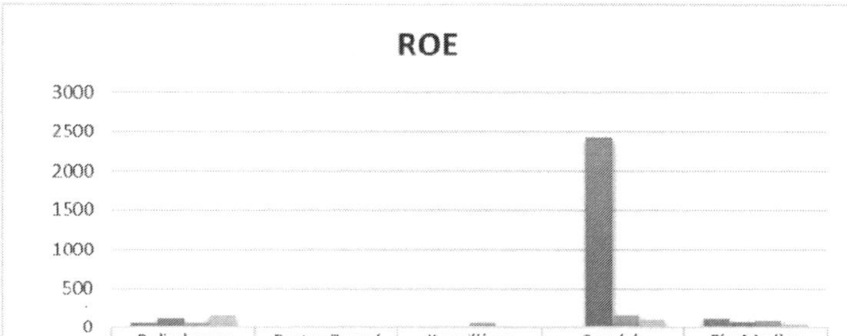

	Belladonna	Paster Zavod	Konzilijum	Beo lab	Bio Medica
2016	59.78	0	20.43	0	111.01
2017	108.41	0	19.22	2422.73	67.64
2018	53.41	0	56.64	152.14	86.04
2019	154.48	0	19.96	103.95	44.67

Figure 10-3. Values of return on equity
Source: Tables 10:1–4

Beo Lab achieved the highest ROE in 2018 and 2017 (152.14 and 2,422.73, respectively). Thus, per 100 monetary units of equity, Beo Lab realized 152.14 monetary units of net profit in 2018 and 2,422.73 monetary units of net profit in 2017. The highest ROE in 2016 was achieved by Bio Medica, which realized 111.01 monetary units of net profit per 100 monetary units of equity. The lowest ROE during the analysed period was achieved by Paster Zavod.

Earnings before interest and taxes (EBIT) is independent of the financial decisions of management and tax regulations and is used to assess the performance of the company; EBITDA represents earnings before interest, taxes, depreciation, and amortization. In the analysed period 2016–2019, Bio Medica and Konzilijum achieved the highest EBIT and EBITDA.

The level of indebtedness in the observed period is highest in Beo Lab and shows how many dinars (Serbian currency) of equity capital are covered by each dinar of borrowed capital, which is especially important in the case of low profitability and increased business risk. The high value of this ratio implies that the largest part of Beo Lab's asset (fixed and current) financing comes from debt. Indebtedness can also be measured by the ratio of debts and capital (financial leverage), and during the analysed period, Beo Lab recorded the highest values of financial leverage, which indicates that this company relies more on debt to finance its assets.

According to the operating profit per employee indicator, growing productivity was recorded at Bio Medica and Konzilijum, while for the remaining companies, productivity was maintained at approximately the same level during the analysed period. The highest productivity was recorded by Bio Medica and Konzilijum, and the lowest in Paster Zavod. Figure 10-4 represents an overview of this indicator with the appropriate values.

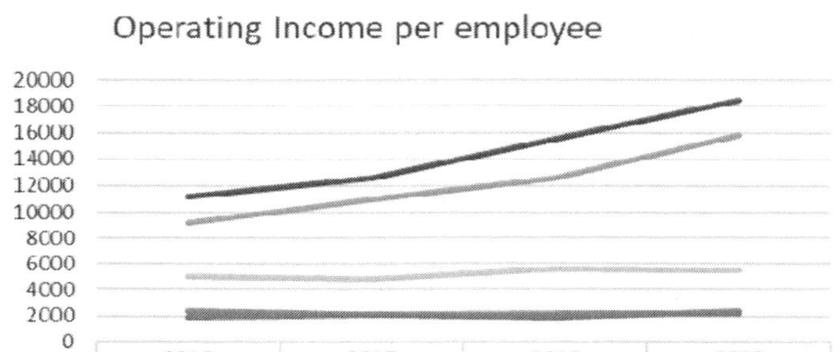

	2016	2017	2018	2019
Belladonna	2343.33	2056.8	2153.73	2232.6
Paster Zavod	1927	2058.42	1879.54	2386.82
Konzilijum	9189.19	11011.85	12632.31	15834.31
Beo lab	4999.63	4797.88	5632.31	5457.37
Bio Medica	11175.42	12613.77	15495.58	18450.94

Figure 10-4. Values of the operating income per employee
Source: Tables 10:1–4

The financial statements of the observed companies summarize the economic consequences of their business activities. Financial metrics play a key role in controlling the operations of companies so the presented and interpreted indicators of companies can be used for that purpose, as well as for planning the future performance of private laboratories.[24]

4. Conclusion

This study is one of the first analyses of the key financial performance indicators of private laboratories, describing some of the most important factors and comparing five laboratories (firms) in the Serbian healthcare

[24] Knežević, S., Mitrović, A., Vujić, M., Grgur, A. *Analysis of Financial Statements*, author's edition. Belgrade, Serbia, ISBN: 978-86-901336-0-4.

system. Indicators used to evaluate financial performance have been confirmed as being of significant importance for the financial business of companies. Besides its pilot characteristic, this study has some limitations. Units of analysis belong to two classification groups, and this is a limitation. There could be more space for analysing additional potential factors of financial performance. Furthermore, there is also the importance of comparison between financial performance indicators and overall business performance indicators, such as the efficiency and efficacy of performed laboratory tests. Also, this study analyses only five private laboratories as a case series study. Further investigations with a larger sample are needed to create a clearer picture of the current status of the performance of companies whose impact on the overall healthcare system of almost every country in the world is increasing. Finally, this research may be of interest to investors who are interested in investing in this form of business.

References

Bhunia A., Chand F., Harbour D. Financial performance analysis – A case study. *Current Research Journal of Social Science* 3 (2011): 269–275.

Business Registers Agency. Available at: www.apr.gov.rs.

College of American Pathologists 2019 – QTracks [cited 2019 Aug]. Available from: https://estore.cap.org/OA_HTML/ibeCCtpSctDspRte.jsp?section=10498&sitex=10020:22372:US

Dowdle W. R. "The future of the public health laboratory." *Annual Review of Public Health* 14 (1993): 649–664.

Dowdle W. R. "The public health laboratory: Does it have a role in the future?" *Current Issues in Public Health* 1 (1995): 25–29.

Eljelly, Abuzar. "Liquidity – profitability tradeoff: An empirical investigation in an emerging market." *International Journal of Commerce and Management* 14, no. 2 (2004): 48–58.

Hill, H. W. "Public laboratories vs. private laboratories." *American Journal of Public Hygiene* 19, no. 4 (1909): 705.

IFCC. "Quality indicators in laboratory medicine" [cited 2020 Sep]. Available from: http://217.148.121.44/MqiWeb/Page_QualityIndicators.jsf

Knežević, S., Mitrović, A., Vujić, M., Grgur, A. *Analysis of Financial Statements*, author's edition, Belgrade, Serbia, ISBN: 978-86-901336-0-4.

Lazaridis, Ioannis, and Dimitrios Tryfonidis. "Relationship between working capital management and profitability of listed companies in the Athens stock exchange." *Journal of Financial Management and Analysis* 19, no. 1 (2006): 26–35.

McDade, Joseph E., and William J. Hausler. "Modernization of public health laboratories in a privatization atmosphere." *Journal of Clinical Microbiology* 36, no. 3 (1998): 609–613.

Morer, Rosa Ruiz, Mercè Ibarz, M. Antonia Llopis, Alicia Martínez-Iribarren, Carmen Biosca, Núria Serrat Orús, Ma Isabel Llovet et al. "Quality indicators for extra-analytical processes in clinical laboratory: Ten years' experience." *Revista del Laboratorio Clínico* 9, no. 4 (2016): 147–158.

Myšková, Renáta, and Petr Hájek. "Comprehensive assessment of firm financial performance using financial ratios and linguistic analysis of annual reports." *Journal of International Studies* 10, no. 4 (2017): 96–108.

Padachi, Kesseven. "Trends in working capital management and its impact on firms' performance: An analysis of Mauritian small manufacturing firms." *International Review of Business Research Papers* 2, no. 2 (2006): 45–58.

Panwala, Manisha. "Dimensions of liquidity management – A case study of the Surat Textile Traders Co-Operative Bank Ltd., Surat." *National Journal of System and Information Technology* 2, no. 1 (2009): 69–78.

Penman, S. *Financial Statement Analysis and Security Valuation*. McGraw-Hill Irwin, New York. (2001).

Rafuse, Maynard E. "Working capital management: An urgent need to refocus." *Management Decision* (1996).

Rajesh, M., and V. Reddy. "Impact of working capital management on firm's profitability." *Global Journal of Finance and Management* 3, no. 1 (2011): 151–158.

Shahangian, Shahram, and Susan R. Snyder. "Laboratory medicine quality indicators: A review of the literature." *American Journal of Clinical Pathology* 131, no. 3 (2009): 418–431.

Shcolnik, Wilson, Carla Albuquerque de Oliveira, Adriana Sá de São José, César Alex de Oliveira Galoro, Mario Plebani, and David Burnett. "Brazilian laboratory indicators program." *Clinical Chemistry and Laboratory Medicine (CCLM)* 50, no. 11 (2012): 1923–934.

The Royal College of Pathologist. *Key Performance Indicators for Laboratory Services: Recommendations from the Royal College of Pathologists 2013* [cited 2019 Sep]. Available from: https://www.rcpath.org/uploads/assets/uploaded/131d8206-d7be-4d9b-a29e4f90a35eba15.pdf

CHAPTER ELEVEN

ANALYSIS OF NON-PERFORMING LOANS OF NON-BANK FINANCIAL INSTITUTIONS IN ALBANIA

ALBAN KORBI[1]
LLESH LLESHAJ[2]

Abstract

Non-bank financial institutions (NBFIs) provide services that are not necessarily suited to banks, serve as competition to banks, and specialize in sectors or groups. Individual NBFIs may specialize in a particular sector, gaining an informational advantage and promoting competition within the financial services industry. Generally, NBFIs deal with clients directly, with lower costs, fees, and rates. As a part of the financial system, NBFIs have these main advantages: alternative source of funding and credit; direct contact with clients, eliminating intermediaries; liquidity for the finance system, etc. Currently, in Albania there are NBFIs that offer payment and money transfer service activities, lending, microcredit, financial leasing, factoring, foreign exchange services, and foreign exchange advisory services. The loan portfolio for this entity accounts for 5.7% of the banking system in Albania, and its development potential is vast. The analysis in this study is based on quarterly time intervals from 2010 to 2020 with three variables: TPL (total loan portfolio of NBFIs), NPL (non-performing loans of NBFIs/outstanding loans); and NPLB (non-

[1] PhD (Doc.) in Finance, vice Dean at Faculty of Economy, University of Tirana, Albania

[2] PhD in Statistics, Department of Finance, Faculty of Economy, University of Tirana, Albania

performing loans of banks/outstanding loans). The methodology applied for data processing is the co-integration method of NPL-NBFIs and NPL-banks. The credit risk in NBFIs is co-integrated to the credit risk of the banking system but it is lower, indicating a stability of this segment of the financial market that is very promising for the future. For forecasting the TPL values, the exponentially weighted moving average (EWMA) model is applied.

Keywords: *non-bank financial institution, non-performing loans, leasing portfolio forecasting*

1. Introduction

A non-bank financial institution (NBFI) is a financial institution that does not have a full banking license and cannot accept deposits from the public. However, NBFIs do facilitate alternative financial services such as investment (both collective and individual), risk pooling, financial consulting, brokering, money transmission, and cheque cashing. NBFIs are a source of consumer credit (along with licensed banks). According to the World Bank, NBFIs include insurance firms, venture capitalists, currency exchanges, some microloan organizations, and pawn shops. These institutions provide services that are not necessarily suited to banks, serve as competition to banks, and specialize in sectors or groups.

NBFIs supplement, and sometimes compete with, banks by providing such financial services to individuals and firms. While banks may offer a set of financial services as a package deal, NBFIs unbundle these services and tailor them to particular groups. Additionally, individual NBFIs may specialize in a particular sector, thus gaining an informational advantage. By this unbundling, targeting, and specializing, NBFIs promote competition within the financial services industry.

Not only do NBFIs provide alternate sources, but they also offer more efficient ones. Compared with banks, NBFIs generally deal with clients directly, with lower costs, fees, and rates. Providing financing and credit is important for keeping the money supply liquid. Figure 1 lists some of the main advantages and disadvantages of NBFIs.

Advantages	Disadvantages
Alternate source of funding, credit	Non-regulated, not subject to oversight
Direct contact with clients, eliminating intermediaries	Non-transparent operations
Liquidity for the finance system	The systemic risk to the financial system, economy

Figure 11-1. The main advantages and disadvantages of NBFIs

After the economic crisis in 2008, sustainable development has become an important issue. The non-bank financial sector has attracted considerable global interest and a number of studies have aimed to quantify its size. In the studies focusing on the USA,[3,4] and in Bouveret[5] for studies focusing on Europe, it is often referred to as the shadow banking sector. In addition, policymakers and regulators are reviewing how to strengthen the oversight of the sector and reduce its opacity.[6]

The role of financial intermediaries such as NBFIs is to channel savings to investors. As competition declines, firms can earn more rent on their loan markets by charging higher interest on the loans. Higher loan rates would imply a higher bankruptcy risk for bank borrowers.[7] Carey and Stulz[8] suggest that many financial institutions have a substantial franchise

---

[3] Noeth, Bryan J., and Rajdeep Sengupta. "Is shadow banking really banking?" *The Regional Economist* 10 (2011): 8–13.

[4] Pozsar, Zoltan, and Manmohan Singh. *The Nonbank-Bank Nexus and the Shadow Banking System*. IMF Working Paper No. 11/289 (2011).

[5] Bouveret, Antoine. "An assessment of the shadow banking sector in Europe." *Available at SSRN 2027007* (2011).

[6] European Commission. "Non-bank financial institutions: Assessment of their impact on the stability of the financial system." *Economic Papers* 472 (2012).

[7] Boyd, John H., and Gianni De Nicolo. "The theory of bank risk-taking and competition revisited." *The Journal of Finance* 60, no. 3 (2005): 1329–343.

[8] Carey, Mark and Rene M. Stulz. *The Risk of Financial Institutions*, NBER Working Paper Series 11442 (2005). http://www.nber.org/papers/w1142

value that could be lost if they are viewed as being too risky. Merton[9] emphasized that risk management is uniquely important for financial institutions because, in contrast to firms in other industries, their liabilities are a source of wealth for their shareholders.

This study analyses the performance of NBFIs and the portfolio of financial leasing in Albania between 2010 and 2020 (in quarterly time intervals). It uses analyses based on co-integration techniques of finance leasing and other forms of medium-term and long-term financing as well as the EWMA method for forecasting.

There are several reasons why this study focuses on finance leasing. Firstly, it is a very good financing tool for small and medium businesses in Albania (on average, 95% of national enterprises are small or medium businesses). Secondly, the development of the financial sub-sector (NBFIs) advances the growth of the financial sector and the economy in general.

2. Performance of NBFIs in Albania

In December 2019, there were 32 non-bank financial institutions (NBFIs), 2 more institutions than in 2018, in Albania that offer:

- ✓ Payment and money transfer service activities
- ✓ Lending
- ✓ Microcredit
- ✓ Financial leasing
- ✓ Factoring
- ✓ Foreign exchange services
- ✓ Foreign exchange advisory services

In December 2019, the total assets of NBFIs amounted to ALL58.1 billion, up by around ALL11.8 or 25.4% compared with the previous year. The credit portfolio accounts for the main share in the structure of NBFIs assets; around 50.4%. The rest of the assets are oriented towards liquid assets (24.5%) and variable-income securities (8.7%). The main funding sources continue to be borrowings (52% of liability) and capital items (39% of liability), whereas borrowing through bond issuance constitutes 0.7% of liabilities. Most of the exposure portfolio of non-bank financial

[9] Merton, Robert C. *Operation and Regulation in Financial Intermediation: A Functional Perspective*. Harvard Business School Press, Boston, MA. 1993.

institutions is held by lending and microcredit entities (73.5%), followed by financial leasing entities (25%) and factoring entities (1.5%). The loan portfolio for this entity accounts for 5.7% of the banking system (Bank of Albania, 2019). Figure 11-2 shows the performance of NBFIs by activities.

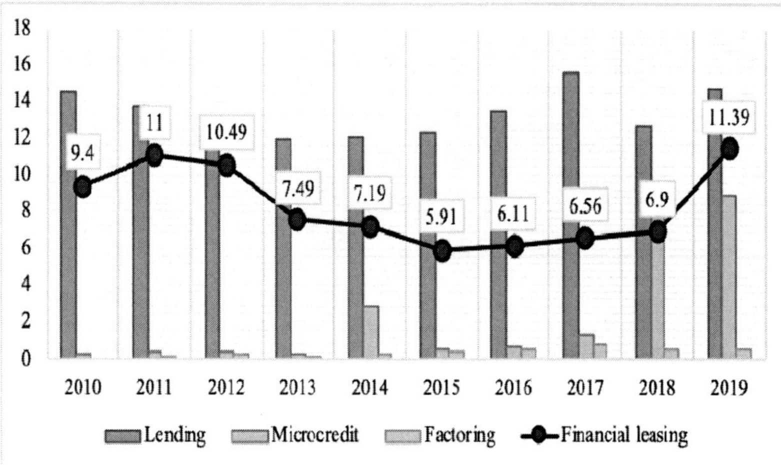

Figure 11-2. NBFI performance of gross portfolio by activity (billion ALL), 2010 – 2019

As can be seen from figure 11-2, NBFIs are dominated by lending and financial leasing. From 2011 to 2015, financial leasing showed a decreasing trend, which changed to an increasing trend from 2016 to 2019. This happened for two reasons: firstly, before 2015, the leasing financing market of these financial entities and their products was in the launch phase; secondly, after 2015, some of the leasing entities were absorbed by commercial banks. According to the stress test conducted by the Bank of Albania, the leasing market became more optimistic. According to Bank of Albania (2019), at the end of 2019, the activities of lending and financial leasing entities remain business-oriented, with around 71% and 82%, respectively, while the factoring portfolio is carried out entirely for business purposes. Compared with 2018, there was an increase of loans to households against enterprises (29% vs 20%), which was mainly due to microcredit activity. The most financed sectors are "Other services activities" (40%), "Trade, vehicles repair, and household items" (23%), and "Agriculture, Forestry, Fishing" (14%); whereas for financial leasing activity, the sectors "Other services activities" (31%), "Trade, vehicles repair, and household items" (20%), "Construction" (13%), and "Real estate activities (7%) are listed.

To analyse the relationship between the non-performing loans of NBFis and those of banks between 2010 and 2018 (in quarterly intervals), first we analyse the trend of these variables, as in figure 3.

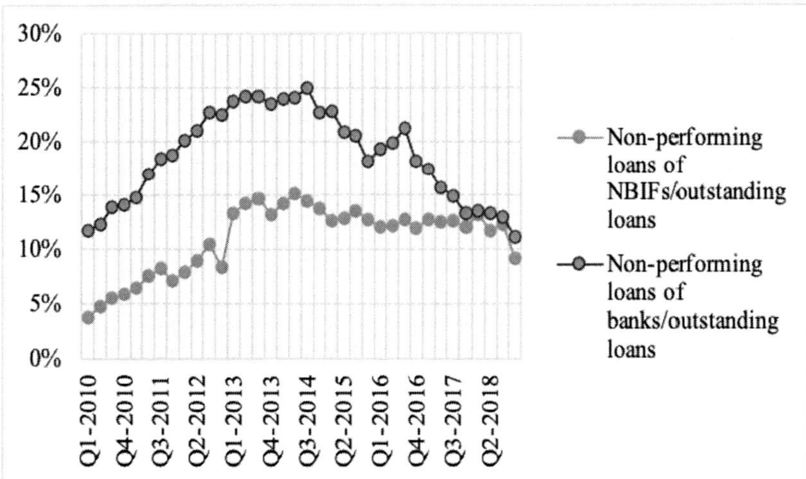

Figure 11-3. The trend of non-performing loans of NBFIs and banking system in Albania, 2010 – 2019

As can be seen from figure 11-3, NBFis had a consistently lower level of non-performing loans compared to the banking system in Albania. So, the credit risk in NBFIs is lower than in the banking system. As a result, the level of regulatory capital in NBFIs is lower, as well as the value of provisions, indicating a very promising stability for the future of this segment of the financial market.

3. Research methodology

The techniques and analysis of the exponentially weighted moving average (EWMA) model and co-integration with some macro-financial variables are used in this study. The data are taken from official statistics published in statistical reports and institutional studies. These data represent a 3-month time series between 2010 and 2020. The analysis begins with finding significant statistical relationships between the unit root, co-integration, and EWMA parameter estimation.

ADF Test of Unit Root: This test is the fundamental testing of the series and the return to a stationary series. To realize this, we used the augmented Dickey-Fuller test (ADF),[10] to test whether a time series of data is influenced by its initial value, the trend of time, or both simultaneously. The basic equation of the ADF test linked with the constant and the trend (first order integral) is:

$$\Delta X_t = \lambda_0 + \lambda_1 t + \lambda_2 X_{t-1} + \sum_{i=1}^{p-1} \lambda_i \Delta X_{t-1} + \varepsilon_t$$

There are three cases for the specification of the AR(p) model above: Case 1: No constant term (no drift) and no linear trend in the model; Case 2: Constant term (drift) but no linear trend; and Case 3: Constant term (drift) and linear trend. This equation shows a time series (variable in the study) in the form of the first difference $\Delta X_t = X_t - X_{t-1}$ in the period t, where λ_0 is the constant and t is the trend, with the null hypothesis, H0: $\lambda_2 = 0$ (time series data is nonstationary).

Johansen test for co-integration: After addressing the issue of unit root, the co-integration test can be applied to establish the long-term relationship among the variables. To identify these long-term relationships, we will use the trace test for co-integration and its maximum eigenvalue statistic (Johansen, 1991). Theoretically, the Johansen test is based on matrix theory and the theory of its eigenvalue. Let $k > 2$ be the number of nonstationary and integral first order series I(1) included in the model, and r the number of vectors that co-integrate with each other, where $r \in [0; k - 1]$, then the co integration hypothesis is: $r \geq 1$ (there is at least one cointegrating pair). Trace test and Max-Eigen values are lower than the critical values and the p-values for them are also insignificant, which asserts the vector error correction.

Exponentially weighted moving average (EWMA) model: This is widely used for modelling and forecasting volatility. Introduced by RISKMETRICS, this model assigns weight λ to previous quarterly

[10] Dickey, David A., and Wayne A. Fuller. "Distribution of the estimators for autoregressive time series with a unit root." *Journal of the American Statistical Association* 74, no. 366a (1979): 427–431.

variance and (1-λ) to previous quarterly news measured by the square of the variable. The EWMA formula is:

$$S_t = \lambda S_{t-1} + (1-\lambda)x_{t-1}$$

S_t is the time series variable forecast previous time (quarterly) and x_t is the value of variable in the previous time (in our study this variable is the total loan portfolio of NBFIs).

4. Empirical analysis and results

The analysis of this study is based on quarterly time intervals from 2010 to 2020 in the official publication data (Bank of Albania). The variables in the model are TPL (total loan portfolio of NBFIs, measured in billion ALL), NPL (non-performing loans of NBFIs/outstanding loans, measured in percentages); and NPLB (non-performing loans of banks/outstanding loans measured in percentages).

We applied the Dickey-Fuller test to analyse the stationarity of these time series. Table 1 shows the unit root test results for each series. The Dickey-Fuller approach is used to apply the unit root tests.

Table 11-1. Time series stationarity test

ADF-test	*Level*		*First difference*	
Unite root test	*t-stat.*	*Prob.*	*t-stat.*	*Prob.*
Variable NPL; I(1)				
Intercept	-2.4350	0.1399	-6.7836	0.0000
Trend and intercept	-1.2548	0.8826	-7.7758	0.0000
None	0.0452	0.6906	-6.7819	0.0000
Variable NPLB; I(1)				
Intercept	-1.6751	0.4320	-5.5661	0.0001
Trend and intercept	-2.2760	0.4329	-5.5906	0.0005
None	-2.8793	0.0057	-6.4523	0.0000

Source: Data proceeding in EViews 11 by authors. Note: I(1) shows that the series is first-order integral (i.e., it is stationary with first difference)

According to the ADF test, all variables are found out to be non-stationary for level form; however, their first difference turns these series into stationary ones. These time series are influenced by the effect of the trend, i.e., they are non-stationary at the level, so the Johansen test is applied to find their long-term (equilibrium) relationship. With Johansen and Juselius' approach, we have only two possibilities: a co-integrating relationship or no co-integration. This approach suggests two kinds of statistical tests: the trace test and the maximum eigenvalue test. First, we must determine the optimum lag (time retrospective of the variable); the results of which are in table 11-2.

Table 11-2. Lag order optimal selection criteria

Lag	LogL	LR	FPE	AIC	SC	HQ
0	134.8204	NA	8.51e-07	-8.301276	-8.209668	-8.270911
1	197.9630	114.4459*	2.11e-08*	-11.99769*	-11.72286*	-11.90659*
2	200.9538	5.047055	2.26e-08	-11.93461	-11.47657	-11.78279
3	202.8854	3.018019	2.60e-08	-11.80533	-11.16407	-11.59278
4	208.3123	7.801270	2.41e-08	-11.89452	-11.07004	-11.62123

* indicates lag order selected by the criterion
LR: sequential modified LR test statistic (each test at 5% level)
FPE: Final prediction error
AIC: Akaike information criterion
SC: Schwarz information criterion
HQ: Hannan-Quinn information criterion

Source: Authors' calculation in EViews 11

We chose the "lag" equal to 4 because the most of criteria suggest it. This lag is the best economically (the data are quarter of year). According to the optimal criterion, we found that lag = 1. Now we need to identify the co-integration pairs, the results of which are shown in table 3.

Table 11-3. Estimations of co-integration rank test (trace) and rank test (maximum eigenvalue)

Hypothesized No. of CE(s)	*Rank Test (Trace)*		*Rank Test (Maximum Eigenvalue)*	
	Trace Statistic	*Prob.*	*Max-Eigen Statistic*	*Prob.*
None	18.9103	0.0147	17.2772	0.0162
At most 1	1.6331	0.2013	1.6331	0.213

Source: Authors' calculation in EViews 11.

We found there is a long-term (equilibrium) relationship between these two variables. This means that an increase in non-performing loans in the banking sector is expected to increase the non-performing loans by NBFIs. Non-performing loans in the banking sector have recently increased as a result of the earthquake in December 2019 (6.4 magnitudes) and the COVID-19 pandemic, and this trend would have resulted in an increase in the non-performing loans of NBFIs.

The relationship for forecasting according to the empirical analysis for the EWMA model of the total loan portfolio of NBFIs in Albania is shown in table 11-4.

Table 11-4. Parametric estimation of EWMA of variable "TPL"

Sample: 2010Q1 2018Q4		
Included observations: 36		
Method: Holt-Winters No Seasonal		
Original Series: TLP		
Forecast Series: TLPSM		
Parameters:	Alpha	0.7400
	Beta	0.2300
Sum of Squared Residuals		17.40724
Root Mean Squared Error		0.695366
End of Period Levels:	Mean	25.96182
	Trend	0.742578

Source: Authors' calculation in EViews 11

The general EWMA forecasting equation for the TLP variable is

$$S_t = 0.74S_{t-1} + 0.23TLP_{t-1}$$

where S_t is the previous forecasting value of the total loan portfolio of NBFIs. These parameters, show that the forecast is very good fit.

Figure 11-5. The general EWMA forecasting equation for the FLP variable

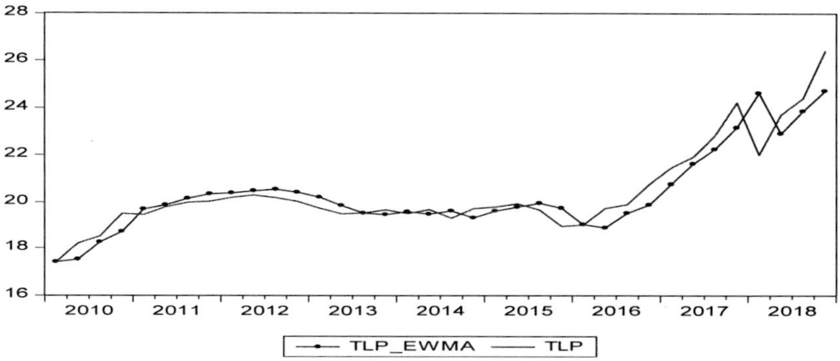

Authors' calculation in EViews 11

According to the EWMA model, if the forecasting quarterly current value is multiplied by the coefficient 0.74 and the current value of the "total loan portfolio of NBFIs" e multiplied by 0.23, we obtain the forecasting value for the following quarter with an on average 97% certainty.

5. Conclusions

NBFIs provide services that are not necessarily suited to banks, serve as competition to banks, and specialize in sectors or groups. Individual NBFIs may specialize in a particular sector, thus gaining an informational advantage and promoting competition within the financial services industry. Generally, NBFIs deal with clients directly, with lower costs, fees, and rates. As a part of the financial system, NBFIs have these main advantages: alternative source of funding and credit; direct contact with clients, eliminating intermediaries; liquidity for the finance system, etc.

Currently, in Albania there are NBFIs that offer payment and money transfer service activities; lending; microcredit; financial leasing; factoring; foreign exchange services; and foreign exchange advisory services. The loan portfolio for this entity accounts for 5.7% of the banking system portfolio in Albania, and its development potential is vast. Most of the exposure portfolio of non-bank financial institutions is held by lending and microcredit entities (73.5%), followed by financial leasing entities (25%) and factoring entities (1.5%).

Analysing the time series data from 2010 to 2020 (at quarterly intervals) with the variables: (1) total loan portfolio of NBFIs; (2) non-performing loans of NBFIs/outstanding loans; and (3) non-performing loans of banks/outstanding loans, the results are:

- There is a long-term (equilibrium) relationship between the non-performing loans of NBFIs/outstanding loans and the non-performing loans of banks/outstanding loans. This means that an increase in non-performing loans in the banking sector is expected to increase the non-performing loans by NBFIs as well.
- If the forecasting quarterly current value is multiplied by the coefficient 0.74 and the current value of the "total loan portfolio of NBFIs" by 0.23, we obtain the forecasting value for the following quarter with an on average 97% certainty.

Taking all statistical analysis, findings, and conclusions into account, we conclude that it is essential that the Central Bank, commercial banks, central and local government institutions, financial advisory institutions, and stakeholders consider the findings of this scientific paper for decision-making in this promising financial sub-sector.

The main limitation of this study derives from the shortcomings of data for the individual NBFIs and their funding/serves amounts by sectors of the economy. As consequence, this study did not use the method of finding endogenous and exogenous factors for developing this financial sub-sector.

References

Bank of Albania (2008, 2009, … 2020). Monthly Statistical Report.

Bank of Albania (2018). *Annual Supervision Report.* https://www.bankofalbania.org/Publications/Periodic/Monthly_Statistical_Report/

Bank of Albania (2019). *Annual Supervision Report.* https://www.bankofalbania.org/Publications/Periodic/Supervision_Annual_Report/

Berger, Allen N., and Gregory F. Udell. *A More Complete Conceptual Framework for Financing of Small and Medium Enterprises*. Vol. 3795. World Bank Publications, 2005.

Bierman, Harold. *The Lease Versus Buy Decision*. Prentice-Hall, 1982.

Bouveret, Antoine. "An assessment of the shadow banking sector in Europe." *Available at SSRN 2027007* (2011).

Boyd, John H., and Gianni De Nicolo. "The theory of bank risk-taking and competition revisited." *The Journal of Finance* 60, no. 3 (2005): 1329–343.

Burgess, Deanna Oxender. "Buy or lease: The eternal question." *Journal of Accountancy* 187, no. 4 (1999): 25.

Carey, Mark and Rene M. Stulz. *The Risk of Financial Institutions*, NBER Working Paper Series 11442. (2005). http://www.nber.org/papers/w1142

Contino, Roberto. *Negotiating Business Equipment Leases*. McGraw-Hill Inc. 2004.

Dickey, David A., and Wayne A. Fuller. "Distribution of the estimators for autoregressive time series with a unit root." *Journal of the American Statistical Association* 74, no. 366a (1979): 427–431.

Merino, Barbara D. "The lease/buy decision: A simplified guide to maximizing financial and tax advantages in the 1980s." *Journal of Accountancy (pre-1986)* 151, no. 1 (1981): 85.

European Commission. "Non-bank financial institutions: Assessment of their impact on the stability of the financial system." *Economic Papers* 472. 2012.

Goldman, Emanuel. *Lecturer Notes: Data Analysis in Finance*. Pace University, 2020.

Gujarati, Damodar N., and Dawn C. Porter. *Essentials of Econometrics*. Vol. 2. Singapore: Irwin/McGraw-Hill, 1999.

Mao, Wen, and Peter Zaleski. "The effect of leasing versus buying on entry deterrence." *Managerial and Decision Economics* 32, no. 5 (2011): 325–331.

Merton, Robert C. "A functional perspective of financial intermediation." *Financial Management* (1995): 23–41.

Merton, Robert C. Operation and Regulation in Financial Intermediation: A Functional Perspective. Harvard Business School Press, Boston, MA., 1993.

Myers, Stewart C., and Nicholas S. Majluf. "Corporate financing and investment decisions when firms have information that investors do not have." *Journal of Financial Economics* 13, no. 2 (1984): 187–221.

Noeth, Bryan J., and Rajdeep Sengupta. "Is shadow banking really banking?" *The Regional Economist* 10 (2011): 8–13.

Pozsar, Zoltan, and Manmohan Singh. "The nonbank-bank nexus and the shadow banking system." IMF Working Paper No. 11/289 (2011).

Adrian, T., and H. S. Shin. "The shadow banking system: Implications for financial regulation." Banque de France FSR, no. 13 Sept. (2009).